Lecture Notes of the Institute for Computer Sciences, Social Informatics and Telecommunications Engineering 276

More information about this series at http://www.springer.com/series/8197

Navin Kumar · R. Venkatesha Prasad (Eds.)

Ubiquitous Communications and Network Computing

Second EAI International Conference
Bangalore, India, February 8–10, 2019
Proceedings

 Springer

Editors
Navin Kumar
Amrita University
Bangalore, Karnataka, India

R. Venkatesha Prasad
Delft University of Technology
Delft, The Netherlands

ISSN 1867-8211 ISSN 1867-822X (electronic)
Lecture Notes of the Institute for Computer Sciences, Social Informatics
and Telecommunications Engineering
ISBN 978-3-030-20614-7 ISBN 978-3-030-20615-4 (eBook)
https://doi.org/10.1007/978-3-030-20615-4

This Springer imprint is published by the registered company Springer Nature Switzerland AG
The registered company address is: Gewerbestrasse 11, 6330 Cham, Switzerland

Preface

We are delighted to introduce the proceedings of the second edition of the 2019 European Alliance for Innovation (EAI) International Conference on UBIquitous Communications and NETwork Computing (UBICNET). This conference has brought together researchers, developers, and practitioners on one platform to discuss the advances in various fields of communication, like 5G and interconnected systems. The theme of the conference was "Global Connectivity."

The technical program of UBICNET 2019 comprised highly selective 20 full papers for oral presentation in the main conference tracks. Basically, the track was arranged in different sessions: Security- and Energy-Efficient Computing; Software-Defined Networks and Cloud Computing and Internet of Things Applications; and Advanced Communication Systems and Networks. Besides the high-quality technical paper presentations, the technical program also featured six keynote speeches and a workshop/special session. Many excellent keynotes speeches by experts from industry focused on highly challenging objectives of the country to build 100 smart cities in the next 4 years. Various challenges on safety, security, and the time frame were also discussed. However, converting these challenges into opportunities was the key feature of discussion to motivate the audience and encourage them to start working toward this goal. Similarly, the keynote speeches on advanced and efficient communication systems and 5G networks for ubiquitous communication received acclamation. Many challenges and associated opportunities were discussed. In addition, the conference also incorporated three special sessions on dip dive into machine learning, 5G networks, and global survivability of optical fiber networks. It can be said that the conference was very successful.

The success was due to the well-structured coordination with the steering chair, Imrich Chlamtac. Dr. Amuda J. and Prof. Murty helped us to compile the high-quality technical program. The Technical Program Committee co-chair, Dr. Arpita, played an important role in getting papers reviewed on time. Special mention should be made of our local chairs, Prof. Sagar B. and Prof. Sreebha B., who ensured each and every conference requirement was properly arranged. The conference management and EAI staff were quick in responding to the queries, which is another reason for the success of the conference. We sincerely appreciate their constant support and guidance. It was also a great pleasure to work with such an excellent Organizing Committee, who worked very hard in organizing and supporting the conference, and in particular the Technical Program Committee. We are grateful to the conference managers, Radka P. and Kitti Szilagyiova, for their continuous support. In addition, we are very grateful to all the authors who submitted their papers to the UBICNET 2019 conference.

We strongly believe that the UBICNET conference provided a good forum for all researchers, developers, and practitioners to discuss the relevant issues related to technology, research, and development. We are sure that future editions of the

UBICNET conference will be as successful and stimulating as indicated by the contributions presented in this volume.

April 2019   Navin Kumar
                                                                                          R. Venkatesha Prasad

Organization

Steering Committee

Imrich Chlamtac (Chair)	European Alliance for Innovation
S. G. Rakesh	Amrita School of Engineering Bangalore, Amrita Vishwa Vidyapeetham, India

Organizing Committee

General Chair

Navin Kumar	Amrita School of Engineering Bangalore, Amrita Vishwa Vidyapeetham, India

General Co-chairs

Mohan Kankanhalli	National University of Singapore, Singapore
Amuda J.	Amrita School of Engineering Bangalore, Amrita Vishwa Vidyapeetham, India

TPC Chair and Co-chairs

Arpita Thakre	Amrita School of Engineering Bangalore, Amrita Vishwa Vidyapeetham, India
Qi Luo	University of Kent, UK
Venkatesha Prasad	Delft University of Technology, The Netherlands

Program Chairs

N. S. Murty	Amrita School of Engineering Bangalore, Amrita Vishwa Vidyapeetham, India
Sithu D. Sudarsan	ABB India

Sponsorship and Exhibit Chair

Suresh Babu	Amrita School of Engineering Bangalore, Amrita Vishwa Vidyapeetham, India

Local Chairs

Sagar Basavaraju	Amrita School of Engineering Bangalore, Amrita Vishwa Vidyapeetham, India
Sreebha Bhaskaran	Amrita School of Engineering Bangalore, Amrita Vishwa Vidyapeetham, India

Workshops Chairs

T. K. Ramesh   Amrita School of Engineering Bangalore, Amrita
                                Vishwa Vidyapeetham, India
Amod Anandkumar M.   Mathworks Inc., India

Publicity and Social Media Chairs

N. Rakesh   Amrita School of Engineering Bangalore, Amrita
                                Vishwa Vidyapeetham, India
Shruthi N. V.   Monash University, Australia
Savita Patil   Ohlone, San Francisco, USA
Nidhi Gangrade   Amrita School of Engineering Bangalore, Amrita
                                Vishwa Vidyapeetham, India
Sunny Sanyal   Chongqing University of Posts
                                and Telecommunications, China

Publications Chair

Reema Sharma   Visvesvaraya Technological University, Belagavi,
                                India

Tutorials Chairs

Kaustav Bhowmick   Amrita School of Engineering Bangalore, Amrita
                                Vishwa Vidyapeetham, India
Vamsi Krishna   PES University, Bangalore, India

Technical Program Committee

Sambit Patra   Accenture, India
Ganeshan Tiagaraja   MMRFIC, Bangalore, India
Anand M.   CDoT, India
Soma Pandey   Reliance Jio, India
Miguel Almeida   Nokia, Portugal
Sunil Kumar   California University, USA
Claudio Sacchi   UNITN, Italy
Mayur Dave   Reliance Telecom, India
Dharma P. Agrawal   University of Cincinnati, USA
Indranil Saha   IIT Kanpur, India
Suvra Sekhar Das   IIT Kharagpur, India
Niranth Amogh   Huawei, India
Vladimir Poulkov   Technical University, Sofia, Bulgaria
Preetam Kumar   IIT Patna, India
Ashutosh Dutta   AT&T, New Jersey, USA
Kalyan Sundaram   Sai Technologies, India
Sanjay Kumar   BIT, Mesra, India
T. V. Prabhakar   IIT Kanpur, India

Contents

Performance Analysis of Femtocell on Channel Allocation

Mahesh Lalapeta$^{(\boxtimes)}$, Sagar Basavaraju, and Navin Kumar (ID)

Department of Electronics and Communication Engineering,
Amrita School of Engineering, Bengaluru,
Amrita Vishwa Vidyapeetham, Bengaluru, India
maheshl.1994@gmail.com, navinkumar@ieee.org

Abstract. Femtocell channel assignment is an important design criteria in cellular systems. In femtocell, access mechanisms are classified in to three classes: open access, closed access and, hybrid access. Additionally, the subscribers in the femtocell network are divided into two groups: subscriber group (SG) and non-subscriber group (NSG). Normally, some channels are reserved for SG. In this paper, five channel assignment models are briefly discussed and analyzed. The performance parameters such as blocking probability for each case is derived and analyzed. Furthermore, other parameters such as bit error rate (BER), the capacity for different path loss condition are also analyzed. We also identified the optimum reserved percentage of channel for SG so that performance remains the highest. The results show that the increase in offered traffic increases the blocking probability. Also, as the base stations increase, BER decreases and the capacity increases.

Keywords: Femtocell · Hybrid access · Channel allocation ·
Blocking probability · SG · NSG

1 Introduction

Femtocell [1] is a low powered base station that is placed in homes to increase the signal strength of the macro base station near cell edge areas. By using this femtocell, the coverage of the signal can be increased and the number of users also increased, giving the better quality of service (QoS) [2]. Femtocell base stations (also called as femto access point (FAP)) being plug and play devices [2], provided by the network operator; enhances the throughput of the macro base station coverage.

The different aspects of femtocell are access modes [3] and the channel allocation [4, 5]. The access modes differentiate the subscribers to access the femto network. For example, under open access, any user is given access to the network. Channel allocation is one of the most important aspects in the femtocell. In this, the channels are allocated to femtocell to give access to the subscribers. The channel allocation also increases the capacity. Additionally, the macrocell reliability is increased. The channel allocation is accomplished in two ways [6, 7]: (i) one being from macrocell to femtocell and (ii) from femtocell to the user. Placing a macro cell base station at the cell edges to increase the

N. Kumar and R. Venkatesha Prasad (Eds.): UBICNET 2019, LNICST 276, pp. 1–16, 2019.
https://doi.org/10.1007/978-3-030-20615-4_1

signal strength is proven to be a costlier than placing a suitable femtocell base station network. This induces cost benefit for the user as well as the network provider.

The channels which are existing in macrocell can be given to the femtocell to increase the QoS and coverage at the edges of the macrocell region where the signal strength of the macrocell is less. When the set of channels are allocated to the femtocell, then there will be interference between the femtocell and macrocell which degrades the macrocell QoS. The interferences exist between the femtocell to femtocell or femtocell to macrocell. There are two types of interferences [5]: (i) the co-channel interference and (ii) the adjacent channel interference. Co-channel interference is the interference between the femtocell and macrocell whereas the adjacent channel interference is the interference between the femtocell and the femtocell. As the same set of channels is allocated to macrocell and femtocell, there will be co channel interference between the femtocell and macrocell. This is one of the main challenges in the channel allocation of femtocell. However, allocation of channels follows different methods for different users (subscribers).

The subscribers of the femtocell are divided into the two groups: subscriber group (SG) and nonsubscriber group (NSG) [8, 9]. The numbers which are stored in the FAP are the customers as SG and the user numbers which are not stored at FAP are customers as NSG. The total service rate is considered as 3-min. The different models are analyzed for the blocking probability and number of occupied channels. In this paper, parameters like blocking probability [8], BER, capacity [10, 11] for the femtocell network is investigated and the corresponding results are presented. The result obtained in this work is different from the existing work and suitable conclusion is drawn. We have also found the optimum reserved channels for the SG users. It is observed that if assignment of reserved channel is varied, the QoS varies. Therefore, it becomes necessary to identify the optimum number of SG users. As per our knowledge, such study and results are not available in the literature. Other performance parameters like bit error rate (BER), capacity is also analyzed and discussed.

Contents of the rest of the paper is as follows. Section 2 presents the system configuration and architecture of femtocell network. Section 3 discusses the methodological model overview where models for most of the methods are described. Results are presented and discussed in Sect. 4 examines and analyses the results. Section 5 presents the conclusion and future scope.

2   System Configuration

This section describes a brief explanation of the architecture of femtocell network.

Architecture of Femtocell Network
The architecture of the femtocell network [8] is as shown in the Fig. 1. The architecture defines how the femtocell is placed in the macrocell region and how it works in the region without any problem.

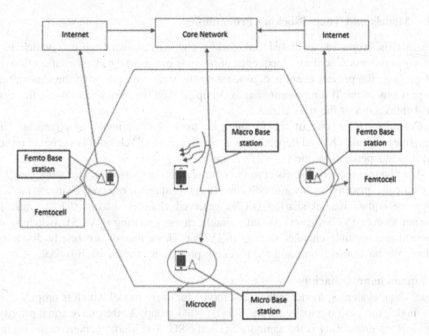

Fig. 1. Architecture of the femtocell network

Normally, the femtocell base station is placed at the edge of the macrocell region. There can be one or many femtocell base stations along the cell edge of the macrocell. This femtocell base station is also known as the Femto Access Points. These FAP's are connected to the core network of a provider by using the Internet broadband connection. These FAP's can be accessed by the users as they are plug and play devices. The main contribution is of these FAPs are to increase the signal strength near macrocell edge areas and improve the QoS. FAP's can use the same frequency set that of macrocell or other set of frequencies. Normally, they use less power transmission and therefore, coverage area of FAP is small. However, there are few challenges like interference, blocking probability, etc.

The characteristics and performance depends on various factors such as number of FAPs, number of channels allocated and so on. To understand the performance, we should understand the models. In the next section, we analyze various models for the channel allocation and derive for the some of these performance parameters.

3 Design and Analysis

In this section, we discuss the mathematical model of different channel allocation techniques of femtocell network. Most of the models are based on Markov chain.

3.1   Models and Their Blocking Probabilities

The models proposed are based on Markov chain as shown in Fig. 2 which is a stochastic process describing a sequence of possible events in the channel allocation. In this process, the present event is dependent on the state (occupancy of the channel) of the previous event. If the present state is occupied then the user will move to the next event (allocation of the next channel).

Consider, '*n*' is one of the channels in total of '*s*' number of channels. The occupancy of 'nth' channel depends upon whether $(n-1)^{th}$ channel is occupied or not and it is independent on the $(n-2)^{th}$ channel.

The channel models discussed in the next sections are based on two strategies [8]: (i) with equal priority for SG and NSG and (ii) percentage of reserved channels for SG. They are equal channel sharing (ECS), reserved channel sharing (RCS), variable channel sharing (VCS), reserved and variable channel sharing (RVCS), switching of reserved and variable channel sharing (SRVCS). These models are briefly discussed below. We have also found and the blocking probability for the each model.

A. Equal channel sharing

Equal channel sharing model is the basic model for every model which is proposed. In this model, there is no priority for the SG and NSG group. As they have equal priority, the blocking probability is the same for SG and NSG. The Markov chain model for the ECS is as shown in the Fig. 3.

For the analysis of ECS model, total *s* number of channels is considered which are for SG and NSG group together. There is no priority for the groups. To find the total probability, we need to know the zeroth probability and state probability. Zeroth probability is defined as P_o and state probability is mentioned as P_j and is given by:

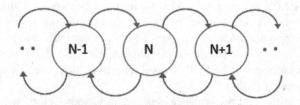

Fig. 2. Markov chain model

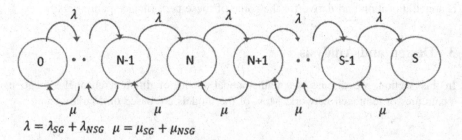

$$\lambda = \lambda_{SG} + \lambda_{NSG} \quad \mu = \mu_{SG} + \mu_{NSG}$$

Fig. 3. Markov chain model for ECS

$$P_j = \frac{\left(\frac{\lambda_{SG} + \lambda_{NSG}}{\mu_{SG} + \mu_{NSG}}\right)^j}{j!} P_o \qquad (1)$$

where

$$\lambda_{SG} = \rho * \mu_{SG} \qquad (2)$$

$$\lambda_{NSG} = \rho * \mu_{NSG} \qquad (3)$$

ρ is defined as the offered traffic and is given by the total number of channels in the femtocell, μ_{SG} and μ_{NSG} is the service rate for the user (SG and NSG). Its value is considered as 3 min. As we know that total probability is always equal to 1 by using that property we find the zeroth probability and total state probability:

$$\sum_{j=0}^{s} P_j = 1 \qquad (4)$$

From the Eqs. (1) and (4), the zeroth probability is calculated and it is given as:

$$P_o = \frac{1}{\sum_{i=0}^{s} \frac{\left(\frac{\lambda_{SG} + \lambda_{NSG}}{\mu_{SG} + \mu_{NSG}}\right)^i}{i!}} \qquad (5)$$

Now, solving (1) and (5), the blocking probability is calculated. Replacing j by s, the blocking probability is given by P_s:

$$P_s = \frac{\frac{\left(\frac{\lambda_{SG} + \lambda_{NSG}}{\mu_{SG} + \mu_{NSG}}\right)^s}{s!}}{\sum_{i=0}^{s} \frac{\left(\frac{\lambda_{SG} + \lambda_{NSG}}{\mu_{SG} + \mu_{NSG}}\right)^i}{i!}} \qquad (6)$$

The blocking probability is the same for SG and NSG subscribers as there is equal priority for both categories of subscribers and it is given by:

$$P_{bSG} = P_{bNSG} = P_s \qquad (7)$$

B. Reserved channel sharing

In the reserved channel sharing, some channels are reserved for the SG users. Even the reserved channel is unused, they will not be offered to NSG users. The Markov chain model for the RCS is as shown in Fig. 4.

Consider again that there are total of s number of channels in these $(n + 1)$ to s number of channels is reserved for the SG users. That is, 0 to n channels are occupied by both SG and NSG users whenever they want the service. The remaining $(n + 1)$ to s channels are for SG users. If the reserved channels are occupied and if more SG users

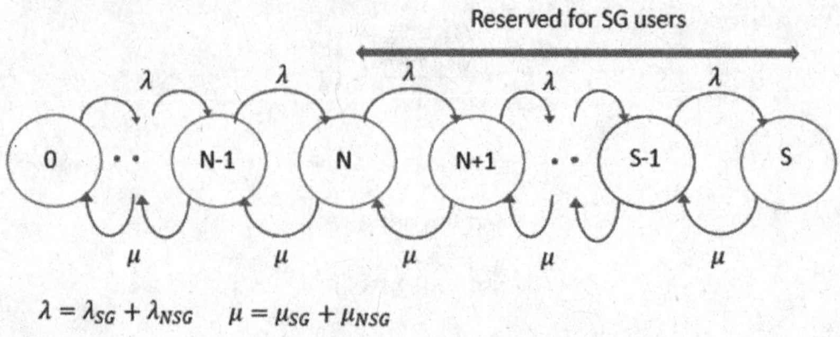

Fig. 4. Markov chain model for RCS

needed the service, then from the remaining channels it can be allocated to the SG user. The blocking probability is then calculated.

The state probability for reserved and unreserved channels are:

$$p_j = \frac{\left(\frac{\lambda_{SG} + \lambda_{NSG}}{\mu_{SG} + \mu_{NSG}}\right)^j}{j!} p_o \quad (0 < j \leq n) \tag{8}$$

$$p_j = \frac{(\lambda_{SG})^{(i-n)} (\lambda_{SG} + \lambda_{NSG})^n}{i!(\mu_{SG} + \mu_{NSG})^i} P_o \quad (n < j \leq s) \tag{9}$$

And, the total state probability is given as:

$$p_s = \frac{\left(\frac{\lambda_{SG} + \lambda_{NSG}}{\mu_{SG} + \mu_{NSG}}\right)^s}{s!} + \frac{(\lambda_{SG})^{(s-n)} (\lambda_{SG} + \lambda_{NSG})^n}{s!(\mu_{SG} + \mu_{NSG})^s} P_o \tag{10}$$

The zeroth probability is given as:

$$P_o = \frac{1}{\sum_{i=0}^{n} \frac{\left(\frac{\lambda_{SG} + \lambda_{NSG}}{\mu_{SG} + \mu_{NSG}}\right)^i}{i!} + \sum_{i=n+1}^{s} \frac{(\lambda_{SG})^{(i-n)} (\lambda_{SG} + \lambda_{NSG})^n}{i!(\mu_{SG} + \mu_{NSG})^i}} \tag{11}$$

Therefore, the blocking probability can be expressed as:

$$p_s = \frac{\frac{\left(\frac{\lambda_{SG} + \lambda_{NSG}}{\mu_{SG} + \mu_{NSG}}\right)^s}{s!} + \frac{(\lambda_{SG})^{(s-n)} (\lambda_{SG} + \lambda_{NSG})^n}{S!(\mu_{SG} + \mu_{NSG})^s}}{\sum_{i=0}^{n} \frac{\left(\frac{\lambda_{SG} + \lambda_{NSG}}{\mu_{SG} + \mu_{NSG}}\right)^i}{i!} + \sum_{i=n+1}^{s} \frac{(\lambda_{SG})^{(i-n)} (\lambda_{SG} + \lambda_{NSG}g)^n}{i!(\mu_{SG} + \mu_{NSG})^i}} \tag{12}$$

The blocking probability for each categories (subscriber) in RCS is:

$$p_{bSG} = p_S \; and \; p_{bNSG} = \sum_{n}^{S} p_j$$

The disadvantage of this model is that sometimes no channel may remain for the NSG in the reserved channels.

C. Variable channel sharing

In this model, all the channels are variable. That is, all channels are shared among the SG and NSG users. There is no priority for the SG and NSG users. The variable channel sharing depends upon the value c, the presence of NSG users whose value is considered between the 0 and 1. Here, 0 implies no NSG user while 1 implies NSG user. The Markov model for the VCS is shown in the Fig. 5.

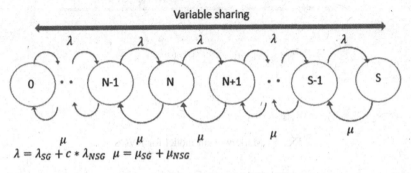

Fig. 5. Markov chain model for VCS

For variable channel sharing let us again consider that a total s number of channels are present. The variable c defines the presence of NSG user, when $c = 0$, then there is no NSG user and $c = 1$ defines the presence of NSG user with equal priority. So, when the variable $c = 1$, the variable channel sharing is equal to equal channel sharing model. The blocking probability is then calculated.

The state probability for s channels is given as:

$$p_j = \frac{\left(\frac{\lambda_{SG} + c\lambda_{NSG}}{\mu_{SG} + \mu_{NSG}} \right)^j}{j!} P_0 \tag{13}$$

For zeroth probability and replacing j by i, it follows:

$$p_o = \frac{1}{\sum_{i=0}^{s} \frac{\left(\frac{\lambda_{SG} + c\lambda_{NSG}}{\mu_{SG} + \mu_{NSG}} \right)^i}{i!}} \tag{14}$$

The total state probability is defined as:

$$p_s = \frac{\frac{\left(\frac{\lambda_{SG}+c\lambda_{NSG}}{\mu_{SG}+\mu_{NSG}}\right)^s}{s!}}{\sum_{i=0}^{s}\frac{\left(\frac{\lambda_{SG}+c\lambda_{NSG}}{\mu_{SG}+\mu_{NSG}}\right)^i}{i!}} \tag{15}$$

The SG blocking probability is given as:

$$p_{bSG} = p_s$$

The NSG blocking probability when the channels are variable when c = 0, there will be the maximum blocking probability for NSG.

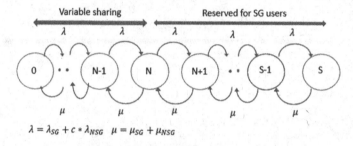

$$\lambda = \lambda_{SG} + c * \lambda_{NSG} \quad \mu = \mu_{SG} + \mu_{NSG}$$

Fig. 6. Markov chain model for RVCS

D. Reserved and variable channel sharing

This model is improved version of the VCS model. It is a combination of RCS with high priority for the SG users so that SG users do not want their QoS to be affected. In this model, some channels are reserved for the SG users and remaining channels are available for SG and NSG users with the variable sharing. The Markov chain model for the RVCS is as shown in Fig. 6.

Let us consider, s be the total number of channels. In this total (n + 1) to s channels are reserved for SG users. From 0 to *n* channels are variable and these channels can be occupied by the SG and NSG users. The blocking probability for RVCS is calculated as below.

The state probability for the (0 to n) channels is:

$$p_j = \frac{\left(\frac{\lambda_{SG}+c\lambda_{NSG}}{\mu_{SG}+\mu_{NSG}}\right)^j}{j!}P_o \quad (0 < j \le n) \tag{16}$$

The state probability for $(n + 1)$ to s channels is given as:

$$P_j = \frac{(\lambda_{SG})^{(i-n)}(\lambda_{SG} + c\lambda_{NSG})^n}{i!(\mu_{SG} + \mu_{NSG})^i}P_o \quad (n < j \leq s) \tag{17}$$

The total state probability for s channels is:

$$P_s = \frac{\left(\frac{\lambda_{SG} + c\lambda_{NSG}}{\mu_{SG} + \mu_{NSG}}\right)^s}{s!} + \frac{(\lambda_{SG})^{(s-n)}(\lambda_{SG} + c\lambda_{NSG})^n}{s!(\mu_{SG} + \mu_{NSG})^s}P_o \tag{18}$$

The zeroth probability is calculated as:

$$P_0 = \frac{1}{\sum_{i=0}^{n}\frac{\left(\frac{\lambda_{SG} + c\lambda_{NSG}}{\mu_{SG} + \mu_{NSG}}\right)^i}{i!} + \sum_{i=n+1}^{s}\frac{(\lambda_{SG})^{(i-n)}(\lambda_{SG} + c\lambda_{NSG})^n}{i!(\mu_{SG} + \mu_{NSG})^i}} \tag{19}$$

The blocking probability for RVCS is:

$$p_{bSG} = \frac{\frac{\left(\frac{\lambda_{SG} + c\lambda_{NSG}}{\mu_{SG} + \mu_{NSG}}\right)^s}{S!} + \frac{(\lambda_{SG})^{(s-n)}(\lambda_{SG} + c\lambda_{NSG})^n}{S!(\mu_{SG} + \mu_{NSG})^s}}{\sum_{i=0}^{n}\frac{\left(\frac{\lambda_{SG} + c\lambda_{NSG}}{\mu_{SG} + \mu_{NSG}}\right)^i}{i!} + \sum_{i=n+1}^{s}\frac{(\lambda_{SG})^{(i-n)}(\lambda_{SG} + c\lambda_{NSG})^n}{i!(\mu_{SG} + \mu_{NSG})^i}} \tag{20}$$

whereas, $P_{b,NSG} = \sum_{n}^{s}P_j$ is the blocking probability for the RVCS model.

E. Switching based reserved and variable channel sharing

The SRVCS is an extension of model's VCS and RVCS. It states the switching capability to provide channels to NSG users or not. There are two cases which exist in this model; the one is $c = 0$ and $c \neq 0$.

For the case $c = 0$, this model works normally as VCS and RVCS where as for $c \neq 0$, SRVCS completely turns into SG mode where all NSG users are blocked. So, $P_{bNSG} = 1$ and blocking of SG users will be minimum. The blocking probability for SG users is as then calculated.

The blocking probability for SRVCS when $c = 0$ using VCS model is:

$$P_s = \frac{\frac{\left(\frac{\lambda_{SG}}{\mu_{SG} + \mu_{NSG}}\right)^s}{s!}}{\sum_{i=0}^{s}\frac{\left(\frac{\lambda_{SG}}{\mu_{SG} + \mu_{NSG}}\right)^i}{i!}} \tag{21}$$

The blocking probability for SRVCS when c = 0 using RVCS model is given as:

$$P_S = \frac{\frac{\left(\frac{\lambda_{SG}}{\mu_{SG}+\mu_{NSG}}\right)^s}{s!} + \frac{(\lambda_{SG})^{(s-n)}(\lambda_{SG})^n}{S!(\mu_{SG}+\mu_{NSG})^s}}{\sum_{i=0}^{n}\frac{\left(\frac{\lambda_{SG}}{\mu_{SG}+\mu_{NSG}}\right)^i}{i!} + \sum_{i=n+1}^{s}\frac{(\lambda_{SG})^{(i-n)}(\lambda_{SG})^n}{1!(\mu_{SG}+\mu_{NSG})^i}} \tag{22}$$

The above blocking probability completely blocks NSG users when c = 0. When c = 1, SRVCS will act as VCS or RVCS model.

3.2   Other Performance Parameters

A. Signal to interference plus noise ratio (SINR)

This is one of the most important quality of service parameters. The mathematical form for the SINR [12,13] is given as:

$$SINR = \frac{P_{fbs}G_{fbs}}{\sigma + \sum P_{fbs} + \sum P_{mbs}} \tag{23}$$

where, P_{fbs} is the transmission power of femtocell station; P_{mbs} is the transmission power of macrocell station; G_{fbs} is the channel gain and σ = noise power.

B. Path Loss (P_L)

Path loss is defined as the obstacles between the transmitter and receiver and it is different for the indoor and outdoor.

Case I: Pathloss [14, 15] between the macro base station and an user equipment is:

$$P_L = 15.3 + 37.6\log(d) + L_{ow} \tag{24}$$

where d is the distance between the transmitter and receiver and L_{ow} is outer walls for the case of outdoor it is set to zero.

Case II: Pathloss between the femto base station and an user equipment is:

$$P_L = \max(15.3 + 37.6\log(d), 38.46 + 20\log(d)) + 0.2d_{indoor} + 18.3n^{\left(\frac{n+2}{n+1}\right)-0.46} + qL_{iw} + L_{ow1} + L_{ow2} \tag{25}$$

where n = number of penetrated floors

q = number of walls separating apartments between the femto base station n and the user equipment.

d_{indoor} = distance inside the house.

L_{ow} and L_{iw} penetration loss of an outdoor and indoor wall which are set to 20 dB and 5 dB respectively.

C. Bit error rate (BER)

The BER of Shannon channel capacity is expressed as:

$$BER = 0.2exp\left(\frac{1.5SINR}{2^k - 1}\right) \tag{26}$$

where SINR is the signal to interference plus noise ratio, and k is the number of users.

D. Capacity or throughput

Capacity [16, 17] is the tight upper bound on the rate at which information can be reliably transmitted over a communication channel.

To calculate the capacity, we use:

$$C = B * \log_2(1 + \alpha SINR) \tag{27}$$

where B is the bandwidth, and $\alpha = \frac{-1.5}{\ln(5BER)}$

4 Results and Discussion

In this section, we summarize the results obtained for the different models for different performing parameters. For all the simulation of models mentioned in the Sect. 3 parameters that are considered are total number of channels are 50, offered traffic is equal to total number of channels considered, total service rate is set to the 3 min. For RCS and RVCS 70% of channels are reserved for the SG users. For the simulation of SINR, BER the parameters considered are micro transmit power is 43dBm, femtocell transmit power is 10dBm, noise power −174dBm/Hz, number of femtocell and microcell considered as 10 and 1.

Figure 7 illustrates the blocking probability for the equal channel sharing model for both categories of users. It is seen that the blocking probability for ECS model is same for SG and NSG because in this model there is no priority for SG or NSG users. In the figure, we also have RCS SG when 70% of the channels are reserved for SG. From the Fig., we see that out of 40 number of channels, when 5 channels are occupied; the blocking probability for the ECS is less that is performance is better. As the number of channel's occupation increases, the blocking of another user also increases. 70% of reserved channel in case of RCS is considered because, it is found to be approximately optimum. If, we reserve more percentage of channels, there is very small increment in the performance.

The result of VCS and RVCS is as shown in Fig. 8. The plot is drawn for the two cases, when c = 0 and c = 0.5. When c = 0, most of the NSG users will be blocked while SG users will experience minimum blocking (as can be seen in the Fig.). However, when c = 0.5, VCS and RVCS of both categories of user experience the almost same blocking.

Figure 9 illustrates the blocking performance for RVCS model for different values of c with 70% channel reservation for SG users. We have used c values from 0 to 0.8. As stated, c = 0 implies no NSG user while c = 1 implies presence of NSG user. It is seen that for smaller value of c, the blocking for SG users is minimum.

The performance of SRVCS is shown in Figs. 10 and 11. Figure 10 shows the performance for different values of c using VCS model for only SG blocking. It can be seen that when c = 0, blocking for SG users is minimum, as no NSG users are present. While, c = 0.5, the blocking of SG user increases since there will be presence of NSG users.

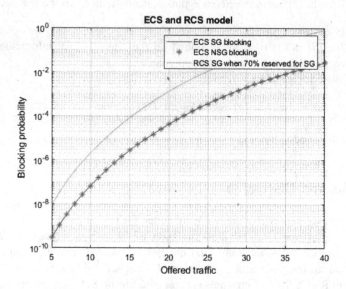

Fig. 7. Blocking probability of ECS and RCS (70%)

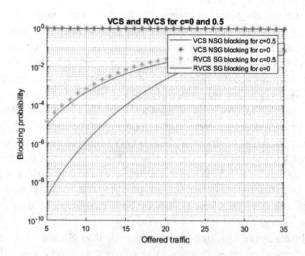

Fig. 8. Blocking probability of VCS and RVCS

Figure 11 shows the blocking probability for SRVCS using RVCS model when 70% of the channels are reserved for SG users in both cases (c = 0 and c = 0.5). It is seen that the performance in both cases are almost same except that when offered traffic is less, the SRVCS blocking performance for c = 0 is slightly better.

Figure 12 shows the BER performance over the number of femtocells. We considered some fixed value of path loss that is 0.2 and 0.5. It is seen that as the number of femtocell base station increases, the BER is decreased and it is slightly poorer when path loss is higher (0.5).

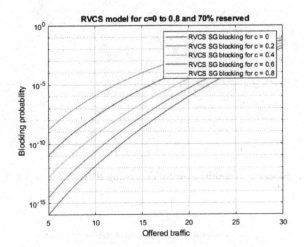

Fig. 9. Blocking probability of RVCS for different 'c'

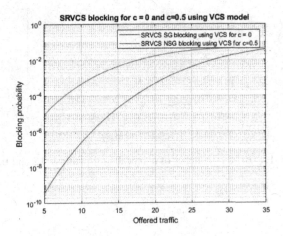

Fig. 10. Blocking probability for SRVCS using VCS for c = 0 & c = 0.5

Figure 13 shows the relation between the number of femtocells and the capacity (bit/Hz). It is seen that as the number of femtocell base station increases the capacity also increases. Of course, that seems obvious. However, when number of FAPs is less the difference in the capacity between path loss of 0.2 and 0.5 is small. But this difference in performance increases when FAPs are more.

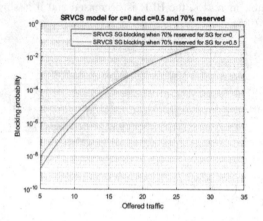

Fig. 11. Blocking probability for SRVCS using RVCS for c = 0 & c = 0.5

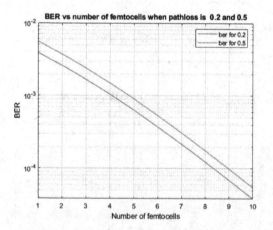

Fig. 12. BER vs Number of femtocells for pathloss 0.2 and 0.5

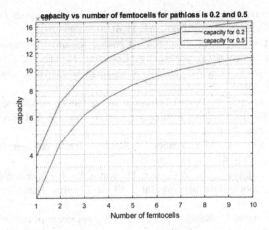

Fig. 13. Capacity vs Number of femtocells for pathloss 0.2 and 0.5

5 Conclusion

In this work various models of channel allocation for femtocell is studied and investigated for different cases like, presence of NSG users, percentage of reserved channel of SG and so on. It is found that 70% of reserved channel for SG is optimum. If we reserve more channel than 70%, the performance does not change significantly. It is also observed that when number of femtocell base stations is increased, the capacity as well as bit error performance is increased. However, interference is a limiting factor in this performance. The exact amount of limitation or effect by interference is not studied, but can be undertaken to observe the performance between QoS and number of FAPs which cause interference. Deployment of FAPs is another area of investigation which might be macrocell dependent and coverage area of it after actual field measurement.

References

1. Chandrasekhar, V., Andrews, J.G.: Femtocell networks: a survey. IEEE Commun. Mag. **46**(9), 59–67 (2008)
2. Elleithy, K., Rao, V.: Femto-cells: current status and future directions. Int. J. Next Gener. Netw. (IJNGN) **3**(1) March 2011
3. Zhang, Y.: Resource sharing of completely closed access in femtocell networks. In: IEEE Communications Society, April 2010
4. Cheung, W.C., Quek, T.Q.S., Kountouris, M.: Throughput optimization, spectrum allocation, and access control in two-tier femtocell networks. IEEE J. Sel. Areas Commun. **30**(3), 561–574 (2012)
5. Zhang, H., Jiang, D., Li, F., Liu, K., Song, H., Dai, H.: Cluster-based resource allocation for spectrum-sharing femtocell networks. IEEE Access **4**, 8643–8656 (2016)
6. Liu, Z., Li, S., Yang, H., Chan, K.Y., Guan, X.: Approach for power allocation in two-tier femtocell networks based on robust noncooperative game. IET Commun. **11**(10), 1549–1557 (2017)

7. Niu, C., Li, Y., Hu, R.Q., Ye, F.: Femtocell-enhanced multi-target spectrum allocation strategy in LTE-A HetNets. IET Commun. **11**(6), 887–896 (2017)
8. Usman, M.R., Usman, M.A., Shin, S.Y.: Channel resource allocation and availability prediction in hybrid access femtocells. Phys. Commun. **24**, 112–122 (2017)
9. Kim, J.-S., Lee, T.-J.: Handover in UMTS networks with hybrid access femtocells. In: ICACT, February 2010
10. Akinlabi, O.A., Joseph, M.: Signal behaviour in an indoor environment: femtocell over macrocell. In: 16th International Conference on Environment and Electrical Engineering (EEEIC). IEEE, June 2016
11. Ulhaq, S.A., Patidar, A.: Maximization of SINR in femto cell network. Int. J. Electr. Electron. Comput. Eng. **6**, 114–117 (2017)
12. Chiranjeevi, D., Rajakumar, B., Devender, M., Kiran, B.: Performance evaluation of LTE femtocell in an indoor cellular network. Int. J. Electr. Electron. Data Commun. **3**(2), 20–23 (2015)
13. Kurda, R., Boukhatem, L., Kaneko, M.: Femtocell power control methods based on Users context information in two-tier heterogeneous networks. EURASIP J. Wireless Commun. Network. **129**, 1–17 (2015)
14. Chaudhary, K.R., Arya, R.: Comparison of SINR in femtocell & macrocell network in macrocell environment. Int. J. Eng. Comput. Sci. **2**(8), 2476–2480 (2013)
15. Bouras, C., Kavourgias, G., Kokkinos, V., Papazois, A.: Interference management in LTE femtocell systems using an adaptive frequency reuse scheme. In: Wireless Telecommunications Symposium. IEEE, August 2012
16. Estrada, R., Jarray, A., Otrok, H., Dziong, Z.: Base station selection and resource allocation in macro–femtocell networks under noisy scenario. Wireless Netw. **20**(1), 115–131 (2014)
17. Akinlabi, O.A., Paul, B.S., Joseph, M., Ferreira, H.C.: A pricing policy to mitigate interference management in femtocell network. Int. J. Comput. Theor. Eng. **7**(3), 181–186 (2015)

System Level Performance Analysis of Designed LNA and Down Converter for IEEE 802.11ad Receiver

S. Pournamy and Navin Kumar[✉]

Department of Electronics and Communication Engineering,
Amrita School of Engineering, Amrita Vishwa Vidyapeetham, Bengaluru, India
navinkumar@ieee.org

Abstract. A low noise amplifier (LNA) operating at millimeter wave (mmWave) frequency and a down converter suitable for IEEE 802.11ad receiver is designed in a 65 nm radio frequency (RF)-CMOS low leakage (LL) process. These designed blocks are integrated in a super heterodyne receiver architecture and the overall performance of the receiver is analyzed. The designed LNA gives a performance metric of 20 dB of gain, 1.7 dB of noise figure (NF) and −7.78 dBm of IIP3. Modified Gilbert cell topology is used for down converter which gives a conversion gain of 1.5 dB from 57 GHz to 66 GHz, input P_{1dB} of −7.8dBm and IIP3 of 8.78 dBm with RF at 57.24 GHz from a 1.2 V supply voltage and a 1Vpp of local oscillator (LO) drive. The obtained IIP3 is 10.08 dB higher than the conventional Gilbert cell and offers an error vector magnitude (EVM) improvement of −23 dB at the receiver. This work provides RF designers a comprehensive understanding of system and circuit level on pre silicon base.

Keywords: Low noise amplifier · Radio frequency · Error vector magnitude

1 Introduction

The millimeter wave (mmWave) IEEE 802.11ad standard operating at 60 GHz offers very high throughput of multi Giga bit data [1]. The standard specifies 4 channels each with a bandwidth of 1.08 GHz and uses higher order (even up to 1024) of modulation. Although, mmWave based 5G cellular design would be quite different but developers and designers might use the skills and evaluation/measured data from this 802.11ad standard to understand the functionality of new generation networks [2]. The circuit and radio designer would consider some of the parameters and fine tune the circuits to operate perfectly in cellular system. With multi Giga bit data, the standard is likely to penetrate the indoor environment, hot-spot, airport like location; making it ubiquitous. However, the communication range is very limited to 10 m or so. Additionally, radio frequency (RF) components such as low noise amplifier (LNA), mixer in receiver and power amplifier in the transmitter chain play important role in the overall performance of the system.

© ICST Institute for Computer Sciences, Social Informatics and Telecommunications Engineering 2019
Published by Springer Nature Switzerland AG 2019. All Rights Reserved
N. Kumar and R. Venkatesha Prasad (Eds.): UBICNET 2019, LNICST 276, pp. 17–32, 2019.
https://doi.org/10.1007/978-3-030-20615-4_2

Design of RF components in this mmWave frequency with wide bandwidth, high linearity is challenging. RF impairments in each building block of the receiver would greatly affect the overall performance [3]. Furthermore, any block in the RF chain is heavily dependent on the other circuits [4]. Thus, a system level analysis becomes essential in order to satisfy the requirements of error vector magnitude (EVM) for the wireless standard 802.11ad. EVM measures the distance of the received signal points from the ideal location in a signal constellation and is used to quantify the performance of a transmitter or receiver. Additionally, the higher modulation schemes are adversely affected by RF impairments and reduce the acceptable data rate. This work mainly concentrates on design of RF components in the receiver such as LNA and down converter. The suitability of the designs is analyzed at system level for 802.11ad standard. Particular attention is paid to improve the noise figure, linearity and gain flatness of the receiver blocks.

In this work, a complete direct conversion and heterodyne architecture based transceiver is developed for IEEE 802.11ad [5] using our designed LNA and mixer. Common source (CS) cascade topology is used for LNA. Modified Gilbert cell topology is used for down converter. Various improvements, such as; gain, linearity and isolation are obtained by fine tuning the design. These values are improved from any existing design available in the literature. Furthermore, analysis of each module is carried out for the suitability of IEEE 802.11ad standard. The system level heterodyne receiver including the designed LNA and RF down converter offers an EVM of −32.24 dB for 802.11ad 16QAM baseband signal. A detailed RF budget analysis is carried out to validate the performance of the designed components of LNA and the mixer. The overall NF is 5.377 dB for a heterodyne receiver. IIP3 and SNR of the whole system is −9.688 dBm and 28.26 dB respectively.

The contents of the rest of the paper are as follows. Design of RF components such as LNA and down converter and its nonlinearity issues are described in Sect. 2. System level of heterodyne receiver for 802.11ad wireless standard and specification of each block are presented in Sect. 3. Simulation results and impact of nonlinearity of down converter on EVM are explained in Sect. 4 while, Sect. 5 concludes the paper.

2 Design of Receiver Components

2.1 Design of Low Noise Amplifier

LNA is an important component in any RF receiver and used for amplifying the signal level without increasing the noise floor. One of the key specifications of an LNA is its noise figure. The noise factor is the ratio of actual output noise to that which would remain if the device itself did not introduce noise. The noise figure is the noise factor expressed in decibels (dB) [6]. A common source cascode topology is used for implementing LNA. Though, the topology is common, modification is incorporated to fine tune and obtain enhanced performance. The schematic of 60 GHz LNA is shown in Fig. 1. The design is completed using 65 nm UMC low leakage, low threshold voltage, CMOS RF transistors (N_12_LLLVTRF). Important design equations of LNA are [7, 8]:

$$Z_{in} = j\omega\left(L_{dg} + L_{TL}\right) + \frac{1}{j\omega C_{gs}} + \frac{g_m L_{TL}}{C_{gs}} \tag{1}$$

$$LL_1 = \frac{1}{\omega^2(CC + C_{ds})} \tag{2}$$

where, Z_{in} is the input impedance. L_{TL} is the inductance corresponds to the transmission line, at the input (tlinp in Fig. 1), which is used to tune out $\mathrm{Im}\{Z_{in}\}$ along with degenerative inductor L_{dg}. C_{gs} and C_{ds} are the parasitic capacitances at the gate and drain. CC is the coupling capacitor between stages. Load inductance LL_1 resonates with CC and C_{ds} at the operating frequency ω.

The dimension of the transistors M_0, M_1 are $22 \times 1\,\mu m \times 60\,nm$. The second stage transistors are sized a bit larger in order to provide higher gain. Size of M_2 and M_3 is $26 \times 1\,\mu m \times 60\,nm$. A high transconductance g_m is obtained by maintaining high aspect ratio. Two middle inductors L_{m1} of 87pH and L_{m2} of 73pH are connected in the midway of the cascode structure. Together with parasitic capacitances of the transistors, it increases the unity current gain frequency, f_T to 260 GHz. Figure 2 shows the improvement in f_T with the presence of L_m. The inductors LL_1 of 160pH and LL_2 of 190pH are designed to resonate at fundamental frequency together with c_{ds} of M_1 and M_3 as in Eq. (2) [9]. L_i of 139pH is used for blocking the RF signal from going to the bias circuit. A 97pH of L_{dg} is connected as a degenerating inductor at the source of M_0.

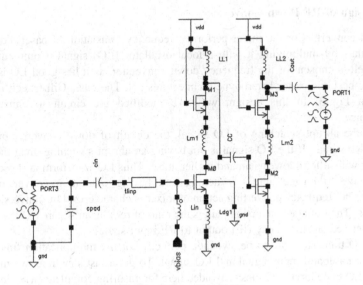

Fig. 1. Schematic of LNA

L_{dg} plays an important role in gain and the stability. A padding capacitance of 25fF, input and output capacitance of 55fF and 38fF respectively are selected as part of the matching network. A coupling capacitor between the stages is chosen to be 210fF to resonate at the operating frequency as in Eq. (2). The presented circuit is designed for a V_{DD} of 1.2 V.

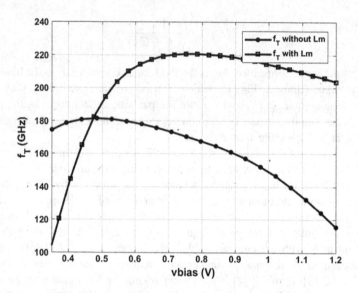

Fig. 2. Improvement on f_T with the presence of L_m.

2.2 Design of RF Down Converter

RF down converters or the mixer performs frequency translation of baseband modulated signals by multiplying it with a local oscillator (LO) signal. Commonly used Gilbert cell is chosen for the frequency down conversion as it has good LO isolation and is the best choice for heterodyne architectures [4]. The basic Gilbert cell mixer is shown in Fig. 3. In this design, we have modified the circuit to enhance the performance.

With the abrupt switching of LO signal, the circuit of down converter produces spurs of RF signal. If the LO signal is not having an abrupt switching, then the down converter will suffer a lower gain and higher noise. Thus LO waveform is chosen to be square wave to ensure abrupt switching and having maximum conversion gain (CG) [4]. The frequency converting action of mixer is characterized by conversion gain or the loss. The voltage conversion gain is the ratio of root mean square (RMS) voltage of the intermediate frequency (IF) output to RF input signal.

The LO transistors are to be switched perfectly for the multiplication function of modulated baseband input signal and LO signal. To get a fast slew rate, we made the swing of LO to be large. LO bias is avoided here for ensuring complete switching off of the balanced pair. Thus, the first step in the design was to device a switching transistor which gives an abrupt switching characteristics.

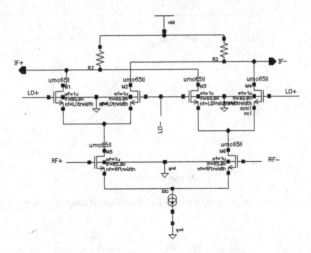

Fig. 3. Basic Gilbert cell down converter

The design uses 65 nm UMC low leakage low threshold voltage, CMOS RF transistors (N_12_LLLVTRF). Each transistor is chosen to have a length of 65 nm and width per finger of 1 μm. The analysis of switching characteristics is done for the carrier frequency of 58.32 GHz as LO frequency, the central frequency of channel 1 in IEEE802.11ad and assured a low rise time. The width of LO transistors (M_1, M_2, M_3, M_4) in Fig. 3 is chosen to be 13 μm with an LO peak to peak of 1 V.

The next step in the design of a down converter is to determine the appropriate size of the RF transistors to trade off noise figure and maximum frequency of oscillation (f_{max}). Maximum frequency of oscillation is commonly used as a figure of merit of the transistors and is defined as the frequency at which the extrapolated power gain falls to unity. The value of f_{max} depends on sizing, bias conditions, as well as transistor resistive loss and layout parasitic [9]. Figure 4 shows the tradeoff of f_{max} and NF.

The RF transistor width is varied from 0.5 μm to 50 μm. Figure 4 shows minimum noise figure and maximum unity gain frequency which can be achieved for a finger width of 17 μm to 30 μm. A supply voltage of 1.2 V and a bias voltage of 0.5 V is chosen [10]. After fixing the bias voltage and number of fingers for minimum NF and maximum f_{max}, the g_m of the RF transistors are made high to get a high conversion gain. The requirement has to be satisfied for a low V_{ds}. Since the power supply is only 1.2 V, there is no enough head room for the V_{ds} of the RF transistors to vary. The transistors are made in saturation region in order to obtain high g_m and low C_{gd} values. Thus as a conclusion, we need to choose a large width for providing high g_m, which will intern help to saturate the transistors at low V_{ds}. For low noise also, large width is preferred. Thus the width of the RF transistors is fixed at 28 μm.

Modified double balanced Gilbert cell is used to achieve high linearity and better return loss. The schematic diagram of the modified Gilbert cell is shown in Fig. 5. A pair of PMOS transistor M_7 and M_8 are used as active load and in order to achieve sufficient bandwidth and gain with the limited voltage head room available. These load transistors are biased to strong inversion region with a width of 29 μm.

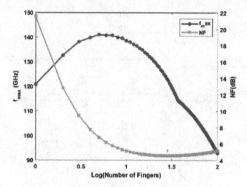

Fig. 4. f_{max} and NF variation with respect to Number of fingers of the RF transistor

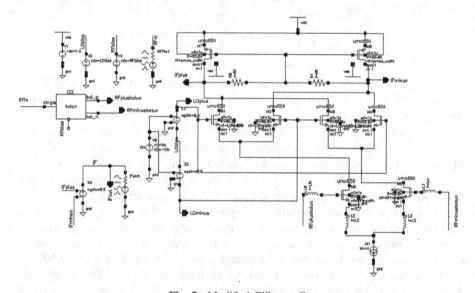

Fig. 5. Modified Gilbert cell

Feedback resistances, R_f is used at the load for high output impedance. This will prevent any decease of CG at low LO power. Degenerative inductors L_2, L_3 and L_0, L_1 at the RF input are used for matching the differential input 50 Ω. The design equation of the matching circuit is given as:

$$Z_{in} = j\omega L_2 + \frac{1}{j\omega C_{gs}} + \frac{g_m L_2}{C_{gs}} + j\omega L_0 \tag{3}$$

where, the variables have usual meaning. Equation 3 is derived with the assumption that C_{gd} is negligible and assume that node between source resistors is at virtual ground. For a perfect match and resonance, equate $\frac{g_m L_2}{C_{gs}}$ to 50 Ω and $\omega^2 = \frac{1}{(L_2 + L_0)C_{gs}}$, along with a transconductance, $g_m = 20.73$ m and $C_{gs} = 28.57$fF, L_2 and L_0 are calculated to be $2.0796 * 10^{-10} H$ and $1.891 * 10^{-11} H$ respectively.

2.3   Nonlinearity Issue of Down Converter

In this paper, the linearity issue in down converter is studied in detail. These RF impairments can be compensated only by the proper designing of RF components. For predicting the effect of RF impairments on receiver performance, a detailed analytical study is required. EVM, a measure of how far the constellation points are from the ideal locations can be evaluated using Eq. (4). The actual constellation points will deviate from its ideal locations by various imperfections in the implementation of transmitter and receiver.

$$EVM = \sqrt{\frac{E|v_o - v_{ref}|^2}{E|v_{ref}|^2}} \tag{4}$$

where v_o is the output of down converter and v_{ref} is the reference signal without any imperfections. Here the EVM variation due to the no idealities of the down converter is considered. Any non-linearity in the output of the down converter signal can be expressed as its baseband equivalent signal.

$$v_0 = a_1(v_I + jv_Q) + a_3\left(v_I^3 + jv_Q^3\right) \tag{5}$$

where a_1 and a_3 represent the linear and third order nonlinearity of the I/Q signal gains. IIP3 of a circuit and these gains are related to:

$$IIP3 = \sqrt{\frac{4}{3}\left|\frac{a_1}{a_3}\right|} \tag{6}$$

The reference signal will be compressed due to the nonlinearity present in the circuit.

$$v_{ref} = C(v_I + jv_Q) \tag{7}$$

where C is the compression factor and is defined as [11, 12]:

$$C = \sqrt{a_1^2 + 2a_1a_3k + a_3^2k^2} \tag{8}$$

and

$$k = \frac{v_I^3 + jv_Q^3}{v_I + jv_Q} \tag{9}$$

Substituting (7), (8) and (9) in to (4),

EVM due to IIP3 can be estimated as

$$\text{EVM}_{\text{IIP3}} = \frac{1}{C}\sqrt{(a_1 - C)^2 + 2(a_1 - C)a_3 k + a_3^2 k^2} \tag{10}$$

when there is no nonlinearity present, $a_3 = 0$ and $C = a_1$; and $\text{EVM}_{\text{IIP3}} = 0$ as expected.

Each impairment affects the overall EVM. The net EVM in a receiver is the contributions due to these circuit no idealities.

$$EVM_{overallR}^2 = EVM_{\Delta IQ}^2 + EVM_{LO}^2 + EVM_{IIP3}^2 \tag{11}$$

EVM due to the components in transmitter are not considered here. For example the EVM due to power amplifier's AM-AM conversion and AM-PM conversion are not included in the analysis. EVM degradation due to LO leakage is also discarded as it affects for direct conversion receivers only.

3   System Level Development of IEEE 802.11ad Receiver

A system level simulation of heterodyne receiver is carried out to suit the IEEE802.11ad standard. The frequency allocation of the four channels in 802.11ad and its central frequencies are as shown in Fig. 6. The channel extends from 57.24 GHz to 65.88 GHz and having four channels. Each channel is 1.08 GHz wide and having central frequencies as in Fig. 6. The analysis of RF components and the receiver are carrier out to ensure satisfactory performance in these four channels.

The performance metric of the receiver are error vector magnitude (EVM), signal to noise ratio (SNR), linearity, and the noise figure.

The main challenge in the design of RF components is to reduce EVM by reducing the RF impairments. A stand-alone LNA or down converter design is no longer meaningful as its performance heavily depends on the other circuits in the RF chain.

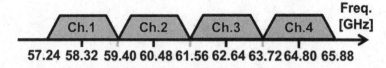

Fig. 6. Channels defined in IEEE 802.11ad standard

Figure 7 shows the architecture of the receiver and its analysis setup for the measurement of EVM in cadence virtuoso environment. The models and the measurement components are chosen from the rfLib.

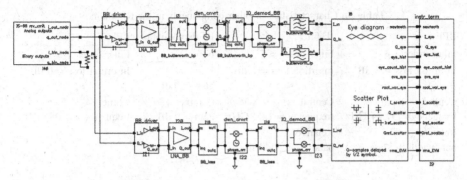

Fig. 7. Architecture of the receiver for IEEE 802.11 ad/ay and a system level performance analysis simulation set up for EVM.

System level receiver is analyzed with designed components and components from references. The obtained receiver EVM with the designed LNA along with mixers in the references are tabulated in Table 1. Table 2 lists the EVM of the receiver with designed down converter and some LNAs from literature. These values are tabulated for channel 1 of IEEE 802.11ad with an LO frequency of 58.32 GHz.

Table 1. Estimated EVM for the receiver with designed LNA along with mixers in references.

Designed LNA specifications	Down converter 1 specifications [5]	Down converter 2 specifications [13]	Down converter 3 specifications [14]
Gain = 20 dB	CG = 1 dB	CG = 0 dB	CG = 2 dB
NF = 1.7 dB	NF = 17 dB	NF = 16 dB	NF = 3 dB
IIP3 = −7.78 dBm	IIP3 = −7.5 dBm	IIP3 = 9.5 dBm	IIP3 = −8 dBm
EVM	−20.4087 dB	−27.5540 dB	−21.9024 dB

Table 2. Estimated EVM for the receiver with designed down converter along with mixers in references.

Designed down converter specifications	LNA 1 specifications [15]	LNA 2 specifications [16]
CG = 1.5 dB	Gain = 14.6 dB	Gain = 18.7 dB
NF = 7 dB	NF = 5.5 dB	NF = 5.2 dB
IIP3 = 8.78 dBm	IIP3 = −6.8 dBm	IIP3 = −6.5 dBm
EVM	−34.1053 dB	−31.9145 dB

The EVM is found to be −32.24 dB using the designed LNA and down converter along with other RF components. Specifications of the RF components other than LNA and down converter are listed in Table 3.

Table 3. Characteristics of other components in the RF chain.

BPF	IF filter	IQ demodulator	LPF
Filter order = 3	Filter order = 3	NF = 2	Filter order = 3
Insertion loss = 3 dB	Insertion loss = 1 dB	I mixer gain = 0 dB	Insertion loss = 0 dB
Central frequency = 57.24 GHz	Central frequency = 1.08 GHz	Q mixer gain = 0 dB	Corner frequency = 1.08 GHz
Relative bandwidth = 37 m	Relative bandwidth = 49 m		

4 Results and Discussions

4.1 Performance of LNA and Down Converter

The designed LNA has a uniform gain of 20 dB around the required band of interest as shown in Fig. 8(a). Input and output return losses S_{11} and S_{22} are both less than -10 dBm in 57–66 GHz band. Wide band matching is achieved using transmission lines. NF is

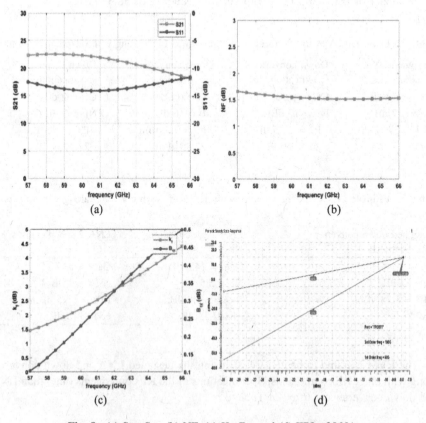

Fig. 8. (a) S_{21}, S_{11}, (b) NF, (c) K_f, B_{1f} and (d) IIP3 of LNA

approximately 1.7 dB as plotted in Fig. 8(b). Figure 8(c) shows that the stability factor (Rollet factor) k_f which is greater than 1 and the alternate stability factor B_{1f} is less than unity for the entire band of interest. Thus, the designed LNA has a very good stable characteristic as it satisfies the stability criteria [8, 17]. IIP3 of LNA is plotted in Fig. 8(d) and is found to be at −7.78 dBm.

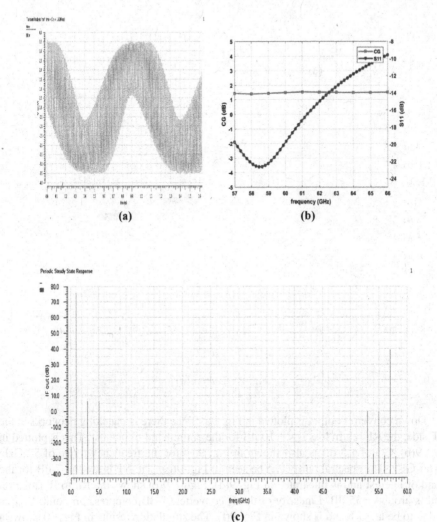

(a)

(b)

(c)

Fig. 9. (a) Mixer output and its spectrum, (b) CG vs RF frequencies and RL, (c) Spectrum of IF output signal, (d) NF for the down converter, (e) RF-IF isolation and (f) P_{1dB} of mixer

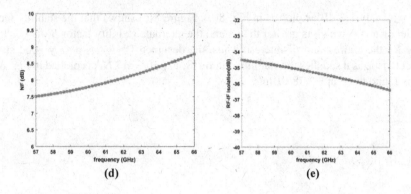

(d)   **(e)**

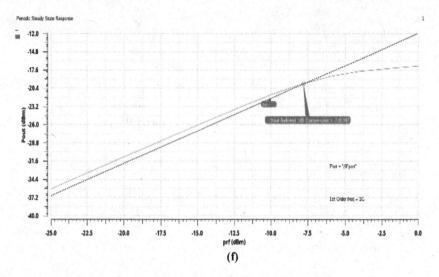

(f)

Fig. 9. (*continued*)

Down converter output is plotted in Fig. 9a. Since there is matching networks at the RF side, the RF return loss is < −10 dB for the entire band of interest. This is plotted in Fig. 9(b). CG of 1.5 dB is also shown in Fig. 9(b) for the frequency range of 57 GHz to 66 GHz. The spectral purity can be seen in Fig. 9(c). The NF is around 7 dB for the band of interest and is illustrated in Fig. 9(d). Figure 9(e) shows the RF to IF isolation and is around −35 dB. Linearity of down converter, 1 dB compression point, P_{1dB} is found to be at −7.8 and is shown in Fig. 9(f). The simulation results in Fig. 10 shows a significant linearity improvement of IIP3 while maintaining good CG and wide IF bandwidth. The IIP3 of the modified double balanced down converter is found to be at 8.78 dBm and is 10.08 dB more in compared to the conventional Gilbert cell topology having an IIP3 of −2.3 dBm.

Tables 1 and 2 in Sect. 3 also show the comparison of previously reported LNA and RF down converters in various technologies and topologies with the designed LNA and down converter.

4.2 Impact of Nonlinearity of Down Converter on Receiver Performance

The IIP3 of the down converter has been improved from −2.3 dBm to 8.78 dBm by modifying the commonly used Gilbert cell configuration. The EVM was found to be −9.213 dB, for an IIP3 of −2.3 dBm. By improving the linearity of the down converter to an IIP3 of 8.78 dBm, EVM has been reduced to −32.24 dB.

Figure 11 shows the simulated and analytical EVM improvement with respect to different IIP3 values. The deviation in graph is due to the contributions of other components such as EVM due to I/Q imbalance, $EVM_{\Delta Q}$, phase noise of local oscillator, EVM_{LO} as in Eq. (11). Those contributions can be considered as an additive term to the present EVM variation.

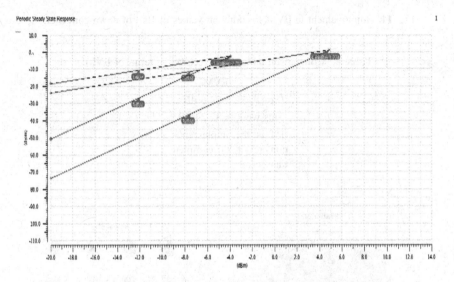

Fig. 10. IIP3 improvement in modified down converter

The constellation of 16QAM signal for EVM of −9.213 dB is shown in Fig. 12(a) and the constellation corresponding to an EVM of −32.24 dB is given in Fig. 12(b).

Table 4 shows the comparison table of receiver in terms of EVM for IEEE 802.11ad channel 1 for 16QAM with the results in [5]. In [5] a complete transceiver is implemented and the measured EVM was −24.6 dB, −23.9 dB, −24.4 dB and −26.3 dB for channel 1, 2, 3 and 4 respectively for 64QAM. For 16QAM, the EVM for the entire transceiver was measured to be −24.6 dB, −24.1 dB, −24.6 dB, −27.0 dB and −17.2 dB for channel 1, 2, 3, 4 and channel 1 to 4 bonding. A 7 dB improvement is observed in comparison with [5].

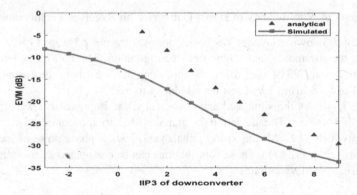

Fig. 11. Improvement in EVM for different values of IIP3 of down converter.

Table 4. Comparison table of the receiver in terms of EVM

	EVM
[5]	−24.6 dB
This work	−32.24 dB

[a][5] is the implementation result of complete transceiver.

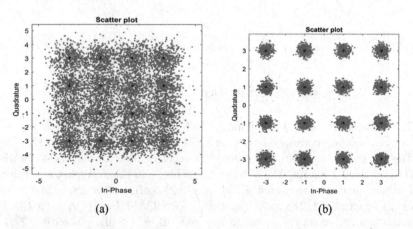

(a)   (b)

Fig. 12. Constellation of 16QAM for EVM of (a) −9.213 dB and (b) −32.24 dB.

RF budget is calculated for the cascaded receiver in Fig. 7 and is displayed in Fig. 13. The IIP3, NF, Gain of the entire receiver is −10.68 dBm, 5.597 dB and 14.83 dB respectively. SNR of the entire receiver is 28.04 dB. This is reasonably good for a 16QAM modulation to get a bit error rate of 10^{-15} [18].

```
           InputFrequency:  58.32 GHz
    AvailableInputPower:    -50 dBm
        SignalBandwidth:    1.08 GHz
             AutoUpdate:   true


Analysis Results
     OutputFrequency:  (GHz) [58.32    58.32    58.32     1.08     1.08]
         OutputPower:  (dBm) [  -30   -30.66  -33.66   -32.16   -35.17]
      TransducerGain:   (dB) [   20    19.34    16.34    17.84    14.83]
                 NF:   (dB) [  1.7      1.7    5.484    5.597    5.597]
               OIP3:  (dBm) [12.22    11.56    8.565    7.161     4.15]
               IIP3:  (dBm) [-7.78    -7.78    -7.78   -10.68   -10.68]
                SNR:   (dB) [31.94    31.94    28.16    28.04    28.04]
```

Fig. 13. RF budget of the receiver

5 Conclusion

An EVM of -32.24 dB is observed for 16QAM in channel 1 of IEEE802.11ad standard. SNR of the entire receiver is 28.04 dB. This is reasonably good performance for a 16QAM modulation to get a bit error rate of 10^{-15}. These performances are supported by flat gain characteristics of LNA and down converter. Designed LNA and down converter has a linearity of -7.78 dBm and 8.8 dBm of IIP3. A return loss lesser than -10 dB ensures the stability criteria. NF of 1.7 dB for LNA and 7 dB for the down converter is also observed. These are improved and optimum performance parameters (based on exhaustive simulation and analysis) for the standard with the modified LNA and mixer. However, with fabricated chip, the performance needs to be evaluated.

Funding Information.. This research work was supported by the Women Scientists Scheme A (WOS-A) SR/WOS-A/ET-82/2016 from Department of Science and Technology (DST), Government of India.

References

1. Kumar, C.S., Priyadharsini, A.R.A., Babuthirumangaialwar, E.: A multi giga bit speed wireless communication standard – IEEE 802.11ad. Int. J. Innov. Res. Sci. Eng. Technol. **3** (3), 1598–1601 (2014)
2. Radio Electronics. https://www.radio-electronics.com/info/wireless/wi-fi/ieee-802-11ad-microwave.php. Accessed 6 July 2018
3. Nitsche, T., Cordeiro, C., Flores, A.B., Knightly, E.W., Perahia, E., Widmer, J.C.: IEEE 802.11ad: directional 60 GHz communication for multi-Gbps Wi-Fi. IEEE Commun. Mag. **52**, 132–141 (2014)
4. Razavi, R.: RF Microelectronics, 2nd edn. Prentice Hall Communications Engineering and Emerging Technologies Series from Ted Rappaport (2013)
5. Wu, R., Minami, R., Tsukui, Y., Kawai, S., Seo, Y., Sato, S.: 64QAM 60 GHz CMOS transceivers for IEEE 802.11 ad/ay. IEEE J. Solid State Circuits **52**(11), 2871–2889 (2017)

6. Chen, H.K., Lin, Y.S., Lu, S.S.: Analysis and design of a 1.6–28-GHz compact wideband LNA in 90-nm CMOS using a π-match input network. IEEE Trans. Microw. Theory Tech. **58**(8), 2092–2104 (2010)
7. Prameela, B., Daniel, A.E.: Design of low noise amplifier for IEEE standard 802.11b using cascode and modified cascode techniques. Procedia Technol. **25**, 443–449 (2016)
8. Pournamy, S., kumar, N.: Design of 60 GHz broadband LNA for 5G cellular using 65 nm CMOS technology. In: 7th International Conference on Communication Systems and Network Topologies (CSNT), Nagpur, pp. 320–324 (2017)
9. Pozar, D.: Microwave engineering, 3rd edn. Wiley, Hoboken (2012)
10. Singh, S., Vasudevamurthy, R., Kumar, N.: Design of wideband 5G millimeter wave mixer in CMOS 65 nm. Accepted in 7th International Conference on Advances in Computing, Communications and Informatics (ICACCI 2018), pp 19–22, September 2018
11. Nassery, A., Ozev, S., Slamani, M.: Analytical modeling for EVM in OFDM transmitters including the effects of IIP3, I/Q imbalance, noise, AM/AM and AM/PM distortion. In: 2013 18th IEEE European Test Symposium (ETS), Avignon, pp. 1–6 (2013)
12. Gupta, A.K., Buckwalter, J.F.: Linearity considerations for low-EVM, millimeter-wave direct-conversion modulators. IEEE Trans. Microw. Theory Tech. **60**(10), 3272–3285 (2012)
13. Zhu, F., Hong, W., Chen, J.-X., Jiang, X., Wu, K.: A broad band low power millimeter wave CMOS down conversion mixer with improved linearity. IEEE Trans. Circuits Syst. **61**(3), 138–142 (2014)
14. Zhang, F., Skafidas, E., Shieh, W.: A 60 GHz double balanced Gilbert cell down conversion mixer on 130 nm CMOS. In: 2007 IEEE Radio Frequency Integrated Circuits (RFIC) Symposium, Honolulu, HI, USA. IEEE (2007)
15. Lee, C.-H., Choi, W., Kim, J.-H., Kwon, Y.-W.: A 77 GHz 3-stage low noise amplifier with cascode structure utilizing positive feedback network using 0.13 μm CMOS process. JSTS: J. Semicond. Technol. Sci. **8**(4), 289–294 (2008)
16. Yao, T., Gordon, M., et al.: Algorithmic design of CMOS LNAs and PAs for 60-GHz radio. IEEE J. Solid State Circuits **42**(5), 1044–1057 (2007)
17. Kraemer, M., Dragomirescu, D., Plana, R.: A low-power high-gain LNA for the 60 GHz band in a 65 nm CMOS technology. In: 2009 Asia Pacific Microwave Conference, Singapore, pp. 1156–1159 (2009)
18. Homepage Dsp log, http://www.dsplog.com/2007/12/09/symbol-error-rate-for-16-qam/, last accessed 2018/7/6

Optimizing Multi Gateway Wireless Mesh Networks for Throughput Improvement

Soma Pandey[1]([⊠]), Govind Kadambi[1], and Vijay Pande[2]

[1] Faculty of Engineering and Technology, MSRUAS, Bangalore, India
soma.p@ieee.org
[2] School of Engineering, Amrita Vishwa Vidyapeetham, Bangalore, India

Abstract. This paper applies the concept of subnet virtualization to the edge network comprising of the multi-gateway Wi-Fi mesh. A necessary and sufficient condition for improving the throughput of Wi-Fi mesh network (WMN) is proposed in the paper. A holistic approach of optimizing the mesh topology by fair distribution of gateways (GW) is developed. Subnets (partitions) are created within the mesh such that each partition has one GW and approximately equal amount of Mesh Routers. Thereafter an overload estimation process is defined which indicates the instance when the WMN is overloaded and a Load Management Scheme (LMS) has to be applied. A Steady State Load equation is derived based on the current processing load of each GW. Thereafter a stability condition is defined which can avoid triggering chain of load transitions from one neighbor GW to another. Simulation studies presented in the paper show that after providing a conventional WMN with the features of the proposed LMS, the throughput became more than double, there was a decrease of 22% in the average packet delay and a decrease of 90% in the number of packets dropped.

Keywords: Wi-Fi mesh · IEEE802.11s · Optimizing mesh networks ·
Multiple gateway load balancing · Virtualization

1 Introduction

The IEEE 802.11s [1, 2] Wi-Fi mesh standard has still not been able to gain the kind of popularity that is enjoyed by its low data rate counterpart; the sensor mesh networks. The main focus of mesh networks is to extend the coverage of Wi-Fi through use of routers. IEEE 802.11s standard gave lot of hope to increase coverage of Wi-Fi broadband but could not gain much traction. Some of the reasons for the standard not gaining popularity are following

- Throughput drops with increase in number of hops [3]
- There is no guarantee of minimal Quality of Service (QoS) support in order to present it as a commercial network
- The standard proposes multiple Internet Access Points (Gateways). Increasing the number of GWs need not increase the throughput necessarily. In fact, in some cases multiple GWs might reduce throughput at some of the MRs due to GW contention issues as proved in [4]

© ICST Institute for Computer Sciences, Social Informatics and Telecommunications Engineering 2019
Published by Springer Nature Switzerland AG 2019. All Rights Reserved
N. Kumar and R. Venkatesha Prasad (Eds.): UBICNET 2019, LNICST 276, pp. 33–52, 2019.
https://doi.org/10.1007/978-3-030-20615-4_3

Devising a suitable MR-GW association process which also incorporates load management amongst multiple GWs is important to achieve better throughput and thereby better QoS in WMNs. This process should be efficient enough to be able to fairly allocate MRs to GWs with low time complexity. Various methods for load balancing and allocation of GWs are available in literature. Some of the papers on load balancing include [5–8]. The main disadvantage of these schemes is their requirement to calculate and save all possible alternative paths to the available GWs. Implementing such schemes results in creating large overheads in both time and space.

In this paper the concept of load sharing in WMNs is proposed. The major advantage of load sharing over load balancing is the elimination of repeated path computations between the MRs and GWs. Conventional load management in WMN is performed continuously thereby consuming the resources actually meant to be used for Internet traffic. Such schemes have high computational time complexity. Therefore there is need for a load aware GW scheduling mechanism. The major challenges in load aware GW scheduling are

- High computational time complexity of scheduling algorithm
- Large packet processing and queuing delays

This paper proposes to overcome these challenges by 'fixed partitioning' and 'load sharing'. Instead of the conventional method of combining the GW scheduling with load balancing, this paper proposes to perform both of these processes independently. Initially partitioning is performed to define a GW and its associated MRs. If load demand of a partition exceeds maximum capacity of its GW, then some MRs are shifted/transited to a less loaded neighbouring partition. This process is called load sharing amongst the GWs.

Another novelty of this paper lies in the fact that none of the literature presents such a detailed study on effect on the throughput of network when the number of Mesh Routers (MRs) is fixed and the number of GWs is increased systematically. Similarly the study also investigates the change in throughput of WMN when number of GWs is kept fixed and number of MRs is increased. This kind of simulation study is very valuable for network planning and designing and correct assessment of change in throughput values with change in number of load generating MRs and load processing GWs.

Section 2 of the paper presents a brief overview of the present IEEE 802.11s mesh architecture. Thereafter it is explained how this architecture can be optimised by the work proposed in this paper. A comparison of the present and the optimised mesh architecture is provided in Figs. 1 and 2. The next Sect. 3 builds the framework to optimise the WMN through Partitioning and load management procedures. Section 3.1 describes partitioning procedure and Sect. 3.2 describes the load management scheme for load optimisation and load sharing within the WMN. Lost nodes and redundant nodes are a possibility when nodes are transited from one partition to another during load management. Section 3.3 extends the proposed partitioning and LMS to map it onto a matrix representation. This matrix representation helps in validating maintaining integrity of mesh topology by providing a check on lost nodes or redundant nodes. Section 4 provides a comparative performance analysis of the mesh throughput obtained in the existing IEEE 802.11s WMN as compared to the throughput obtained in a WMN which is optimised after applying the proposed LMS. In the end, Sect. 5 and Sect. 6 provide conclusions on this work and future extensions of the proposed LMS respectively.

2 Proposed Architecture

This paper proposes city wide Wi-Fi mesh based on IEEE 802.11s standard for WMNs. This standard is compatible to any Wi-Fi (IEEE 802.11x) based end node. The only changes needed will be on the routers and the Network Operation Centre (NOC). The solution addresses QoS provisioning within the WMN through load management. The novelty lies in the proposed architecture as it serves the purpose of deploying single WMN for entire city.

This is achieved in this paper as explained next. First a topology is defined for the WMN which addresses the GW parenting issue. The topology is based on well-defined partitions/service clusters around the GWs. A partitioning algorithm is developed by modifying the Ciarlet and Lamour's graph partitioning algorithm [9] for WMNs with multiple GWs. This was published in [4] by the authors. This partitioning algorithm leverages the matrix representation of graphs for marking and collecting MRs for each partition. To achieve this a node marking algorithm is developed [10]. The partitioning algorithm defines partitions with the GW and a set of MRs around it. The algorithm ensures that each partition has exactly one GW and a set of nodes (MRs) which will be serviced by the GW. The algorithm also computes and assigns nearly same number of MR to each GW to ensure fairness in GW scheduling. This is explained in Sect. 3.1 of this paper.

Once the partitions are in place a mechanism has to be drafted to prevent overloading of the partitions. For this each partition has to be monitored for load. A load monitoring and overloading condition called the Steady State Load (SSL) condition is defined based on the load on each GW. If the SSL condition is violated then load management has to be performed. Overload is managed by moving some MRs from one partition to another. This is achieved by updating the routing table entries managed at each GW. This is explained in Sect. 3.2 of the paper.

The partitions generated by the partitioning algorithm are further mapped onto the matrix model of the WMN graph. The purpose of mapping partitions onto a single WMN matrix is to provide a unified model to represent the partitions of the WMN. A validation equation is formulated which is required to ensure that there are no lost nodes/partitions [18]. The purpose of maintaining a matrix model, is to monitor a subnet GW connectivity and link through the adjacency matrix of the subgraph. This solution also proposes using of validation equation defined on the matrix model of the partitioned WMN. Violation of the validation equation means there are lost nodes or redundant nodes in the system. The validation equation also keeps check on the security aspect of the network wherein no additional malicious MRs can be added to the network. This is explained in Sect. 3.3 of the paper.

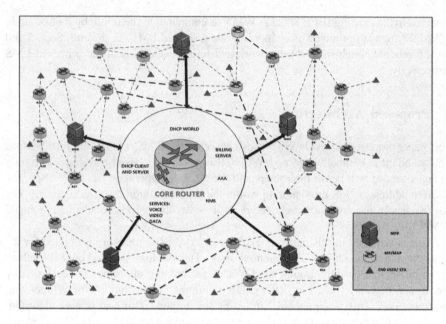

Fig. 1. A generic 802.11s network. (Color figure online)

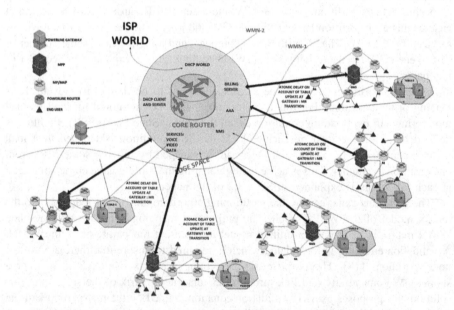

Fig. 2. Optimized 802.11s network with QoS guarantees. (Color figure online)

Figures 1 and 2 give an idea of the topology of Conventional WMN and the WMN obtained after applying the proposed LMS. Figure 1 presents a generic 802.11s network as defined by the IEEE. One may observe that a generic 802.11s network has

Mesh Portal Points (this is IEEE 802.11s term for gateway) shown as boxes in Fig. 1, connect to the Internet through a high bandwidth wired connection. On the other side these MPP are connected to the Mesh Points (this is IEEE 802.11s term for MRs) and Mesh access Points (this is IEEE 802.11s term for those MR which also cater to Wi-Fi clients or end devices) through wireless links. The green color triangles denote the end user devices which can be laptop, smart phone or any other Wi-Fi enabled service. The concept here is to show that the generic IEEE 802.11s can connect distant devices to Internet through multiple wireless hops thereby increasing the coverage area of the Wireless Local Area Network. This property allows for installation of city wide networks.

Figure 2 presents the proposed architecture which attempts to optimize the existing 802.11s mesh network so as to accommodate diverse networks with QoS guarantees. Unlike Fig. 1; Fig. 2, has well defined groups of Mesh Points/Mesh Access Points. In this paper Mesh Points/Mesh Access Points will be collectively called the MRs. Each group has been provided a dedicated Mesh Portal Point (GW) to serve. Therefore these are called the partitions. In a similar extension these partitions can also be thought of composed of other networks also. This network is generically denoted as WMN.

3   Optimizing the IEEE 802.11s WMN

Partitioning of WMN such that each GW has well defined service set, results in better throughput [4]. But since these multiple GWs have their own service set therefore they cannot serve other MRs outside their service set even when they are idle and other GWs are overloaded. This results in unfair scheduling of multiple GWs [20]. In order to have efficient use of all resources and to prevent overloading and drop in QoS it is suggested to manage load amongst the GWs. Load management will be dealt with in later sections. The next section describes the partitioning of WMN.

3.1   Partitioning the WMN

The initial arrangement of partitioned WMN, obtained after applying the modified Ciarlet and Lamour algorithm [9], is taken as reference point. This partitioning of network can be done in planning and deployment phase. Partitioning is done over Graph model of WMN wherein the MRs represent the vertices (nodes) of the graph and wireless links between the vertices represent the graph edges [12]. Network is partitioned by performing graph walk using Breadth First Search [12]. This procedure is called 'node marking'. Node marking has been explained in detail in [10]. An innovative method of node marking especially defined for wireless networks is available in [10].

Every time a partition is to be created the graph walk begins from an unmarked GW node and ends when fair number of nodes required to create a partition are marked and collected. These MRs along with the GW constitute one partition. This procedure is repeated for every unmarked GW till all the GWs have formed a partition with required number of MRs. This greedy procedure for partition formation is summarized in next paragraph.

Let total number of partitions required be k, number of nodes per partition will be $n_i = \lfloor \frac{n}{k} \rfloor$, where n_i is number of nodes in partition i then, $n = \sum_{i=1}^{k} n_i$. In order to differentiate GW nodes from ordinary nodes, they are pre-marked and are kept in a list of GWs (GW_list). Let V_i be the set of nodes in i^{th} partition (analogous to the ordered set S in NMA). The greedy procedure for partition formation is summarized as follows

1. Select a GW node (already marked in the adjacency matrix) from the GW_list
2. Create this node as start node for the partition in question
3. Accumulate descendants of the GW for the partition in question using the NMA
4. Stop if total number of accumulated nodes = $\lfloor \frac{n}{k} \rfloor$

Detailed algorithm along with pseudocode and comparison study is available in [4]. After partitioning the network is booted up and the GWs start processing network data packets. The normal functioning of WMN continues until one of the GWs gets congested and overloaded. In such a condition load sharing has to be performed. In coming sections we first define congestion of GWs and derive a mathematical equation to define overloading of GWs. Thereafter we present a load management scheme based on load sharing among the GWs.

3.2 Load Management Scheme (LMS) Among the Partitions of WMN for QoS

In this section a LMS is devised through which the GWs can be utilized efficiently and overloading among the GWs can be prevented. The LMS is aimed at maintaining nominal load for GW. Each GW has processing load of the packets being directed to it through the MRs which are assigned to its partition. Initially a steady state load (SSL) condition is derived. If this condition is violated then it implies overloading of one or more of the WMN GWs. Load management is done by identifying and reducing the load of the overloaded GWs by shifting its MRs to a neighboring partition having GW with lesser load. The next subsection defines process for computing load of each partition.

Load Monitoring and Overload Condition
Following assumptions on load and traffic will apply for the rest of the paper

- **Full Coverage:** The term full coverage means that all the MRs must be served by a GW. This requires each MR to be assigned only one GW. Further no MR should be left isolated so that no GW is assigned to it. The assigned GW is treated as the default GW by the MR and it routes all its traffic through it until the assigned GW gets overloaded. On overloading of the assigned GW, the MR is assigned another less loaded GW by the proposed LMS. But at no point, is there a situation where an MR is not covered by a GW.
- **GW Throughput:** All GWs can process data as per their maximum throughput W_{gw}, defined by the Eq. (2) in next paragraph. When the MRs and their traffic demand increases, the corresponding GWs become overloaded. In such circumstances, the proposed LMS moves some MRs from the overloaded GW partition to another partition which has GW with a load lesser than its capacity.

- **MR Throughput:** Similar to the GWs, even the MRs have a maximum throughput. As indicated in Fig. 3, all the MRs direct their local traffic as well as the relay traffic towards their assigned GWs. Since the MR has multiple paths to reach the GW, it can always select the best alternative with the help of Air Time Link Metric (ATLM) computed by the path selection process of the routing protocol. In case a particular MR gets congested and overloaded, it need not accept the relay traffic. In such a situation, the relay traffic can be rerouted through other MRs having better ATLM. The process of reducing congestion at the MRs is far simpler as it is an inbuilt mechanism by which packets are not routed through a neighbor if its ATLM is poor. MR congestion being a localized problem can be solved by the underlying path selection mechanism easily and does not significantly disturb the mesh traffic and its topology.

It is assumed that the NICs associated with each of the m edges of the network graph, denoting wireless links can have separate transmit and receive frequency bands of operation. The physical location of a vertex (GW or MR) $v_i \in V$ is static after deployment and its co-ordinates are denoted by (X_i, Y_i). Additionally each vertex $v_i \in V$ is connected to a power supply which is not subjected to power constraint. Representation of number of non-interfering channels through a notation in set theory can be written as Eq. (1)

$$CH = \{1, 2, \ldots, c\} \tag{1}$$

Where c is the number of non-interfering channels in the wireless system which varies from one wireless standard to another (for IEEE 802.11b value of $c = 3$). Two vertices (MRs or GWs) are connected by an edge if and only if they are within the transmission range of each other and they can communicate on the same channel.

Capacity of a GW: In a WMN, the maximum capacity of a GW is

$$W_{gw} = \sum_{i=1}^{|\rho(v_{gw})|} w_i \tag{2}$$

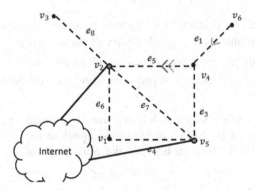

Fig. 3. A WMN graph and its traffic. (Color figure online)

Where, w_i bits/s is the data rate of channel $i \in CH$ and $|\rho(v_{gw})|$ is number of wireless interfaces configured on a GW denoted by $v_{gw} \; \forall \; gw = 1 \cdots k$. This is because at a given time slot, there are at most $|\rho(v_{gw})|$ (where, $|\rho(v_{gw})| \leq c$) interfaces in a GW that can simultaneously transmit and receive data packets to/from its neighbouring MRs.

Given an MR $v_i \in V$, its traffic may include two parts as shown in Fig. 3.

- Local Internet traffic: This traffic is generated by various mobile devices such as laptops and smartphones which use the MRs as AP.
- Relayed Internet traffic: This is the traffic that is generated by other MRs which are further away from the GW as compared to MR v_1. Such MRs route their traffic through v_1 thereby adding to its local load.

In Fig. 3, all traffic is directed towards the GWs v_2 and v_5. For example MR v_6 can send its traffic to Internet through GW v_2 via MR v_4 considering it as an optimal path. In such a case traffic at MR v_4 will be its local Internet traffic which is depicted with a blue color in addition to relay traffic of v_6 depicted in red color.

Therefore the *bandwidth demand* d_i in terms of the local and relay traffic [13–16] is given by

$$d_i = local(v_i) + relay(v_i) \tag{3}$$

And *load on a GW* denoted by R_{gw} is defined as the current processing requirement of the GW and can be computed by Eq. (4).

$$R_{gw} = \sum_{i=1}^{p} d_i \tag{4}$$

Where p is number of MRs assigned to the GW (number of MRs within the partition to which the GW belongs) and d_i is the bandwidth demand at MR v_i.

Derivation of Supergraph for Load Monitoring in a WMN

- A threshold load equation has to be derived which if violated results in invocation of the load sharing process. This section defines a structure called Supergraph from the graph model of WMN to monitor the load state of WMN. The term Supergraph is derived from the fact that it is a graph derived from subgraphs of partitioned WMN.
- A *Supergraph* of G is denoted by G^2 because it can be perceived as a second order graph of G. Formally a super graph $G^2(V^2, \mathcal{E}^2)$ is defined as a graph with set of vertices V^2 which represent each partition (sub graph) and a set of edges $\mathcal{E}^2$ such that an edge uv $\in \mathcal{E}^2$ if and only if partitions u and v are connected to each other by at least one edge.

The process to derive a Supergraph is explained by using the partitioned WMN of Fig. 4. The WMN of Fig. 4 has five GWs and therefore five partitions are created around these five GWs. This implies that the Supergraph of Fig. 5 will have five vertices corresponding to the subgraphs $\mathcal{G}_1, \mathcal{G}_2, \ldots, \mathcal{G}_5$. Therefore $\mathcal{V}^2 = \{\mathcal{G}_1, \mathcal{G}_2, \ldots, \mathcal{G}_5\}$ and there will be 6 edges corresponding to $\mathcal{G}_1\mathcal{G}_2, \mathcal{G}_1\mathcal{G}_3, \mathcal{G}_2\mathcal{G}_3, \mathcal{G}_2\mathcal{G}_4, \mathcal{G}_3\mathcal{G}_5$ and $\mathcal{G}_4\mathcal{G}_5$ since these partitions are connected to each other by one or more edges.

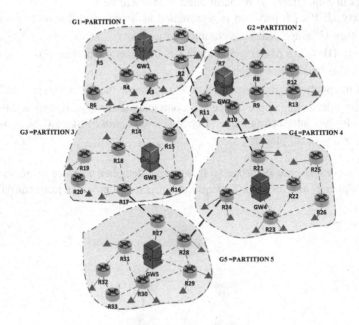

Fig. 4. A partitioned WMN. (Color figure online)

Whereas, there will be no edges connecting $\mathcal{G}_1\mathcal{G}_5$ and $\mathcal{G}_2\mathcal{G}_5$ because they do not have any edges between them. Therefore $|\mathcal{V}^2| = 5$ and $|\mathcal{E}^2| = 6$ and the resultant Supergraph is shown in Fig. 5.

Only the MRs which are in the communication range (denoted by a connecting edge) of a neighbor partition can be transited. In this case, if partition 5 gets overloaded than it can either transit R_{27} to partition 3 or R_{28} to partition 4. Since graph model for load management involves transition of traffic bearing MRs, these MRs are presumed to be active. But before performing load sharing, an overload condition has to be defined. Also to avoid chain transitions for load sharing a stability condition has to be defined. If these conditions are satisfied then only the MRs can be transited to neighborhood. Next sections present these conditions.

It can be noted in Fig. 4 that the actual partitions represent their connectivity using red color edges which represent various wireless links whereas the black color edges represent the connectivity between the partitions. These are virtual links which are further used to create the Supergraph of Fig. 5. It may be noted that each vertex V_i^2 of the supergraph is formed by contraction of a subgraph $\mathcal{G}i$ which has n_i number of nodes. For the WMN and its Supergraph corresponding to Figs. 4 and 5, it may be seen that $\mathcal{G}_1$ has $n_1 = 7$ nodes (1 GW and 6 MRs), similarly $\mathcal{G}_2$ has $n_2 = 8$ nodes (1 GW and 7 MRs) and so on.

Properties of Supergraph

The following properties can be derived for the Supergraph of a partitioned WMN

Property I: A WMN with k GWs will have k partitions and therefore number of vertices in Supergraph $\mathcal{G}^2$ of partitioned WMN will be k.

Property II: If each partition is represented as a node and this node is of degree $k-1$, then $\mathcal{G}^2$ graph will be a complete graph[1].

Property III: $\mathcal{G}$ is a planar graph and $\mathcal{G}^2$ is its Supergraph, then if $\mathcal{G}$ is planar then $\mathcal{G}^2$ will also be a planar graph

About property III: By contradiction let us assume that $\mathcal{G}^2$ is non planar. Then $\mathcal{G}^2$ will have intersecting edges. Since $\mathcal{G}$ is contracted to form $\mathcal{G}^2$, therefore this implies that $\mathcal{G}$ also has intersecting edges. Hence $\mathcal{G}$ is *non-planar*. Since $\mathcal{G}(\mathcal{V}, \mathcal{E})$ is planar, therefore $\mathcal{G}^2$ is also planar.

Note: As a consequence of property II one may decipher a complete graph like K_5 graph (non-planar) as a resultant Supergraph. Property III provides justification on this.

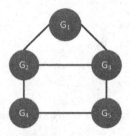

Fig. 5. Supergraph of the WMN of Fig. 4.

SSL and Stability Conditions on Supergraph for Load Sharing

In this section a condition is derived to monitor load imbalance in WMN. This condition is called the SSL condition. Later in this section a stability condition is derived to check if the load sharing can be performed without making the WMN unstable. Suppose $Q(\mathcal{G}_i)$ be the generic service limits[2] defined on subgraph $\mathcal{G}_i$. The generic service limit can be any parameter which might be requiring monitoring and control. The word generic is suggestive of using any threshold value based on formula which can be derived for a combination of various QoS parameters. The floor and ceiling do not imply the strict mathematical operation but these operators indicate those cases wherein the QoS parameters are specified within a range. In such case, the higher range is indicated by the ceiling operator and lower range is indicated by the floor operator. Although load on GWs is one such parameter which is mainly considered in this paper,

---

[1] A complete graph is defined as a simple graph which has connecting edge between all possible pair of vertices.

[2] Generic Service Limit can be QoS with respect to the network under consideration.

but network designers may like to derive some other complex parameter. This is the reason why the discussion on parameters are kept as generic as possible. In this paper the service limit is assumed as the processing capacity of a GW (Eq. 1).

To derive the SSL condition it is needed to define the binary limits on $Q(\mathcal{G}_i)$. The upper and lower limits are also suggestive of defining upper and lower service value which can be derived for a combination of various QoS parameters. Let U_i be the upper service limit where, $U_i = \lceil Q(\mathcal{G}_i) \rceil$. In this case the **maximum capacity** of GW as per Eq. (1) is assumed to be the upper service value. Let L_i be the lower service limit where $L_i = \lfloor Q(\mathcal{G}_i) \rfloor$. **Lower processing limit** can be defined by network planner on the basis of the minimal processing load within the network. This load could comprise of the minimum network management traffic, back-end traffic or protocol related traffic. Mainly it is that processing load of the network which is not generated by end-user. This means that if any vertex of the Supergraph begins to operate at U_i then the GW in partition $\mathcal{G}_i$ must transit some of its MRs to GW of a neighbouring partition $\mathcal{G}_j$ which has operating load of L_j (lower limit of load). But this transition of MRs cannot be done continuously or else it will be an overhead on the system. Therefore a threshold load condition has to be established on the WMN. This is called the *SSL condition* for load monitoring. If this condition is violated then the load sharing process has to be invoked.

SSL Condition for Load Monitoring

Let the existing (present) demand of a partition be denoted by R_i. The inequality $\|R\|^2 \leq \sum_{i=1}^{k} L_i U_i$ must hold true for a WMN to work at the nominal load

Derivation: As it is evident from earlier explanations that $L_i \leq R_i \leq U_i \forall i = 1 \cdots k$ must hold true for all the GWs to work at a nominal load. This implies that for nominal load condition the average[3] demand for all k partitions should satisfy the following inequality

$$R_1^2 \leq L_1 U_1 \tag{5}$$

$$R_2^2 \leq L_2 U_2 \tag{6}$$

$$\vdots$$

$$R_k^2 \leq L_k U_k \tag{7}$$

Summing up the load of individual partitions will give nominal working load for the whole WMN

$$R_1^2 + R_2^2 + \cdots + R_k^2 \leq L_1 U_1 + L_2 U_2 + \cdots + L_k U_k \tag{8}$$

$$\Rightarrow \|R\|^2 \leq L_1 U_1 + L_2 U_2 + \cdots + L_k U_k \tag{9}$$

---

[3] The geometric mean is more appropriate than the arithmetic mean for describing proportional growth like increasing bandwidth demand of Internet [17].

Where, R is the average working load of the whole mesh (WMN). Therefore for SSL operation, nominal load of mesh must satisfy the following inequality

$$\|R\|^2 \le \sum_{i=1}^{k} L_i U_i \tag{10}$$

Therefore the core router which is sending and receiving traffic to the WMN keeps a check on R and the moment value of R violates the Eq. (10), it invokes the load sharing process. In next section, a detailed simulation study is performed to ascertain how far the WMN can continue to remain in steady state with varying load demands. Once the SSL condition to monitor the WMN overloading is determined, a formulation needs to be derived to monitor the WMN systemic stability during MR transitions from the perspective of load sharing. By instability it is meant that an MR transition should not trigger a chain reaction of transitions (ping pong effect). The stability condition established in the next section is used to avoid such a situation.

Bipartite Graph of the Supergraph of WMN

Before presenting the stability condition an overview of bipartite graphs is presented. Formally, a graph $\mathcal{G}(\mathcal{V}, \mathcal{E})$ is said to be bipartite, or 2-partite, if its vertex set can be partitioned into two different sets $\mathcal{V}_1$ and $\mathcal{V}_2$ such that every edge of the graph connects one vertex in $\mathcal{V}_1$ to a vertex in $\mathcal{V}_2$. The two sets $\mathcal{V}_1$ and $\mathcal{V}_2$ are called partite sets.

In simpler words a graph $\mathcal{G}$ called bipartite if its vertex set $\mathcal{V}$ can be decomposed into two disjoint subsets $\mathcal{V}_1$ and $\mathcal{V}_2$ such that every edge in $\mathcal{G}$ joins a vertex in $\mathcal{V}_1$ with a vertex in $\mathcal{V}_2$ and none of the edges in the graph connect vertices of the same set.

Theorem for Stability of Load Sharing in WMN

This theorem is called as the **stability theorem** in this paper. It is stated as:

Stability Theorem: A partitioned WMN can share load by transiting MRs from one GW to another if its Supergraph $\mathcal{G}^2$ is bipartite between S and T where S is the set of nodes in $\mathcal{G}^2$ operating at nominal load (load which is greater than or equal to L_i but less than U_i) and T is the set of nodes in $\mathcal{G}^2$ operating at load which is greater than or equal to the upper load limit U_i.

Proof: Let, $\mathcal{G}^2$ be a Supergraph whose nodes represent WMN partitions. Let the overloaded nodes (partitions/GW) belong to set T and all other nodes belong to set S. Load sharing by MR transition from one partition to another partition can happen if and only if the nodes of Supergraph $\mathcal{G}^2$ form a bipartite graph with S and T.

This theorem is proved as follows:-

Consider that $\mathcal{G}^2$ is non-bipartite for S and T. This implies $\{\mathcal{G}_1 \cdots \mathcal{G}_k\} \in \mathcal{G}^2$ is non-bipartite for S and T. This means that at least one pair of nodes $\mathcal{G}_i$ and $\mathcal{G}_j$ is adjacent to each other and both $\mathcal{G}_i$ and $\mathcal{G}_j$ belong to either S or T.

Case 1. $\{\mathcal{G}_i, \mathcal{G}_j\} \subset T$.
Node transition from one overloaded node to another overloaded node cannot happen, thus proving the theorem.

Case 2. $\{\mathcal{G}_i, \mathcal{G}_j\} \subset S$.

Since both the adjacent partitions are less loaded, they will not resort to the process of transition of MRs as a nominally loaded partition does not have a need for load sharing (MR transition).

This implies that edges connecting vertices belonging to the same set are trivial for load sharing.

3.3 Matrix Model of Partitioned WMN and Its Implementation to Validate Integrity of WMN

The authors have presented a matrix model of WMN in their paper [18]. In this model they represent the partitions in form of neighborhood matrix. The matrix not only provides a mathematical validation equation to perform check on lost MRs and hanging MRs of the network, but also provides a basis to represent MRs which have been moved to other networks for temporary offloading. The validation equation is provided on basis of the graph equation as explained in [18].

A brief explanation in to the matrix equation for the partitioned graph is provided as follows. For any connected self-loop free Graph $\mathcal{G}$ the property $\mathcal{B}C^T = C\mathcal{B}^T = 0 \, (mod \, 2)$ must be true [12]. Where $\mathcal{B}$ is the incidence matrix of graph $\mathcal{G}$ of WMN and C is the cycle matrix of the graph. Therefore for all the connected subgraphs the same property must be true. Extending this property further we can state the following.

For a self-loop free planar graph $\mathcal{G}$ with partitions $\mathcal{G}_1, \mathcal{G}_2 \ldots \mathcal{G}_k$ the partitioned graph is consistent with the original graph if and only if

$$[\mathcal{B}_i] * [\mathcal{C}_i]^T = 0 \, (mod \, 2) \, \forall \, i \in [1 \ldots k] \tag{11}$$

Where $\mathcal{G}_i$ represents the ith partition $\forall \, i = 1, .., k$.

Using Eq. (11) the partitioned graph can be validated for integrity (absence of lost MRs or redundant MRs). This equation is applied every time load sharing happens to ensure that there are no lost MRs or redundant MRs. This is important requirement because every time a MR is moved out of one partition to another there can be chances of lost MRs especially if hand off and hand over from one GW to another does not happen in a seamless manner.

4 Performance Results and Discussion

This section is aimed to analyse the performance of the proposed Load Management Scheme (LMS). In the previous chapter a simulation model of the proposed LMS was developed using MATLAB, and Simulink blocks. This model is used in this chapter to analyse the performance of the proposed LMS. Various test cases for performance analysis are created to compare the performance of the WMN with the proposed LMS and the conventional WMNs with no load management feature. Throughout the simulation process the simulation parameters are kept as per Table 1.

4.1   Analysis of the IMW

This section highlights the importance of the Intelligent Middle Ware (IMW) to invoke the load sharing and internetworking processes for meeting the increased bandwidth demand on a WMN. IMW is the software executing at the core router or the Network Control Centre. This software is supposed to implement the proposed LMS by monitoring the network for overloading. This is done by checking the SSL condition and then proceeding for load sharing if the SSL condition is not satisfied. For the purpose of simulation, the bandwidth demand is increased at randomly chosen MRs. The parameters assumed for simulation are provided in Table 1. As per the MATLAB Simulink model all the packets are routed through the core router to the GWs of the WMN.

Table 1. Simulation parameters.

Parameter	Value
Number of GWs	1–15
Number of MR	Varying from 100–300
Maximum number of mesh clients	250
Mean packet arrival rate	0.01 s (100 packet/s)
Mean hop delay	0.01 s
Flow rate	Markov distribution
Packet size	64 bytes
Core router capacity	100 Mbps
GW Capacity	2 Mbps
Transmission range of MR & GW	250 m
Carrier sensing range	550 m

As shown in Table 1, the increase in bandwidth demand is shown in steps ranging from 0 to 10 Mbps resulting in 10 ranges of bandwidth demand. Each of these was divided to 10 more sub ranges. In all 100 simulations have been performed. In each of these simulations, different MRs are chosen to generate bandwidth demand. Then a count is recorded for number of time the SSL condition is violated for a particular level of bandwidth demand.

The parameters considered for SSL computation are,

U_i = 2 Mbps (GW Capacity)

L_i = 1 Mbps (minimal load)

Then as per SSL condition of Eq. 10,

$$R^2 \leq (k \times U_i \times L_i) = 10 \quad \text{(where k is number of GWs)} \tag{12}$$

Therefore nominal load should satisfy the following inequality

$$R \leq 3.2 \tag{13}$$

It can be seen in Fig. 6 that after the bandwidth demand crosses the 3 Mbps range the WMN load becomes unstable and there is need for load sharing.

Violation of the SSL condition implies overloading of the WMN. Similarly, bipartite reducibility of a graph results in load sharing. Therefore it can be assumed that the numbers of times the Supergraph could be reduced to its bipartite form indicates the number of times load sharing is invoked. In Fig. 6, the X-axis denotes load in Mbps and Y-axis denotes count of number of times an event is invoked for 10 simulations.

Next Fig. 7 compares the throughput obtained in a conventional WMN with the throughput obtained in a WMN with the proposed LMS feature added to it. The results of Fig. 7 are obtained when the throughput of a WMN is compared for the following cases.

- Conventional WMN (no partitioning and load sharing)
- WMN with partitioning
- WMN with partitioning and load sharing.

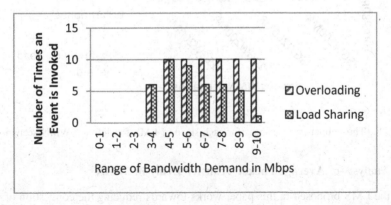

Fig. 6. Frequency of overloading and load sharing with dynamically changing load.

- The simulations have been performed keeping the total number of MRs fixed in each of the WMN scenarios but the number of GWs has been changed. This helps to study the effect of increasing the number of GWs, keeping the number of MRs constant.

Figure 8 depicts throughput improvement in WMN with different number of MR and GWs. The first two bar graph of Fig. 8 reveal that a WMN with the same number of GWs but with a relatively larger total number of MRs, exhibits better throughput performance [19].

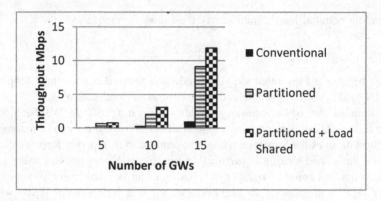

Fig. 7. WMN maximum throughput improvement at each stage of LMS for a 100 MR WMN scenario with increasing number of GW.

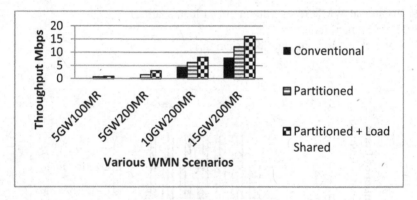

Fig. 8. Throughput performances for each stage of LMS for different WMN scenarios.

4.2 Analysis of Average Packet Transfer Delay in WMN

Since the LMS proposed in this paper works towards reducing the congestion of GWs also, a study of the average packet transfer delay is very important to assess the performance of the LMS.

For the simulation, a WMN with a total number of 100 MRs is considered with the number of GWs being changed from 5 to 10. Figure 9 depicts the average packet delay for the scenario associated with the above stated features. The results are compared with a WMN with no partitioning. The next section studies the effect of the number of packets dropped during each phase of LMS.

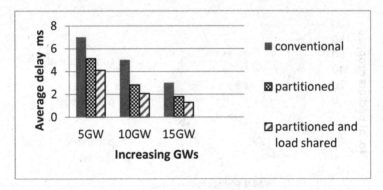

Fig. 9. Average packet delay at each stage of the proposed LMS.

4.3 Analysis of Packet Loss

Packet loss is one of the parameters affecting the QoS. One of the major causes of packet loss in wireless networks is channel congestion. Since the proposed LMS works on relieving the congestion of GWs, it results in a reduced packet loss thereby leading to an overall improved performance of a WMN. For the simulation, a WMN with GWs and MRs is considered. The results of Fig. 10 depict the variation in the packet loss as a function of the elapsed time in 5GW 100 MR WMN. In the simulation, the number of packets lost after a time window of 300 ms. Figure 10 depicts the results obtained for a conventional WMN. The number of packets dropped after 300 ms was found to be 78. Next Fig. 11 captures the packet loss attributed individually to the two basic processes of LMS. For the simulation results showed in Fig. 11, the total number of MRs remain constant at 100 while the number of GWs is varied from 5 to 15.

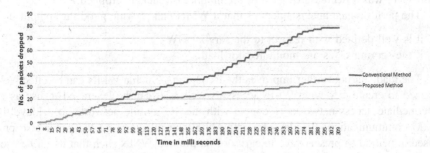

Fig. 10. Packets dropped in 5 GW 100 MR WMN.

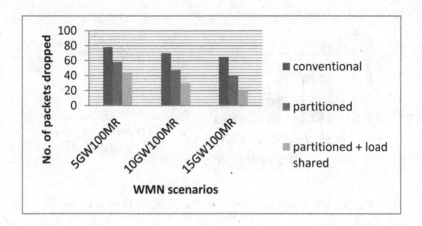

Fig. 11. Number of packets dropped at each stage of the proposed LMS.

5   Conclusions

This paper presented a load management mechanism within a partitioned WMN. Simulation studies indicate that when load on a WMN increases beyond 60% of its capacity, the frequency of occurrence of load sharing increases by 60% and frequency of internetworking increases by 40%. On comparing throughput of a non-partitioned WMN with throughput of a partitioned WMN, it was found that the partitioned WMN showed an average increase of 100% in throughput. Inclusion of the load sharing feature to the partitioned WMN resulted in a throughput improvement of 30%. It was also observed that after providing a conventional WMN with the features of the proposed LMS, on an average, there was a decrease of 22% in the average packet delay. Also there was a decrease of 90% in the number of packets dropped.

The performance analysis depicts that a WMN can provide good throughput if

- it is well defined with respect to the serving GW
- if the serving GWs are monitored for load.

The load sharing further improves the throughput. Such a WMN can be effectively utilized to create city wide Wi-Fi access as well as it can be leveraged to use as an intermediate access networks to couple with the 4G mobile networks to achieve the M2M communication. Besides performing the load management the paper also proposed a method to preserve the integrity of partitioned WMN such that it can be used further for connecting to the Internet of Things as access network. The matrix based platform which is proposed in this paper allows representing disjoint partitions. This representation is leveraged to accommodate other subnets which might be connecting to the WMN access network as part of M2M connectivity infrastructure.

6 Future Work

The paper suggests using the WMN and its subnet representation in form of matrix to address the diversity of Internet of Things (IoT) networks. In this architecture the backhaul for MPPs to the core can be any WAN. Middle mile is achieved through the WMNs which are provisioned with an additional feature of load sharing. Finally the last mile comprise of short range IP and non-IP access networks. In future work non-IP networks should be integrated to the WMN through the matrix based mathematical model. The advantage of such a structure is most appropriate for use with the 4G mobile networks where it gets really difficult to connect sensor based massive IoT networks to the Internet. The architecture should be modified to form a virtualized middle mile network provisioned with load management technique like the one proposed in this paper.

References

1. Institute of Electrical and Electronics Engineers: IEEE Standard for Information Technology–Telecommunications and information exchange between systems–Local and metropolitan area networks–Specific requirements Part 11: Wireless LAN Medium Access Control (MAC) and Physical Layer (PHY) specifications Amendment 10: Mesh Networking, IEEE Std. 802.11s-2011, 10 September 2011
2. IEEE 802.11-2012: IEEE Standard for Information technology–Telecommunications and information exchange between systems Local and metropolitan area networks–Specific requirements Part 11: Wireless LAN Medium Access Control (MAC) and Physical Layer (PHY) Specifications (2012). https://standards.ieee.org/standard/802_11-2012.html
3. Nandiraju, D., Santhanam, L., Nandiraju, N., Agrawal, D.P.: Achieving load balancing in WMN through multiple gateways. In: Mobile Adhoc and Sensor Systems (MASS), pp. 807–812 (2006)
4. Pandey, S., Kadambi, G., Bates, S., Pande, V.: A load sharing and partitioning system for multihop wireless mesh network with multiple gateways. In: IEEE Conference on Open Systems (ICOS), 25–28 September 2011, pp. 369–374 (2011)
5. Sriram, L., Raghupathy, S., Karthikeyan, S.: Multi-gateway association in wireless mesh networks. J. Ad Hoc Netw. **7–3**, 622–637 (2009)
6. Tokito, H., Sasabe, M., Hasegawa, G., Nakano, H.: Routing method for gateway load balancing in wireless mesh networks. In: IEEE Eighth International Conference on Networks, ICN 2009, 1–6 March 2009, pp. 127–132 (2009)
7. Le, A., Kum, D., Cho, Y., Toh, C.: Routing with load-balancing in multi-radio wireless mesh networks. IEICE Trans. Commun. **92**(3), 700–708 (2009)
8. Bruno, R., Conti, M., Pinizzotto, A.: A queuing modelling approach for load-aware route selection in heterogeneous mesh networks. In: Proceedings of IEEE International Symposium on a World of Wireless, Mobile and Multimedia Networks & Workshops, 15–19 June 2009, pp. 1–9 (2009)
9. Ciarlet Jr., P., Lamour, F.: On the validity of a front oriented approach to partitioning large sparse graphs with a connectivity constraint. Technical report 94-37. Computer Science Department, UCLA, Los Angeles, CA (1994)
10. Pandey, S., Pande, V.: A node marking algorithm for partitioning wireless mesh networks. In: IEEE Conference on Open Systems (ICOS), 25–28 September 2011, pp. 363–368 (2011)

11. He, B., Xie, B., Agrawal, D.P.: Optimizing the internet gateway deployment in a wireless mesh network. In: IEEE International Conference on Mobile Adhoc and Sensor Systems, MASS 2007, October 2007, pp. 8–11 (2007)

12. Deo, N.: Graph Theory with Applications to Engineering and Computer Science. Prentice Hall India, New Delhi (1974). Latest Edition 2000

13. Wolf, J., Hevkmuller, S., Wolfinger, B.E.: Dynamic resource reservation and QoS management in IEEE 802.11e networks. In: Proceedings of the International Symposium on Performance Evaluation of Computer and Telecommunication Systems, SPECTS (2005)

14. Wu, H.-T., Yang, M.-H., Ke, K.-W., Yan, L.: Enhanced QoS mechanisms for IEEE 802.11e wireless networks. In: World Academy of Science, Engineering and Technology, vol. 34, pp. 912–916 (2009)

15. Lin, Y., Wong, V.W.S.: An admission control algorithm for multi-hop 802.11e based WLAN. J. Comput. Commun. **31**, 3510–3520 (2008)

16. Lin, H.-T., Lin, Y.-Y., Chang, W.-R., Cheng, R.-S.: An integrated WiMAX/Wi-Fi architecture with QoS consistency over broadband wireless networks. In: Proceeding of the 6th IEEE Consumer Communications and Networking Conference, CCNC (2009)

17. Fleming, P.J., Wallace, J.J.: How not to lie with statistics: the correct way to summarize benchmark results. Commun. ACM **29**(3), 218–221 (1986)

18. Pandey, S., Pande, V., Kadambi, G., Bate, S.: Partitioning and internetworking wireless mesh network with wired network for delivery maximization and QoS provisioning. Procedia Technol. **3**, 18–29 (2012). ISSN 2212-0173

19. Pandey, S., Tambakad, V., Kadambi, G., Vershinin, Y.: An analytic model for route optimization in load shared wireless mesh network. In: Proceedings of the IEEE European Modelling Symposium (EMS), pp. 543–548, 20–22 November 2013

20. Bejerano, Y., Han, S.J., Kumar, A.: Efficient load-balancing routing for wireless mesh networks. IEEE J. Comput. Netw. **51**(10), 2450–2466 (2007)

Direction Finding Capability in Bluetooth 5.1 Standard

Nitesh B. Suryavanshi[1]([✉]), K. Viswavardhan Reddy[1],
and Vishnu R. Chandrika[2]

[1] Department of Telecommunication Engineering,
R.V. College of Engineering, Bengaluru, India
niteshbhupalsuryavanshi@gmail.com
[2] National Instruments R&D, Bengaluru, India

Abstract. Bluetooth technology is a standard prescribed for short-range wireless communication that uses low-power radio frequency at a low cost. It is interoperable with all devices as it consumes a very small amount of energy. The Bluetooth Core Specification provided by Bluetooth Special Interest Group (SIG) will be adding direction finding feature in the Low Energy (LE) standard. This feature will enable a tracker to find the target by estimating the relative angle between the tracker and target. It uses either Angle of Arrival (AoA) or Angle of Departure (AoD) method with multiple antennas switching for direction estimation. To support this feature, the packet structure in LE physical layer is modified. The frames of the LE uncoded packets like the Protocol Datagram Unit (PDU) Header is modified and an additional frame known as Constant Tone Extension (CTE) is added to the LE packet structure. To implement the above ideas, we need to generate a portion of the LE packets in the National Instruments (NI) Bluetooth measurement toolkit. NI Bluetooth measurement toolkit is used for testing and measurement of Bluetooth RF signals. The results show that the CTE, which is needed for direction finding capability, is successfully incorporated in the BLE.5.1 packet structure.

Keywords: Angle of Arrival · Angle of Departure · Bluetooth ·
Constant tone extension · Low Energy · PDU header

1 Introduction to Bluetooth Standard

Direction finding is the measurement or the technique of calculating the direction from which a signal has been transmitted [1]. The basic need of a direction finding system is a directional antenna. Using this antenna system we can find the direction of an incoming signal using phase-based methods, Received signal strength indicator (RSSI) method, triangulation techniques etc. [2]. However more and more accurate methods are still being developed [3–5]. Presently a standardized framework for direction finding has been introduced within Bluetooth. This is based on AoA/AoD estimation i.e. phase-based estimation techniques. Historically direction finding techniques have been developed for as long as electromagnetic waves have been known. There have been many applications of direction finding such as in indoor positioning, asset

N. Kumar and R. Venkatesha Prasad (Eds.): UBICNET 2019, LNICST 276, pp. 53–65, 2019.
https://doi.org/10.1007/978-3-030-20615-4_4

tracking, security services, military intelligence and in intelligent communication systems like Space division multiple access which needs to acquire the direction of waves. For example, asset tracking is an application that is possible due to the direction finding capability in Bluetooth. The object can be tracked by attaching a simple Bluetooth radio tag to it. The tag is continuously transmitting signals and location observers are receiving direction finding enabled Bluetooth signals. As the tag moves, a terminal connected to various location observers computes its location. The asset can also be a user's mobile phone [6].

Another application is indoor positioning. Let us say we have a mobile phone, which has direction finding capability. With the help of an indoor positioning application running on the mobile phone and based on the measured properties of the received direction finding enabled Bluetooth signals coming from another device such as a positioning beacon, one can identify the direction of the beacon. This indoor positioning solution can be very useful in places like hospitals and can provide cm level accuracy and hence improves the navigation experience. Lastly, another application known as service discovery is also possible. This can be used in places where a large number of objects are on display such as a museum. Different objects are equipped with Bluetooth tags that continuously transmit direction finding signals to a mobile phone. Based on the collected signal, the mobile phone enables the user to get more information about the object, which will be collected from the Internet.

These are just some of the applications that are possible with direction finding ability. There are many more yet to be discovered and utilized. Some more applications involve finding a parked car in a crowded parking lot, item finding applications like finding a lost item or searching for a product in a shopping mall and various other IoT applications.

With the growth in usage of the Internet, wireless technology and IoT, Bluetooth evolved as one of the industry standards for Low Rate Wireless Personal Area Networks (IEEE 802.15-LR-WPANs) specially used for short-range wireless communication. As we all know Bluetooth exchanges the information or data between fixed or wireless devices over the unlicensed ISM frequency band of the range 2.4–2.485 GHz. Bluetooth is mainly managed by the SIG. The SIG first emerged with five members: Ericsson Technology licensing, Intel, Nokia, Toshiba, and IBM, prescribed to transfer the data over short distances of range 10–100 m. Moreover many versions have been released like v1.1, v1.2, v2.0, v2.1, v3.0, v4.0 and more recently v5.0 with speeds ranging from 723.1 kbps to 25 Mbps. Bluetooth 5.1 is a recent standard that uses LE packets for transmission. An added feature called direction finding capability shows the location of the Bluetooth device, which is a new feature that is being implemented in the Bluetooth standard [5, 7–10]. For instance, when you want to transfer instructions or signals from one device to many, direction finding capability will be helpful especially if there are a large number of devices and therefore it is an important feature which should be introduced. Two mechanisms for finding the direction in Bluetooth 5 standard has been proposed by the Bluetooth SIG, one using AoA and the other using AoD [6].

In [7] the author has proposed a direction finding method based on sonification, which can be used for search and rescue operations. It proposes the use of a person's cellphone as a localization beacon. Different direction of arrival techniques has been used to determine the location. This was performed on a GSM network but Bluetooth was not used. The authors were able to achieve a method for tracking the signal strength of the user's cellphone. However, the authors state the need for accurate distance estimation techniques due to the urgency related to search and rescue operations. Lymberopoulos *et al.* [8] developed indoor position finding techniques mainly through the use of Wi-Fi. Both infrastructure-less and infrastructure-based (positioning beacons) methods were used. The results showed that indoor positioning was not satisfactorily solved. According to the authors, there did not seem to be a technology that could replicate the results of an outdoor GPS in terms of accuracy and smaller enclosures. From [9] and [10] the authors have used location fingerprinting methods to find the direction of a device using Bluetooth LE and comparisons have been made to its improvement over the use of Wi-Fi. However, the direction estimation is done based on RSSI and on the location of positioning beacons and not on the angle method, which again seems to lead to problems related to accuracy. In [11] the researcher found the location using RSSI signals and trilateration. With this method, a location accuracy of 2 m is achieved. Direction finding using AoA/AoD with legacy Bluetooth devices was carried out in [12]. From the results, it is seen that backward compatibility is possible and doesn't require any extra hardware. [13] details direction finding using angle estimation and compares its advantages over other methods like Time of arrival (ToA) methods. However, no simulation was carried out at the time. In [14], the author has simulated direction finding using AoD, which has yielded promising results. However, no hardware implementation was carried out to verify the results in real time. Based on reviewing the previous literature related to direction finding we can say that there is still a lot of improvements to be done with respect to better estimation using direction finding techniques. We will now have a look at our work, which is based on angle estimation techniques and how it improves upon the previous direction finding techniques especially in terms of accuracy.

In this work, we propose direction finding using Bluetooth 5.1, with angle estimation techniques which can provide accuracies even for indoor applications such as museums, shopping malls etc. For this, we need to make changes in the LE packet to accurately determine the phase difference at the antennas to find the direction. In order to do this, LE data packets have been given as input to an FSK modulator VI (Virtual Instrument file), where the modulated signal varies according to the frequency of the message signal. That means if 1 is given as input to the VI, +250 kHz is added to the RF carrier and if 0 is given, −250 kHz will be added. Later the FSK modulator output is fed to a waveform multiplier where it gets multiplied with an envelope signal and finally a Bluetooth LE waveform is generated. Moreover, the Bluetooth SIG have also given the core specification requirements and the requirements for AoA and AoD estimation [15]. Hence in this work, the implementation of direction finding on hardware and the results associated with it are also discussed.

Section 2 contains the terminologies and methodologies used for direction finding such as the measurement of AoA and AoD. Section 3 details the design and implementation of the overall packet structure including the modifications done to the Bluetooth LE packet structure. Section 4 shows the relevant results obtained after implementing direction finding in Bluetooth and a discussion on this. Section 5 gives a conclusion and some ideas regarding future work that can be done for the better utilization of direction finding.

2 Terminologies and Methodology Used for Direction Finding

In this section, we first discuss the basics of AoA, AoD, roles of the target and tracker, the LE packet format and the CTE.

2.1 General Requirements for Target and Tracker Device

A device assigned with a target role is not required to estimate the direction, but it is required to show its direction to the tracker device based on a trusted relationship. However, direction detection is based on antennas switching in a multi-antenna array. In such a solution the target device is required to support either a single antenna or a multi-antenna array or both. A tracker device should be able to request the target to send directional signals. Therefore, the target and tracker needs to support either a single or multiple transmit antennas depending on whether AoA or AoD is used.

Angle of Arrival
An LE device can make its direction available to a peer device by transmitting direction finding enabled packets using a single antenna. The peer device, consisting of an RF switch and antenna array, switches antennas while receiving part of those packets and captures in-phase (I) and quadrature (Q) samples. The I and Q samples can be used to calculate the phase difference in the radio signal received by different elements of the antenna array which in turn can be used to estimate the AoA.

Consider a receiver device with an antenna array consisting of antennas, separated by a distance 'd' as shown in Figs. 1 and 2.

The transmitter device uses a single antenna to transmit a signal. This can be seen in Fig. 3 where a perpendicular line is drawn from an incoming signal wave front extending to the antenna on the left at the point of intersection to the closest antenna i.e. the antenna on the right. The adjacent side of that right triangle represents the path difference relative to the angle of incidence of that wave front between both antennas. The phase difference, ψ, in the signal arriving at the two antennas is then calculated using Eq. 1.

$$\psi = (2\pi d \cos \theta)/\lambda \tag{1}$$

Where λ is the signal wavelength and θ is the AoA, and it can be derived from Eq. 1.

$$\theta = \cos^{-1}(\psi\lambda/2\pi d) \tag{2}$$

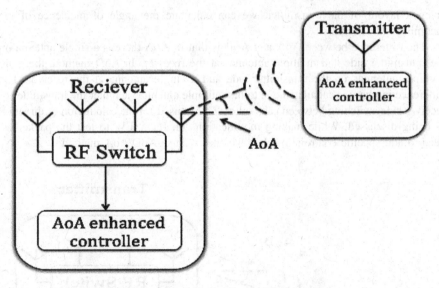

Fig. 1. AoA usage in direction finding [6].

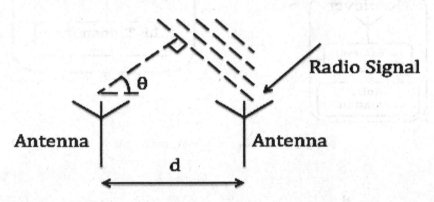

Fig. 2. Measuring the AoA [6].

2.2 Angle of Departure

A device consisting of an RF switch and antenna array can make its AoD detectable by transmitting direction finding enabled packets and switching the antennas during transmission.

The peer device receives those packets using a single antenna and captures I and Q samples. Determination of the direction is based on the different propagation delays of the LE radio signal between the transmitting elements of the antenna array and a receiving single antenna. The propagation delays are detectable with I and Q measurements. Any receiving LE radio with a single antenna that supports the AoD feature can capture I and Q samples and with the aid of profile-level information specifying the antenna layout of the transmitter, we can calculate the angle of incidence of the incoming radio signal.

The difference between AoA and AoD is that in AoA there is a single antenna on the transmitter side and multiple antennas at the receiver. In AoD method, there are multiple antennas on the transmitter side and a single antenna at the receiver. The difference in phase is calculated due to the multiple antennas at either the transmitter or receiver side switching between each other. This is used for the calculation of direction as being discussed. While making modifications on LabVIEW to test the packet we need to add specific controls to select whether we use AoD/AoA method.

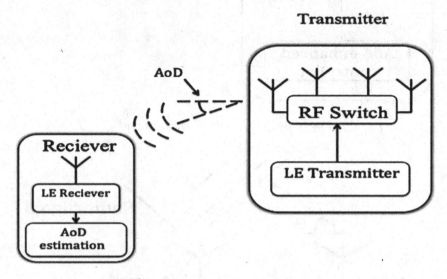

Fig. 3. AoD usage in direction finding [6].

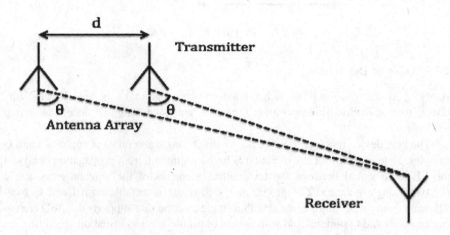

Fig. 4. Measuring the AoD [6].

Consider a transmitter device with an antenna array consisting of antennas, separated by a distance 'd' as shown in Figs. 3 and 4. The receiver device uses a single antenna to receive the signals. The phase difference, ψ, between the signal coming from the antenna on the left and the signal coming from the antenna on the right arriving at the receiver is then calculated using Eq. 3.

$$\psi = (2\pi d \sin\theta)/\lambda \tag{3}$$

Where λ is the signal wavelength and θ is the AoD, and θ is calculated using Eq. 4.

$$\theta = \sin^{-1}(\psi\lambda/2\pi d) \tag{4}$$

3 Proposed Packet Design

The design and implementation of direction finding capability are carried out in LabVIEW using Bluetooth Generation Toolkit v18.0, which generates the test packets. Hence to do this, we considered the LE test packet, modified at some specific places to include the direction finding capability.

Figure 5 shows the packet format of the LE uncoded test packet. It consists of a Preamble of 1 byte, Sync Word or access address of 4 bytes, PDU header and PDU length each of 1 byte (together referred to as the PDU Header), a PDU payload which varies from 37–256 bytes, the Cyclic Redundancy Check (CRC) of 3 bytes and then followed by the CTE of varying length between 2–40 bytes. It is an addition to the packet format for making direction finding possible.

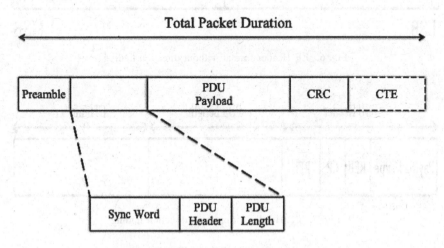

Fig. 5. LE uncoded test packet format

Generally, the PDU Header is of 2 bytes, but for the purpose of our work, we have added an extra 1 byte thus making the total length of the PDU Header 3 bytes. The 1 byte added to the PDU Header is known as CTEInfo consisting of a 5-bit CTETime to specify the length of the CTE, a 1-bit Reserved for Future Use frame (RFU) and a 2-bit CTEType frame. The CTETime field is varied from 2 to 20, which are in units of 8 μs (0.5 μs or 1 μs is the symbol duration). Therefore CTEType is 5 bits long as representation up to at least the number 20 is required. CTEType is used to specify which method of direction finding is used such as AoA or AoD. This one-byte CTEInfo is justified, as the angle estimation method of direction finding is more accurate compared to previous methods and leads to a better calculation of the direction from which the received signal came from [13].

We have modified the payload header to check whether CTE is present or not. To do this, an extra bit called Constant tone extension Present (CP) is included in the RFU as shown in Fig. 7. If the CP bit is marked as 0 then CTE and CTEInfo are absent indicating direction finding is not present. Whereas 1 indicates direction finding is enabled. Figure 6 shows the PDU header and length format without the inclusion of direction finding capability. Also as shown the CTEInfo field is missing.

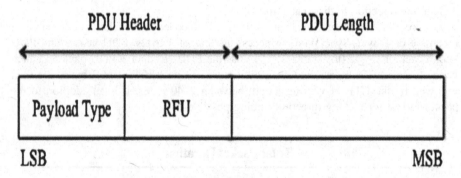

Fig. 6. LE Header format without direction finding

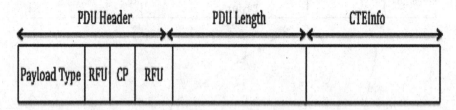

Fig. 7. LE Header format with direction finding

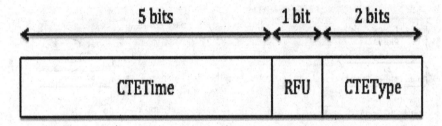

Fig. 8. CTEInfo frame

CP bit as shown in Fig. 7 specifies whether the CTEInfo is present or absent. The CTE is a series of continuous '1's or '0's. Initially, the simulations were carried out in LabVIEW software. The relevant fields i.e. 'VI's' in the LE uncoded packet format were modified and simulated in Bluetooth Generation Toolkit to add this direction finding capability. The CTEInfo frame, which as explained previously, is the additional 1 byte added to the PDU Header to incorporate direction finding and is shown in Fig. 8.

Though the addition of the extra byte produces an overhead the resulting improvement in accuracy more than compensates for this. In RSSI method the accuracy has been shown to be lacking especially in an indoor environment. Another method ToA is present which calculates the time of travel between the transmitting and receiving signal to acquire the distance. However, this method requires a very high clock accuracy to get a good estimation of the distance. Moreover, there is a standardized framework for AoD/AoA methods in Bluetooth [13].

4 Results and Discussion

In this section, we will be discussing how implementation and testing have been carried on NI hardware and the results associated with it. The resulting waveforms will be analyzed and discussed.

Figure 9 shows the front panel of the property controls for the Bluetooth LE packet. Here the payload length, payload sequence type, whitening settings, power ramp settings such as settling time and ramp time etc. can be set. As you can see we have included a special control panel for enabling the CTE. This is responsible for direction finding. Here we can also choose whether we want to use AoA or AoD method and we can also specify the length of the CTE through CTETime. These settings are tweaked accordingly to get the desired length and frame structure. Now to show that direction finding has been implemented we have to show that the CTE frame has been successfully transmitted while testing on hardware. The next sub-section will discuss the results acquired and the change in the packet power spectrum and frequency trace. This difference will be shown with respect to before adding CTE and after adding CTE respectively.

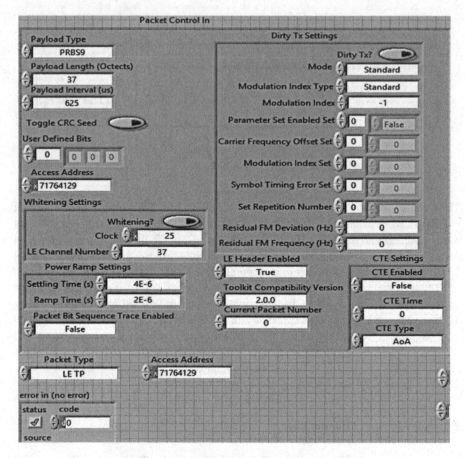

Fig. 9. Specifications of the LE packet.

4.1 Hardware Testing Results for Direction Finding Capability

The hardware testing was done on the NI PXIe hardware. Figures 10a and 10b show the power spectrum traces for LE packet without and with direction finding capability respectively. The x-axis is in frequency (Hz) and the y-axis is in power (dBm). The center RF frequency is 2.408 GHz. When a 1 is transmitted +250 kHz is added and when a 0 is transmitted −250 kHz is added to the center frequency as shown in Fig. 10a. A power spike in the +250 kHz part of the spectrum can be seen in Fig. 10b due to the extra CTE which is a continuous series of 1's. Due to this power spike, we can say that the CTE is present in the frame structure.

The frequency deviation trace for a single LE packet without and with direction finding capability is shown in Figs. 11a and 11b respectively. The x-axis is in time (sec) and the y-axis is in frequency (hertz). In Fig. 11b due to the presence of the CTE frame at the end of the LE packet which contains a continuous series of 1's, the frequency deviation trace shows +250 kHz continuously at the end.

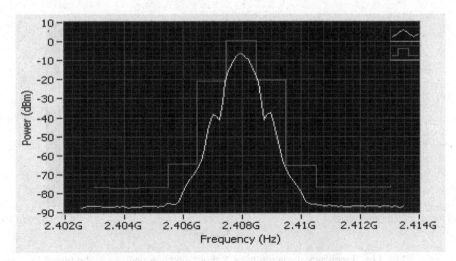

Fig. 10a. Power spectrum traces without direction finding + LE in-band emission channel powers (red line) as per the test specifications. (Color figure online)

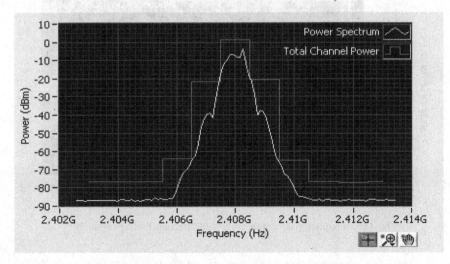

Fig. 10b. Power spectrum traces with direction finding + LE in-band emission channel powers (red line) as per the test specifications. (Color figure online)

From these tests and the resulting analysis, we can say that the CTE has clearly been integrated into the packet frame structure. The long series of '1's of the CTE at the end of the packet makes sure there is no phase change during that time the CTE is received. This ensures that the phase difference between different signals can be calculated without any interference from the packet itself. When there is a change from

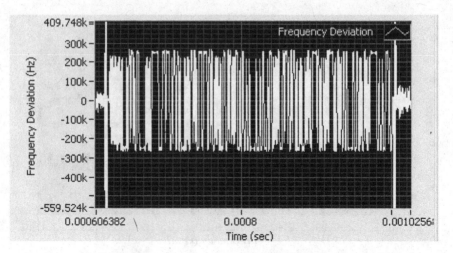

Fig. 11a. Frequency deviation trace without direction finding capability.

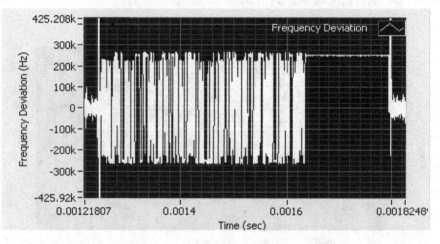

Fig. 11b. Frequency deviation trace with direction finding capability.

0 to 1 or vice versa in the packet frame there is a phase change. This does not happen when the CTE is being received as it only contains a series of '1's and hence doesn't interfere with the calculation of phase difference during antenna switching. Due to this the accuracy of obtaining the direction is greatly increased.

5   Conclusion and Future Work

In this paper, we implement direction finding capability in Bluetooth v.5.1. To implement this, we have modified the LE packet and the packet interval to accurately determine the phase difference in the antennas to find the direction using CTE.

The result for both the simulation and hardware shows that the direction finding is successfully implemented. The phase of the signal can be determined to perceive the direction of the Bluetooth device. Further in future work, the creation of emulated multiple antennas at the receiver side can be done for hardware testing. Also, modifications in the Bluetooth analysis toolkit for receiving the LE packets with CTE should be looked into.

Acknowledgment. This work was carried out at National Instruments R&D, Bengaluru, India, as a part of an internship course. The authors acknowledge the company for providing the resources during the course of the internship, without which the execution of the project would not have been possible. The authors would also like to thank the manager Abraham George for his constant support.

References

1. Tuncer, T.E., Friedlander, B.: Classical and Modern Direction-of-Arrival Estimation, 1st edn. Academic Press, Cambridge (2009)
2. Introduction to Theory of Direction Finding. http://www.rohde-schwarz-usa.com/rs/324-UVH-477/images/TheoryofDF.pdf. Accessed 22 Jan 2019
3. Hart, B.D., Strager, P.J., Pandey, S., Kloper, D., Lyons, D., Silverman, M.A.: Angle of arrival location sensing with antenna array. US20140327579A1, United States, Cisco Technology Inc. (2014)
4. Wang, J.J.-M., Chou, K.-C., Yu, C.-H., Liu, H.-Y.: Direction Finding Antenna format. US20160047885A1, Taiwan, MediaTek Inc. (2016)
5. TU Delft repository, Bluetooth Direction Finding. http://resolver.tudelft.nl/uuid:c07eb3a2-a303-4690-ac3e-e96f0064afcd. Accessed 23 Jan 2019
6. Gunhardson, E.: Indoor positioning using angle of departure information. Linkoping University, Norrkoping, Sweden (2015)
7. Poirier-Quinot, D., Parseihian, G., Katz, B.F.G.: Reduction of perceived instabilities in Parameter Mapping Sonification: application to the real-time exploration of a noisy stream of data. IJHCS, submitted 22 January 2015
8. Lymberopoulos, D., et al.: A realistic evaluation and comparison of indoor location technologies: experiences and lessons learned. In: Proceedings of the 14th International Conference on Information Processing in Sensor Networks (IPSN 2015) (2015)
9. Larsson, J.: Distance estimation and modeling using bluetooth low energy technology (2015)
10. Faragher, R., Harle, R.: An analysis of the accuracy of Bluetooth low energy for indoor positioning applications. In: Proceedings of the 27th International Technical Meeting of the Satellite Division of the Institute of Navigation (ION GNSS + 2014), pp. 201–210 (2014)
11. Proxima.io article page. https://proximi.io/accurate-indoor-positioning-bluetooth-beacons/. Accessed 9 Nov 2018
12. Banerjea, R.: Direction finding for legacy bluetooth devices. US20170201859A1, United States, Qualcomm Technologies International Ltd., Cambridge, GB (2017)
13. Sauli Lehtimaki, Silicon Labs: Understanding advanced bluetooth angle estimation technique for real-time positioning. Embedded World, Germany (2018)
14. Angle of Arrival and Angle of Departure. R.10, in Bluetooth Specification/Version 4.2, Core Specification Working Group (CSWG) (2016)
15. Direction Finding Core Feature Requirements. V10r00, in Bluetooth Specifications (2011)

An Investigation of Transmission Properties of Double-Exponential Pulses in Core-Clad Optical Fibers for Communication Application

Anurag Chollangi, Nikhil Ravi Krishnan, and Kaustav Bhowmick[✉]

Department of Electronics and Communication Engineering,
Amrita School of Engineering, Bengaluru, Amrita Vishwa Vidyapeetham,
Bengaluru, India
k_bhowmick@blr.amrita.edu

Abstract. In this paper, a comparative analysis of the propagation of double exponential and Gaussian ultra-short pulses in fused-silica core-clad optical fibers has been presented. The present study has taken the non-linear propagation parameters from Schrodinger's equation and for silica fiber into consideration. The analysis has been carried out for single-mode and multi-mode fibers, to study the effects of variation in pulse parameters and it has been observed that the double-exponential pulses have a bandwidth-efficiency $\sim 23\%$ over Gaussian pulses and may be useful as femtosecond-laser pulse shapes. It is found that double exponential pulses offer more resistance to dispersive effects than Gaussian pulses at longer distances and retain more power levels for higher input powers, while Gaussian pulses continue to decay. Finally, rapid decay in double-exponential pulses may make them suitable for time-and-wavelength-division-multiplexed passive optical networks (TWDM-PON) applications in optical communication.

Keywords: Double-exponential pulse · Gaussian pulse · Optical fiber

1 Introduction

Pulse shapes play an important role in optical fiber based communication and signal processing applications [1–3] in which non-linear properties of optical pulses [4] and those of the optical fibers [5] contribute significantly. It is a known fact that several useful application can be obtained from non-linear optical fibers carrying or generating pulses e.g., pulse compression, optical fiber communication, optical signal processing and quantum application [6–9]. Due to the increase in use of silica optical fibers due to their special properties, we have considered the fibers in this paper to be fused-silica fibers [5]. Gaussian pulses have thus far been the most common pico-second ultra-short pulse shape used for characterizing and utilizing non-linear properties [10] in an optical fiber, along with its variants e.g. super Gaussian pulses [11]. Various useful and detrimental non-linear properties e.g., chirping, group velocity dispersion or chromatic dispersion leading to pulse broadening etc., in an optical fiber, may be studied using Gaussian pulses. Other than Gaussian, transmission properties of several other pulse shapes e.g., hyperbolic secant, parabolic, etc., in various media, have been studied to some extent [12].

© ICST Institute for Computer Sciences, Social Informatics and Telecommunications Engineering 2019
Published by Springer Nature Switzerland AG 2019. All Rights Reserved
N. Kumar and R. Venkatesha Prasad (Eds.): UBICNET 2019, LNICST 276, pp. 66–79, 2019.
https://doi.org/10.1007/978-3-030-20615-4_5

Another class of pulses called ultra wide band or double-exponential pulses [13] have not yet been studied much in the case of optical fibers, except for in a few medical experiments.

By virtue of the mathematical description of the double exponential function, it may be envisaged that ultra-short and temporally narrow pulses are possible for fiber-optic applications using the double exponential function. Analyses of double-exponential pulses are possible starting from the Schrodinger equation [14, 15]. Thus, in the present work, we have endeavoured a thorough initial study of the characteristics of double-exponential pulse propagation in regular core-clad silica single mode [16] and multimode optical fibers [17]. Throughout the work, the results for double exponential pulse transmission have been compared to the characteristics of Gaussian pulse propagation in optical fibers. The work has been analytically carried out with simulations performed using Matlab package.

Section 2 presents the simulation work and related results. Subsection 2.1 presents a confirmation test for the adopted simulation methods by repetition of published results for Gaussian pulse properties. Subsection 2.2 presents the pulse equations and shapes used in the current paper. Subsections 2.3 and 2.4 presents the simulation of double exponential pulse propagation in silica core-clad single and multi-mode optical fibers respectively. Section 3 discusses obtained results and necessary mathematical results and characteristics. Finally, Sect. 4 concludes the work.

2 Characterization of Gaussian and Double Exponential Pulses

This section presents the step-by-step development of double exponential pulse transmission characteristics via silica communication fibers.

2.1 Verification of Simulation Technique Using Gaussian Pulse

The non-linear effects of silica optical fibers limit their capacity to send signals without degradation [18–20]. These effects include Four Wave Mixing, Self-Phase Modulation and Cross Phase Modulation, which are useful in areas such as wide-band and low-noise optical amplification, supercontinuum (SC) light sources, optical signal processing, strain/temperature sensors, frequency/time/length measurement, and near-infrared spectroscopy [21]. In the present work, a fused silica based optical fiber has been used as a medium for propagation for the Gaussian and double exponential pulses. A step index fiber is considered in this section with refractive indices of the core and cladding, respectively, as 1.447 and 1.444 at 1550 nm wavelength [22]. Waveguide and Material dispersion are both observed in optical fibers. The dispersive effects of interest in this paper are chromatic and modal dispersions [23]. Pulse propagation through such fibers (see Fig. 1) can be simulated using non-linear Schrodinger equation (see Eq. 1) [11].

$$i\frac{\partial A(z,t)}{\partial z} = -\frac{i\alpha}{2}A(z,t) + \frac{\beta_2}{2}\frac{\partial^2 A(z,t)}{\partial t^2} - \gamma|A(z,t)|^2 A(z,t) \qquad (1)$$

Equation (1) describes the propagation of optical pulses inside single-mode fibres [11], where, 'A' is the amplitude of the pulse envelope and 't' is measured in a moving frame of reference (with respect to the group velocity). The terms on the right side of the equation control effects of fibre loss (α), dispersion (β) and non-linearity (γ) such that $\alpha > 0$, $\beta \neq 0$ and is real, $\gamma > 0$. Dispersive or non-linear effects dominate along the fibre depending on the initial values of initial width (T_0) and peak power (P_0) of the initial pulse. The dispersion length L_D $\left(=T_0^2/\beta_2\right)$ and the non-linear length L_{NL} $\left(=1/\gamma P_0\right)$ provide the lengths after which these effects are observed. Herein, β_2 represents pulse dispersion, causing broadening of pulse in time domain by causing a phase shift in frequency domain of the pulse. Again, γ accounts for the material dispersion of the fiber causing a phase shift in time domain leading to frequency shift in frequency domain. For the present work, Split Step Fourier method has been used, which is a pseudo spectral method that employs the use of the Fourier Transform [11].

For the Split-Step Fourier method, the Eq. (1) is rewritten as in Eq. (2):

$$\frac{\partial A}{\partial z} = (L+N)A \tag{2}$$

where, L is a linear operator that accounts for the dispersive effects and N is an operator that accounts for non-linear effects.

We have considered a Gaussian pulse having width $5T_0$ and observed its propagation through an optical fiber with its dispersion parameters $\beta_2 = 1$ and $\gamma = 1$ [11]. We have simulated the said pulse for a distance of one characteristic dispersion length (L_d) (distance where the pulse width increases by a factor of $\sqrt{2}$) and observed the trend in drop in intensity of Gaussian with respect to distance covered, as shown in Fig. 1, in agreement with the result in literature [11], which confirms the correctness of our adoption of the Split-step Fourier transform algorithm.

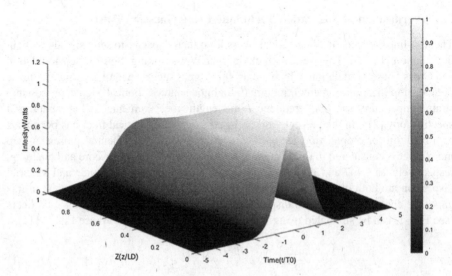

Fig. 1. Simulation of propagation of Gaussian pulse ($\beta_2 = 1$ and $\gamma = 1$).

2.2 Gaussian and Double-Exponential Pulses Used

The pulses of interest- in this study are Gaussian and double exponential pulses. A Gaussian pulse is one in which the pulse envelope is a Gaussian function who's Fourier transform is also a Gaussian function. This is unlike that of a plane wave who's Fourier transform is a Dirac-delta function [24]. This causes the plane wave to have lesser bandwidth than that of a Gaussian pulse, which is why the Gaussian pulse is of use in applications involving wideband communication. The Gaussian pulse is described by Eq. (3):

$$E(z = 0, t) = A \exp\left(-\frac{t^2}{2t_0^2}\right) \tag{3}$$

where, t_0 is standard pulse deviation in picoseconds, A is amplitude, t is time in picoseconds, and z is distance in kilometres.

The motive of this study is to find a clear juxtaposition between the Gaussian and double exponential pulses and explore the capabilities of the double exponential pulses for similar applications. The double exponential pulse can be described using Eq. (4) [13]:

$$E(t) = E_0\left(e^{-\alpha t} - e^{-\beta t}\right) \tag{4}$$

Where, E_0 is the amplitude of the pulse, the rise time and fall time of the pulse are given by α and β, respectively. The rise time is the amount of time taken for a pulse to reach 90% of its maximum value from 10% of its maximum value [13]. The pulse width is the interval of time during which the amplitude of the pulse is higher than 50% of its maximum amplitude. The α and β terms can be calculated using the equation set (5) [25]:

$$\alpha = \frac{\ln(2)}{t_{FWHM}}; \beta = \frac{1}{t_r} \tag{5}$$

t_{FWHM} is the full width half maximum amplitude and t_r is the rise time of the given pulse.

Figures 2 and 3 show the initial conditions for both pulses before propagation. The pulse parameters are chosen in a way that they can be propagated to the maximum extent inside a silica based fiber of maximum operating wavelength = 1550 nm [26]. Figure 2 is the time-domain presentation of the Gaussian and double exponential pulses used in the present study, followed by the wavelength representation of the same in Fig. 3, where both types of pulses are shown to be centred at 1550 nm (~ 1.55 μm).

2.3 Dispersion Characteristics of Double Exponential Pulses in Single Mode Fibers

Dispersion characteristics of double exponential and Gaussian pulses have been observed for a distance of one characteristic dispersion length (L_d) and intensities have been studied with the help of plots to understand the comparative decay of Gaussian and double exponential pulses in a single mode fiber, with core radius ~ 5 μm.

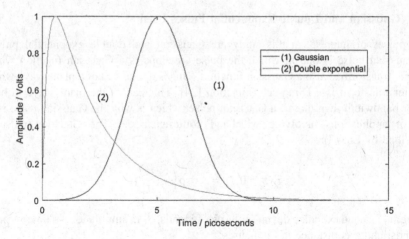

Fig. 2. Comparative time-domain plot of Gaussian and double exponential pulses.

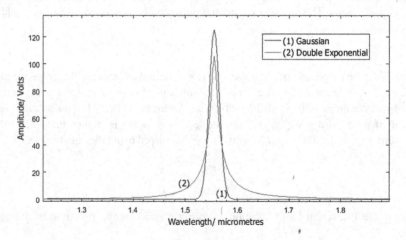

Fig. 3. Center wavelengths of Gaussian and double exponential pulses.

We have observed that rate of decay for a double exponential pulse is higher in the initial stages of propagation (as a function of propagation, 'z') and lower in later stages as compared to Gaussian. These dispersive effects are chromatic in nature. Figure 4 shows the dispersive nature of Gaussian pulse and distance-wise intensity profile of the same along the single mode fiber in consideration. Again, similar study for a double exponential pulse is presented in Fig. 4. We have observed the intensities at z = 0, $0.33L_d$, $0.66L_d$ and L_d. The pulse and fiber parameters are identical to those from [11] ($\beta_2 = 1$ and $\gamma = 1$).

We find a major part of the double exponential pulse gets exhausted from initial stage by comparing Figs. 4(a), (b) and Figs. 5(a), (b), respectively. However, the change in intensity stabilises for double exponential pulse at $\sim 0.8L_d$ (Fig. 5), compared to

Gaussian pulse (Fig. 4), where the latter continues to decay. Double-exponential pulses was generally found to stabilise after decaying over a range of ~ 1 to 5 times of dispersion length, L_d.

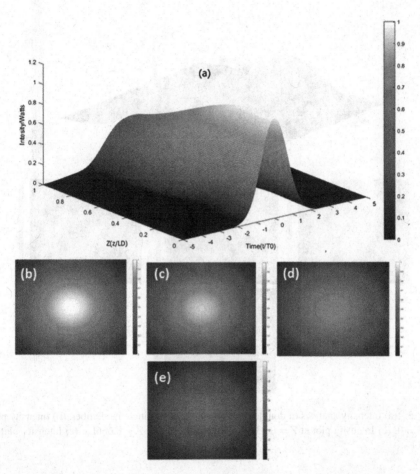

Fig. 4. (a) Intensity analysis of Gaussian pulse in Single mode fiber. (b) Intensity plot at $Z = 0$. (c) Intensity plot at $Z = 0.33L_d$. (d) Intensity plot at $Z = 0.666L_d$. (e) Intensity plot at $Z = L_d$.

2.4 Dispersion Characteristics of Double Exponential Pulses in Multi-mode Fibers

The analysis of dispersive effects in single mode fibers has been carried out in Sect. 2.3. This section deals with the analysis of pulse propagation in multi-mode fibers. Multi-mode fibers have a higher radius than single mode fibers which allow for more number of modes to propagate simultaneously. The β_2 parameter is a function of the modes in this case and the multi-mode fiber dimensions have been adopted from literature [29], with core-radius ~ 25 μm and fiber radius ~ 67.5 μm.

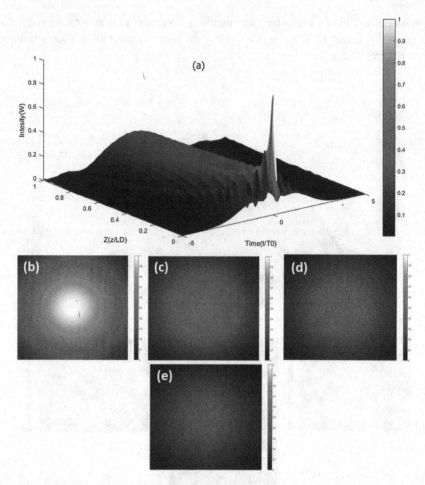

Fig. 5. (a) Intensity analysis of double exponential Pulse in Single mode fiber. (b) Intensity plot at $Z = 0$. (c) Intensity plot at $Z = 0.33L_d$. (d) Intensity plot at $Z = 0.666L_d$. (e) Intensity plot at $Z = L_d$.

In addition to chromatic dispersion, modal dispersion in Gaussian and double exponential pulses is observed. We have considered LP_{02} mode for the purpose of this simulation. A comparative study of the pulse propagation was done as shown in Figs. 6 and 7, representing LP_{02} modes for a Gaussian pulse and a double exponential pulse, respectively. Double exponential pulse is observed to have larger spread compared to Gaussian indicating a larger variation in pulse broadening among the two pulses. From this we infer that the double exponential pulses are better suited for applications involving modal dispersion based sensors [27].

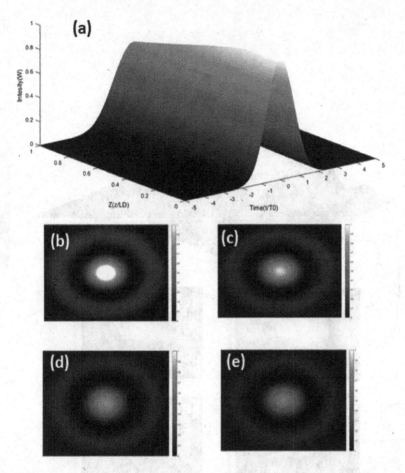

Fig. 6. (a) Intensity analysis of Gaussian pulse in Multimode mode fiber. (b) LP_{02} Intensity plot at Z = 0. (c) LP_{02} Intensity plot at Z = 0.33L_d. (d) LP_{02} Intensity plot at Z = 0.666L_d. (e) LP_{02} Intensity plot at Z = L_d.

3   Results and Discussion

Based on the simulation results presented in Sect. 2, an analysis of bandwidth efficiency has been carried out to draw a comparative conclusion on the effectiveness and area of application for double exponential pulses as compared to Gaussian pulses, transmitting through a non-linear silica fiber.

The Gaussian and double exponential pulse equations have been presented in Eqs. 3 and 4, respectively. Taking Fourier transform of the Gaussian equation (see Eq. 3), the expression in Eq. 6 was obtained:

$$E_g(z, \omega) = F\big(E_g(z, t)\big) = \frac{t_0}{\sqrt{\pi}} A \exp\left(-\frac{t^2}{2t_0^2}\right) \tag{6}$$

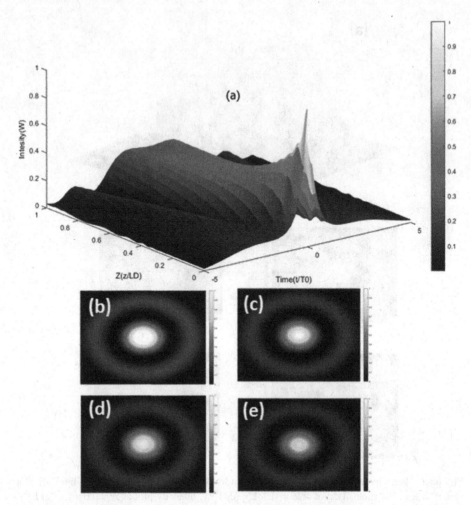

Fig. 7. (a) Intensity analysis of double exponential pulse in Multimode mode fiber. (b) LP_{02} Intensity plot at $Z = 0$. (c) LP_{02} Intensity plot at $Z = 0.33L_d$. (d) LP_{02} Intensity plot at $Z = 0.666L_d$. (e) LP_{02} Intensity plot at $Z = L_d$.

At half power bandwidth, $\mathcal{F}(Eg(z,t)) = Max(\mathcal{F}(Eg(z,t)))/\sqrt{2}$ [30].

Solving for Half-power bandwidth (HPBW) for Gaussian pulse, ω_{HPBW} was obtained as in Eq. (7):

$$(\omega_{HPBW})_{max}^{Gaussian} = \frac{0.832}{t_0} \tag{7}$$

Similarly, taking Fourier transform of Eq. (4), for the double exponential pulse, gives the expression as in Eq. (8):

$$E_e(z, \omega) = F(E_e(z, t)) = \frac{2\alpha}{\alpha^2 + \omega^2} - \frac{2\beta}{\beta^2 + \omega^2} \tag{8}$$

At half power bandwidth, for double exponential pulse, a similar approach as in Gaussian case was followed giving,

$$F(E_e(z, t)) = Max(F(E_e(z, t)))/\sqrt{2}$$

Solving for $(\omega_{HPBW})_{max}^{exponential}$, at $t_r = 0$; $\beta = \infty$ (found by second derivative test), the result was as in Eq. (9),

$$(\omega_{HPBW})_{max}^{exponential} = 0.6434/t_0 \tag{9}$$

For a given pulse-width, the ratio of HPBW for Gaussian to HPBW for double exponential pulse is as in Eq. (10):

$$(\omega_{HPBW})_{max}^{Gaussian} = 1.29(\omega_{HPBW})_{max}^{exponential} \tag{10}$$

From, the relation in Eq. (10), it can be said that double exponential bandwidth is 23% less than Gaussian, for a given pulse width in temporal regime. To observe the effect of pulse width on the pulse propagation we considered the propagation of the Gaussian and double exponential pulses with different pulse width ranging from femto pulse regime to ultra-short pulse regime, i.e., 10–15 to 10–12 s. Table 1 shows the effect of pulse widths on the rate of change in intensity of Gaussian and double exponential pulses over a distance and the effect of decreased pulse width on the pulses through parameters such as rate of change of slope in Gaussian and double exponential pulses, and, distance at which intensity of double exponential pulse is greater than Gaussian intensity.

Dispersion length is the length at which the pulse width increases by a factor of $\sqrt{2}$. Dispersion length is formulated by neglecting the non-linear effects in non-linear Schrodinger equation (NLSE) [28].

$$\frac{\partial A}{\partial z} - j\beta_2 \frac{\partial^2 A}{\partial t^2} = 0 \tag{11}$$

For the Gaussian pulse we solve Eq. (11) by using frequency domain for simpler analysis and then shifting back to time domain through Fourier analysis [28].

$$U(z, T) = \frac{1}{2\pi} \int\limits_{-\infty}^{+\infty} U(0, \omega) \exp\left(j\omega T - \frac{j\beta_2 z \omega^2}{2}\right) d\omega \tag{12}$$

Where $U(z, T)$ is the pulse at time T and position z, giving pulse width at z as,

$$T_1(z) = T_0 \sqrt{1 + \frac{z^2}{L_D^2}} \tag{13}$$

Where z is the distance travelled by the pulse; L_D is the dispersion length of pulse. Using equation and (11) and (12) we derive:

$$L_D^{Gaussian} = \frac{T_0^2}{|\beta_2|} = \frac{0.362 t_{FWHM}^2}{|\beta_2|} \tag{14}$$

For Gaussian pulse with pulse width, T_0, t_{FWHM} is the full wave half maximum time and dispersion coefficient β_2.

For a double exponential pulse the parameters are as in Eq. (15)

$$a = \frac{\ln(2)}{t_{FWHM}} ; b = \frac{1}{t_r} \tag{15}$$

Using Eqs. (11) and (12) we find L_D^{d-exp},

$$L_D^{d-exp} = \frac{1.18 t_p t_{FWHM}}{\beta_2} \tag{16}$$

$$t_p = \frac{\ln\left(\frac{b}{a}\right)}{(b - a)} \tag{17}$$

Table 1. Effect of pulse widths on the rate of change in intensity-slope

T_{FWHM} (pico-secs)	Z/L$_d$	ΔGaussian/(V^2/m)	ΔDouble Exponential/(V^2/m)
0.01	1.7618	0.0023	0.0172
0.1	1.8118	0.0023	0.0175
1	3.7437	0.0023	0.0199

Where, tp is the peak time-instance of the pulse [13]. From this equation we infer that pulse propagates as a function of peak time and pulse width. We infer from the Eq. (16) that double exponential pulse decay depends upon peak time which is a function of its rise time or 'b' (see Eq. 15). When the rise time of the pulse increases, 'b' decreases till a certain value such that the dispersion length of the pulse will be less than that of Gaussian. After a certain order of 'b' we observe an increase in the dispersion length of double-exponential pulse and then it remains nearly constant that is why the double-exponential femto-second pulse has a longer dispersion length compared to pico-second pulse, as shown in Fig. 8.

From Table 1, we have observed that rate of change of slope of double exponential pulse improves with decrease in pulse width, which is graphically shown in Fig. 8. Double exponential pulse attains higher intensity compared to Gaussian faster with decreasing pulse width. This makes double exponential pulses useful as very short pulses, especially in femtosecond regime. TWDM [26] requires pulses with wavelength range in μmeters which boils down to femto second range. Due to the steeper slope and its suggested significance in femto second regime, double exponential pulses can be used to manufacture fiber-laser for TWDM purpose. From the results of the simulation, the decay rate of double exponential pulse is lower as in Figs. 8(a) and (b). We observe that the rate of change of intensity of the Gaussian pulse is higher than the double exponential pulse after a certain distance and rate of change of intensity of double exponential pulse is more than that of Gaussian pulse initially, but when the pulse width is decreased we observe higher amplitudes and lower attenuation of the double exponential pulse as compared to the Gaussian pulse.

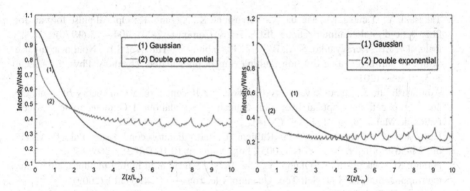

Fig. 8. (1) Gaussian and (2) double-exponential pulses at pulse width (a) 1 picosecond; (b) 0.1 picosecond.

Pico second pules can be used in short range applications such as sensing [28]. TWDM-PON is the main solution to the NG-PON2 standard [26]. This system involves the use of multiple XG-PON systems to improve the bit rates in upstream and downstream and was used to meet the NG-PON2 standards. As observed in Fig. 8(b) femtosecond pulses have high dispersion lengths which is favourable for long range communication. The response to fiber parameters is non-linear and it resists noise better with higher amplitudes. As observed in Fig. 2 in Sect. 2 under Subsect. 2.2, the overlap with consecutive pulses is minimal due to their shape and small pulse width. This enables the Inter symbol interference (ISI) to be low and hence reduces margin for error. As observed from Fig. 4 in Sect. 2 under Subsect. 2.3 the half power bandwidth efficiency of these pulses is 23% hence it favours higher bit rates.

4 Conclusion

The propagation of double exponential and Gaussian pulses in optical fibers were compared for single as well as multimode cases. The effects of dispersion and non-linear effects on the pulses were studied and observations were made. It was found that double exponential pulses are better suited for applications such as femto lasers as it is more resistant to non-linear effects than the Gaussian pulse in that range. But it has a higher half power bandwidth efficiency than that of a Gaussian pulse. The rising and falling edges of the curve are steeper in the case of double exponential pulse and this makes it favourable for applications involving TWDM. The analysis in the case of multimode fibers shows that the Gaussian pulse is more resistant to the Modal Dispersive effects than the double exponential pulses.

References

1. Takasaki, Y., Tanaka, M., Maeda, N., Yamashita, K., Nagano, K.: Optical pulse formats for fiber optic digital communications. IEEE Trans. Commun. **24**(4), 404–413 (1976)
2. Prilepsky, J.E., Derevyanko, S.A., Blow, K.J., Gabitov, I., Turitsyn, S.K.: Nonlinear inverse synthesis and eigenvalue division multiplexing in optical fiber channels. Phys. Rev. Lett. **113**, 013901 (2014)
3. Amiranashvili, S., Bandelow, U., Akhmediev, N.: Recent progress in theory of nonlinear pulse propagation in optical fibers. In: Numerical Simulation of Optoelectronic Devices, Palma de Mallorca, pp. 131–132 (2014)
4. Hirlimann, C.: Pulsed optics. In: Rullière, C. (ed.) Femtosecond Laser Pulses. ADTP, pp. 25–56. Springer, New York (2005). https://doi.org/10.1007/0-387-26674-7_2
5. Hirano, M., Nakanishi, T., Okuno, T., Onishi, M.: Silica-based highly nonlinear fibers and their application. IEEE J. Sel. Top. Quantum Electron. **15**(1), 103–113 (2009)
6. Agrawal, G.P. (ed.): Pulse compression. In: Applications of Nonlinear Fiber Optics, 2nd edn., Chap. 6, pp. 245–300. Academic Press, Cambridge (2008)
7. Agrawal, G.P. (ed.): Fiber-optic communications. In: Applications of Nonlinear Fiber Optics, 2nd edn., Chap. 7, pp. 301–348. Academic Press, Cambridge (2008)
8. Agrawal, G.P. (ed.): Optical signal processing. In: Applications of Nonlinear Fiber Optics, 2nd edn., Chap. 8, pp. 349–396. Academic Press, Cambridge (2008)
9. Agrawal, G.P. (ed.): Quantum applications. In: Applications of Nonlinear Fiber Optics, 2d edn., Chap. 10, pp. 447–492. Academic Press, Cambridge (2008)
10. Santhosh Kumar, C., Kumar, R., Das, D.: Analysis of soliton interaction in optical fiber communication. Int. J. Sci. R. Inventions New Ideas **1**, 15 (2013)
11. Rahimi, E., Nejad, S.M.: Analysis of super-Gaussian ultra-short pulse propagation in nonlinear optical fibers. In: 2008 International Symposium on High Capacity Optical Networks and Enabling Technologies, Penang, pp. 135–140 (2008)
12. Burgoyne, B., Godbout, N., Lacroix, S.: Nonlinear pulse propagation in optical fibers using second order moments. Opt. Express **15**, 10075–10090 (2007)
13. Wu, G.: Shape properties of pulses described by double exponential function and its modified forms. IEEE Trans. Electromagn. Compat. **56**(4), 923–931 (2014)
14. Mori, M., Sugihara, M.: The double-exponential transformation in numerical analysis. J. Comput. Appl. Math. **127**(1–2), 287–296 (2001)

15. Pab Sumesh, E., Elias, E.: Multiwavelet optimized finite difference method to solve nonlinear schrödinger equation in optical fiber. In: IEEE Region 10 Annual International Conference, Proceedings/TENCON, Hyderabad (2008)
16. Gloge, D.: Optical fibers for communication. Appl. Opt. **13**, 249–254 (1974)
17. Gloge, D., Gardner, W.B.: Fiber design considerations. In: Miller, S.E., Chynoweth, A.G. (eds.) Optical Fiber Telecommunications, Chap. 6, pp. 151–165. Academic Press, Cambridge (1979)
18. Gloge, D., Marcatili, E.A.J., Marcuse, D., Personick, S.D.: Dispersion properties of fibers. In: Miller, S.E., Chynoweth, A.G. (eds.) Optical Fiber Telecommunications, Chap. 4, pp. 101–124. Academic Press, Cambridge (1979)
19. Marcuse, D., Gloge, D., Marcatili, E.A.J.: Guiding properties of fibers. In: Miller, S.E., Chynoweth, A.G. (eds.) Optical Fiber Telecommunications, Chap. 3, pp. 37–100. Academic Press, Cambridge (1979)
20. Mitra, P.P., Stark, J.B.: Nonlinear limits to the information capacity of optical fibre communications. Nature **411**, 1027–1030 (2001)
21. Vasilyev, M., Su, Y., McKinstrie, C.: Introduction to the special issue on nonlinear-optical signal processing. J. Sel. Topics Quantum Electron. **14**(3), 527–528 (2008)
22. Malitson, H.: Interspecimen comparison of the refractive index of fused silica. JOSA **55**(10), 1205–1208 (1965)
23. Walmsley, I.A., et al.: The role of dispersion in ultrafast optics. Rev. Sci. Instrum. **72**(1), 1 (2001)
24. Gonçalves, A.M.: Pulse propagation in optical fibers (2012). Online Reference. Accessed 3 Sept 2018
25. Thottappillil, R., Uman, M.A.: Comparison of lightning return stroke models. J. Geophys. Res. **98**(D112), 903–914 (1992)
26. Luo, Y., et al.: Time- and wavelength-division multiplexed passive optical network (TWDM-PON) for next-generation PON stage 2 (NG-PON2). J. Lightwave Technol. **31**(4), 587–593 (2013)
27. Rota-Rodrigo, S., Gonzalez-Herraez, M., Lopez-Amo, M.: Compound lasing fiber optic ring resonators for sensor sensitivity enhancement. J. Lightwave Technol. **33**(12), 2690–2696 (2015)
28. Ladányi, L., Menkyna, R., Mullerova, J.: Analysis of dispersion effects in Gaussian pulses with the various chirp parameters. In: International Conference on Elitech, June, Bratislava (2013)
29. Olshansky, R., Keck, D.B.: Pulse broadening in graded-index optical fibers. Appl. Opt. **15**, 483–491 (1976)
30. Tooley, M.H.: Electronic circuits: fundamentals and applications. Newnes, pp. 77–78 (2006). ISBN 978-0-7506-6923-8

Hybrid Energy Efficient and QoS Aware Algorithm to Prolong IoT Network Lifetime

N. N. Srinidhi[(✉)], Jyothi Lakshmi, and S. M. Dilip Kumar

Department of Computer Science and Engineering,
University Visvesvaraya College of Engineering, Bangalore, India
srinidhinagesh@gmail.com, jyothilakshmi963@gmail.com,
dilipkumarsm@gmail.com

Abstract. The Internet of Things (IoT) consists of large amount of energy compel devices which are prefigured to progress the effective competence of several industrial applications. It is very much essential to bring down the energy utilization of every device deployed in IoT network without compromising the quality of service (QoS). Here, the difficulty of providing the operation between the QoS allocation and the energy competence for the industrial IoT application is deliberate. To achieve this objective, the multi-objective optimization problem to accomplish the aim of estimating the outage performance and the network lifetime is devised. Subsequently, proposed Hybrid Energy Efficient and QoS Aware (HEEQA) algorithm is a combination of quantum particle swarm optimization (QPSO) along with improved non dominated sorting genetic algorithm (NGSA) to achieve energy balance among the devices is proposed and later the MAC layer parameters are tuned to reduce the further energy consumption of the devices. NSGA is applied to solve the problem of multi-objective optimization and the QPSO algorithm is used to gain the finest cooperative combination. The simulation outcome has put forward that the HEEQA algorithm has attained better operation balance between the energy competence and the QoS provisioning by minimizing the energy consumption, delay, transmission overhead and maximizing network lifetime, throughput and delivery ratio.

Keywords: Energy efficiency · IoT · Network lifetime · QoS

1 Introduction

IoT is considered as the future technology for improving the overall efficiency of the industrial and other applications. IoT in its set up consists of large number of reliable M2M devices having lower communication range [1]. Devices used in IoT mainly uses IEEE 802.15.4 compliant devices with IEEE 802.11ah and LoRaWAN to provide communication with other devices through Internet in order to achieve performance efficiency of the application [2].

© ICST Institute for Computer Sciences, Social Informatics and Telecommunications Engineering 2019
Published by Springer Nature Switzerland AG 2019. All Rights Reserved
N. Kumar and R. Venkatesha Prasad (Eds.): UBICNET 2019, LNICST 276, pp. 80–95, 2019.
https://doi.org/10.1007/978-3-030-20615-4_6

In order to provide cellular network to the local short communication range devices capillary networks are used [3]. Capillary networks help in development of IoT technology by leveraging wireless sensor devices (WSN) to use cellular networks with the aid of gateways in between them. In WSN setup the energy and memory constrained devices are arranged in cluster passion. In clustering process individual nodes residual energy, their distance between base station (BS) and other parameters are considered while choosing the cluster head (CH) of the individual cluster [4]. There may be multiple cluster head in the network but the energy consumption of the cluster head is more compared to normal nodes due the information exchange that they carry out between individual nodes and BS. Capillary network lifetime is described as the time period between capillary network deployment to the residual energy of the first nodes drains completely. Gateways help in connecting these nodes to Internet and to cloud platform to notify in case of emergency or to store the data in cloud platform and also to database.

Cooperative communications is meant to improve energy efficiency, reliability and network lifetime in WSN [5]. Cooperative communication called Reliability Improved Cooperative Communication (RICC), scheme is proposed to maximize the reliability of cooperative communication of the random network in case of multi-hop relay WSN without compromising network lifetime. This method uses residual energy of the node to transmit the data and dynamically adjusts the power required for data transmission based on nodes distance with sink node. Remaining energy alerting mechanism uses Distributed cooperative communication nodes control (DCCNC) mechanism [6], this scheme helps in changing the CH whenever their remaining energy falls below the threshold energy level in order to provide reliable data transfer. Cooperative nodes are used to reduce the overload on the CH and large numbers of cooperative nodes are used in non-hotspot area in order to achieve maximum reliability and lesser cooperative nodes are used in hotspot area to maximize network lifetime. This method drains more energy and delays while choosing CH during clustering process. With an objective of improving network lifetime two sensor solution is provided wherein sensors should collaborate and define how much power is required for cooperation [7]. In case of multiple sensor scenarios network lifetime can be maximized by placing cooperative relays in appropriate location to reduce the power requirement of the nodes thereby relay nodes helps to reduce transmission power required by sensor nodes. This cooperative relay mechanism helps in maximizing network lifetime up to 3 times than normal WSN setup. But to improve QoS of the network requires additional energy and this contradicts network lifetime improvement.

Most of the aforementioned works only concentrates on power control and bit error rate rather than improving network lifetime without compromising on QoS. Thus, HEEQA method is proposed with an objective to maintain balance between energy utilization and QoS in case of clustered IoT setup.

Motivation for doing this work are (1) Energy competence or QoS enlargement to further rate of the energy utilization and multi-objective enlargement problem of the operation among QoS and energy competence to enhance IoT network lifetime. (2) A best supportive combination of cooperative node and CH method can be proposed by means of particle swarm optimization inspired with Quantum (QPSO) collective in the company of comprehensive search. The potential CH candidate is determined by comprehensive search. The short computing, instant and quick convergence, small population size and stronger searching ability can be achieved by QPSO, which combines the evolutionary algorithm and the quantum computing theory. (3) The enhanced non dominated categorization of the genetic method is worn to resolve multi-objective enlargement of QoS and energy competence. The congregate improved in obtaining non dominated sorting compared by evolutionary method (EAs) is capable for the maintenance of a better increase of results in NSGA algorithm, QPSO algorithm calculates the fitness values for the selection of various systems as cooperative nodes.

Overall contribution of this work is outlined as

- Improving the IoT network lifetime by harnessing devices energy consumption during data transmission by optimizing provisioning QoS for energy efficient.
- Quantum particle swarm optimization method is used to select potential CH and cooperative nodes.
- Quantum computing theory which optimizes the computing time can have stronger search for potential nodes and reduces the communication overhead.
- Selection of non dominated set of nodes resulted by using non-dominated genetic sorting algorithm to provide QoS in multi-objective optimization perspective.
- Finally, QPSO and NSGA is combined to form hybrid algorithm called HEEQA to calculate the fitness function for QoS.

The rest of the paper is organized as follows. Section 2 presents a summary of various corresponding works with respect to energy conserving and QoS improvement during routing. Section 3 provides the problem statement of the work. Architecture of the method is presented in Sect. 4. The proposed mechanism and its evaluation is presented in Sect. 5. Simulation and Results and conclusion along with future work are presented in Sects. 6 and 7 respectively.

2 Related Work

Many works have been proposed by authors to improve energy consumed during routing of data which includes [8], where authors have proposed an algorithm called Particle Swarm Optimization (PSO) in which they considered flocking of birds, schooling of fishes, theories of swarm and artificial life or biologically derived algorithm. In this algorithm, the g-best and p-best values are calculated based on the velocity of the PSO for the fitness in hyperspace to obtain optimal solution. The advantage of this paper is that the PSO is capable to coach the group in order to reach ninety two percentage of result and this algorithm is still useful for calculating fitness value. The drawback of this work is that in highly discontinuous data surface features it is difficult to optimize function for local optima. Wu et al. in [9], have proposed algorithm for the pareto order, combine and divide law to shape association sets between entity antenna nodes and to overcome the significant problem of scheming mobile antenna networks with the goal of getting better energy competence. This method can make decision about which communication scheme to be used and which CNs should be attached to which CH. But this method is not suitable in case of super-large scale WSNs setup.

Authors in [10], have proposed an algorithm called LEACH in energy competent with transaction protocol for mobile Micro antenna interconnections. Method uses set of rules defined in LEACH protocol for consistent allocation of energy load along with the nodes in the network on the limited cluster support stations like CH. The data aggregation considerably reduces the total amount of information to be sent to the sink node. LEACH decreases transaction energy eight times compared with straight transmission and also reduces transmission energy during routing. In [11], authors have proposed the novel QPSO method which uses quantum computing theory along with standard PSO in order to resolve spectrum allocation issue in radio and this method provides the global optimal solution when different utility functions are being used. Authors in [12], have proposed algorithm called MOR4WSN which uses NSGA-II to provide multi-objective optimization in WSN routing. This method aims to minimize network energy utilization during the process of sensor distribution.

Task phase organization by shared optimisation of wait with energy competence of capillary device to device interconnections with the 5G transmission model have been proposed in [13]. This method provides development of new energy competent and point to point wait task phase, manages design for guiders in the capillary networks controller with the gateway. It formulates a responsibility cycle to organize difficulty with shared optimisation for energy utilization and point to point wait. The proposed model contains of two parts for the communication plan, first part decides the best possible amount of data to be sent among, gateways, M2M systems and coordinators. Second part is a task phase which manages the IEEE 802.15.4. This method is not suited for large network as the model increases overhead when network size increases. Banka et al. in [14], have proposed PSO-MSPA algorithm which is based on PSO and provides efficient method for placing multiple sink nodes present in the WSN network. This method makes use of Euclidean distance between gateway and sink node and also number of hops in between them to reduce energy during data transfer. But this method lacks in addressing various other QoS parameters which are required in increasing network performance. Authors in [15], have proposed EEPR algorithm which uses probabilistic routing mechanism to control packets requesting routes stochastically during packet transmission to maximize network lifetime and to minimize packet loss rate during flooding. In this method ETX metric is used with AODV protocol to achieve the objective. This method lacks in improving overall energy consumed in the network as this method only controls route request packet amount rate and fails to address different factors which drains network energy faster.

3   Problem Statement

IoT nodes have lower communication range, lesser memory and computational capacity and limited energy capacity. These limitations make IoT nodes to be energy efficient in order to prolong IoT network lifetime.

1. The problem is to find out energy efficient path between the source nodes and the sink nodes using the opportunistic routing without compromising QoS parameters like throughput, reliability and end to end delay.
2. To establish balance between network lifetime maximization and QoS parameters through optimization.

This paper emphasize more on establishing balance between network lifetime and QoS provisioning.

3.1   Lifetime of the Network

The overall energy consumed by the nodes during the process of communication is given by

$$k = K_{u+1}(PN^y) + K_{u+1}(PC^y) \qquad (1)$$

where k is the energy consumed by normal node PN during communication and PC represents cluster head. Individual node lifetime is given by

$$LT = \frac{K}{k} \qquad (2)$$

where K denotes the residual energy of the node before clustering process. The lifetime of the nodes is a critical factor in increasing the lifetime of the IoT network.

3.2   QoS Stipulation

QoS is stipulated on the basis of successful packet delivery without much packet loss and with less delay. So QoS of the IoT network relies on throughput, reliability and end to end delay without compromising energy efficiency.

- Throughput TH: It is defined as the total number of packets that are successfully delivered to the destination in a unit time.
- End to End delay ED: It is defined as the time that is taken for transferring packets from source to destination in the network.
- Reliability RL: It is the amount of packets that are generated in the source are successfully delivered to the destination.

Throughput during the steady state is given by

$$TH = uP_sPHh \tag{3}$$

where u is the contention probability in which each node independently sends packet, P_s is the probability of successful packet transfer. PH is the particle-hole symmetry and h is the number of nodes.

Suppose if cooperative node is present at the center of cluster head and gateway then it is given by

$$\sum_{i=0}^{h} PH_i = 1 + \frac{h}{2} \tag{4}$$

End to end delay of ith node when $0 \leq i \leq h$ is given by

$$ED = \sum_{i=0}^{h} (uP_s(1 - PH_{i+1}))^{-1} \tag{5}$$

Overall reliability of network is given by

$$RL = \sum_{i=0}^{h} \frac{d_i(1-\xi)}{d_i + \xi - d_i\xi} \tag{6}$$

where ξ is the probability of packet drop and d_i is the geometric distribution.

Reliability of the node i across i to i + 1 link during time slot t_i is given by

$$re_i = (1 - \xi)^{t_i} \tag{7}$$

So the network lifetime and QoS stipulation problem can be formulated as

$$Max \sum_{i=0}^{h} \{LT\} = Optimal\{TH, ED, RL\} \tag{8}$$

4   Network Architecture

In this section, the network model, energy model and route discovery process is presented.

4.1   Network Model

The nodes are randomly deployed and clusters are formed by clustering process, all the wireless devices perform data collection, aggregation and sends to BS or sink.

1. Sink node collects data from the wireless devices, which have a data to be processed.

2. All devices have same transmission range and are energy constrained, IEEE 802.15.4 protocol is used in the radios for shorter communication.
3. Devices can adjust their transmission range to reach particular destinations.
4. Devices are aware of their locations and energy levels.
5. Devices are classified into nodes, CH, cooperative nodes and capillary gateway. Capillary gateway will provide interface to two different radio network types one radio type is used to communicate with local network and other radio type to connect local network to IoT platform as depicted in Fig. 1.

Here two phases of transmission takes place first by forming clusters using the clustering algorithm. The formation of cluster takes place by nodes belonging to one hop distance, so as to communicate within transmission range. CH is elected based on the high residual energy and each device in the cluster updates its location and knows the detail about CH and cooperative nodes. TDMA protocols schedules the transmission of data collected by nodes. CH is responsible to collect data from nodes through data gathering phase. The data gathered form the nodes is aggregated and sent to all cooperative nodes by CH through broadcasting. Then both CH and cooperative nodes forward data to sink node through long distance mode in order to extend the transmission range and also to reduce the load on cluster head.

4.2 Energy Model

Let consider K_0 be the initial energy of every IoT node powered by non-reachable energy source. Energy model of [16], is followed by the nodes in the network. Cluster head CH, one base station or sink node with h number of nodes are distributed. Each node has direction communication between each other through

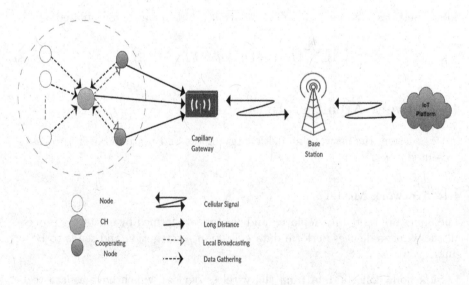

Fig. 1. Network model

radio links within the radio communication range. Every IoT node is uniformly scattered in a terrain of B_t and C_t dimension, wherein i^{th} normal node forwards each packets to the jth cluster head and energy loss while transferring packets between the nodes follows multi-path fading model and free space. Every node in the IoT network consists of transmitter and receiver together called as transreceiver. Energy is dissipated in transmitter by hardware components such as power amplifier and radio components, whereas in receiver energy is dissipated by radio components. Energy is also dissipated during packet transmission and two different models explain this energy dissipation. One model provides for node type whether its head or normal node and other provide based on distance for every packet transferred of size PA_l. After clustering process, the each normal node PN will send data packets to cluster head denoted by PC.

Energy consumed when PA_l bytes of data sent by the normal node is given by

$$K_{los}(PN^y) = K_{elec} * PA_l + K_{fd} * PA_l * ||PN^y - PC^z||^4 \ if ||PN^y - PC^z|| \geq k_0 \quad (9)$$

$$K_{los}(PN^y) = K_{elec} * PA_l + K_{fs} * PA_l * ||PN^y - PC^z||^2 \ if ||PN^y - PC^z|| < k_0 \quad (10)$$

$$k_0 = \sqrt{\frac{K_{fs}}{K_{fd}}} \quad (11)$$

where, K_{elec} is the electronics energy based on factors like modulation, amplifier, filtering and digital coding while, K_{fs} and K_{fd} represents energy of free space and multipath fading model. So the electronics energy is

$$K_{elec} = K_{TRN} + K_{DAG} \quad (12)$$

where K_{TRN} is energy of transmitter and K_{DAG} is energy of data aggregation, $||PN^y - PC^z||$ is the distance between normal node and the cluster head respectively. Each node sends PA_l bytes of data and this sent packet is received by the cluster head. The energy spent by receiver during this process is given by

$$K_{los}(PC^y) = K_{elec} * PA_l \quad (13)$$

Remaining energy of each IoT node is updated after PA_l bytes data is either sent or received

$$K_{u+1}(PN^y) = K_u(PN^y) - K_{los}(PN^y) \quad (14)$$

$$K_{u+1}(PC^y) = K_u(PC^y) - K_{los}(PC^y) \quad (15)$$

This data transfer process continues until every nodes energy becomes zero. The node whose energy is zero is known as dead node.

4.3   Route Discovery Process

The route discovery process works as follows:

1. Routing Information such as source node, destination node and range is taken as an input.
2. Clustering process will takes place and cluster head is selected based on higher residual énergy.
3. Nodes will affiliate to corresponding cluster head which is in its range.
4. The neighbor list will be generated which will contain a list of nodes which are within the transmission range of the source node.
5. The source node will then check cluster head whether the neighbor list contains the destination node with minimum distance. If yes then it will stop the routing process since the destination has reached.
6. If the neighbor list does not contain destination node then the next cluster head is picked up to find the existence of destination node with minimum routing distance.
7. Steps 2 through 6 are repeatedly performed until the destination node with optimal routing distance is reached.

5   Proposed HEEQA Algorithm

In HEEQA, QPSO is used to improve the solution of the candidate iteratively to obtain the objective. During this various attributes like present location, local optima, present velocity and global optima are represented by particles. Cooperative selection is made based on the particle present location. NSGA is used to provide find pareto optimal solution based on objective function. The main objective is to improve network lifetime through cooperative nodes in order to improve energy efficiency of the cluster head. The overall HEEQA algorithm is outlined in below steps.

Step 1: Presume each nodes to be cluster head PC successively and employs following steps to choose the optimal cooperative node for the presumed PC.

Step 2: Initiate the population A_p having qp quantum particles on basis of quantum coding mechanism and add it to Pareto front F.

Step 3: Determine every quantum particle through the fitness sort population A_{pf} according to the non dominated Genetic algorithm to find best energy efficient node.

Step 4: Construct a new population A_{pnew} using QPSO algorithm from the existing population A_p.

Step 5: Analyze every quantum particle of the new population A_{pnew} by combining fitness value of both objectives to obtain $A^*_{pnew} = A_{pnew} \cup A_p$. Classify A^*_{pnew} using NSGA is to provide non dominated solution and assign obtained value to G.

Step 6: Tune up the MAC parameters SIFS, DIFS, CW_{min} and CW_{max} to improve energy efficiency of the nodes.

Step 7: Combine F and G to provide pareto optimal solution set A_{com}.

Step 8: Repeat steps 1 through 7 to find A_{com} of each iteration and add these values for every PC to obtain A_{final}. Classify A_{final} in descending order using NSGA with respect to crowding distance and find optimal solution from sorted A_{final}.

6   Simulation and Results

6.1   Simulation Model

The proposed HEEQA algorithm is evaluated extensively using event driven network simulator NS-2 simulator. The simulation is done on a terrain size of 500 m × 500 m with 30 to 50 nodes deployed randomly with an initial energy of 60 J. The transmission range of the node is set to 250 m. Parameters used in the simulation are given in Table 1. Here, we have compared proposed method with QPSO due to the prevalent functionalities between each other.

6.2   Simulation Results

In this section the performance of the algorithm with respect to residual energy maximization, end-to-end delay, packet delivery ratio (PDR), transmission overhead, network lifetime maximization and throughput is evaluated.

6.3   Variation of Energy Level

Proposed method is efficient in saving the energy of the nodes due to the presence of cooperative node between cluster head and the gateway node which reduces the energy consumption of the node drained during data transmission. The Fig. 2 shows the efficiency of the HEEQA when compared with QPSO.

Table 1. Simulation parameters

Parameter	Value
Number of nodes h	50 nodes
Network size $B_t \times C_t$	500 m ∗ 500 m
Transmission range	250 m
Initial energy K_0	60 J
Propagation model	Two ray ground
Number of rounds	100
Packet size	250 KB
Traffic type	CBR
MAC type	802.11
Antenna type	Omni directional antenna
Examined protocol	HEEQA and QPSO

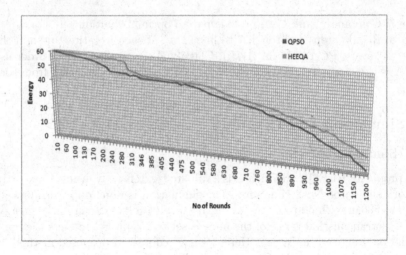

Fig. 2. Residual energy

6.4   Average End-to-End Delay

It is very important for any method to minimize end-to-end delay of the data packets else the reliability of the network decreases. Reduction in end-to-end delay will results in better throughput. In this method data packets are delivered faster due to the use of long distance communication method. Figure 3 provides comparative graph of end-to-end delay.

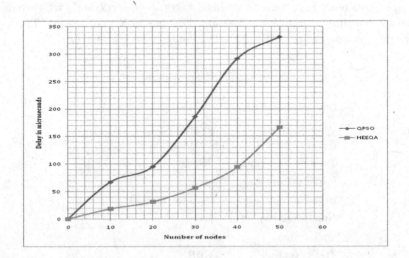

Fig. 3. Average end-to-end delay comparison

6.5 Delivery Ratio

Figure 4 provides the increase in packets delivery ratio achieved by the proposed method. This method achieves notable amount of PDR when compared to QPSA due to presence of cooperative nodes which aid in faster delivery of data packets along with cluster head in long distance mode which avoids congestion in the route due to less channel occupancy.

6.6 Transmission Overhead

Transmission overhead will have negative impact on the overall network lifetime due to the congestion in the transmission route and results in frequent change in the cluster head due to lesser residual energy. Figure 5 shows proposed method outperforms in terms of transmission overhead reduction which is resultant of optimal usage of cluster head residual energy.

6.7 Network Lifetime

It is observed in the Fig. 6 that as the density of the nodes increases then the proposed method outperforms than the QPSO method. Due to different threshold level in outage probability the lifetime of the IoT network increases. It is due to the fact that outage probability provides average unsuccessful rate in transmission by setting up threshold level in the signal to noise ratio. Another factor for improving network lifetime is the use of long distance communication which is about 250 m and this communication method aids in increasing the overall lifetime of the cluster head.

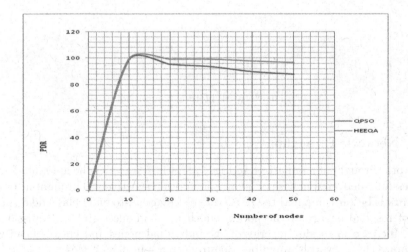

Fig. 4. Packet delivery ratio

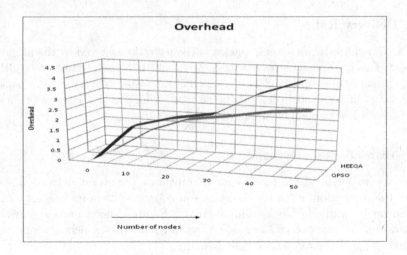

Fig. 5. Comparison of transmission overhead

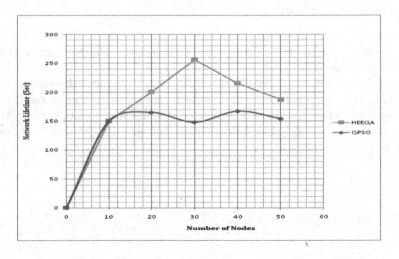

Fig. 6. Network lifetime comparison

6.8   Network Throughput

Network throughput comparison in Fig. 7 and Fig. 8 provides the amount of data successfully delivered in case of 30 and 50 nodes respectively. Throughput of the network is better compared to QPSO due to lesser end-to-end delay and optimal use of residual energy of the nodes, which helps in successful transmission of data. Increase in residual energy of the individual nodes and cluster head will maximize the network throughput due to decrease in dead nodes.

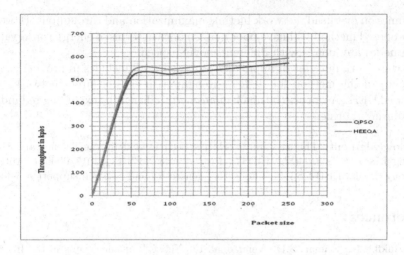

Fig. 7. Throughput comparison for 30 nodes

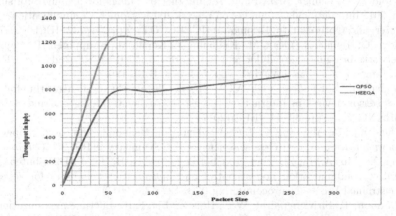

Fig. 8. Throughput comparison for 50 nodes

7 Conclusions and Future Work

Achieving QoS in IoT devices is a major challenge and to prolong lifetime of the devices requires energy balancing. In this paper HEEQA is proposed, which is an energy competent QoS aware model by combining NSGA and QPSO to find the best fitness node with high residual energy for energy efficient communication among the cluster. With the simulation results we have showed that: (i) Use of cooperative nodes will increase the efficiency of cluster heads in terms of optimizing QoS and overall QoS performance is increased due to long communication mode. (ii) Energy consumption of each node in the IoT network is reduced by tuning up of MAC layer parameters. (iii) Proposed method outperforms QPSO in terms of residual energy maximization, end-to-end delay, delivery ratio, transmission overhead, network lifetime maximization and throughput. However the proposed method will have poor performance in terms of energy conservation when nodes are mobile with different moving speed.

Future work in terms of improving proposed work includes improving energy efficiency of the method for higher throughput in case of larger network. The proposed HEEQA can also be made more energy efficient by excluding redundant data during routing.

Acknowledgment. This research work has been funded by the Science and Engineering Research Board (SERB-DST) Project File No: EEQ/2017/000681. Authors sincerely thank SERB-DST for intellectual generosity and research support provided.

References

1. Srinidhi, N., Kumar, S.D., Venugopal, K.: Network optimizations in the Internet of Things: a review. Eng. Sci. Technol. Int. J. **22**(1), 1–21 (2018)
2. Srinidhi, N., Kumar, S.D., Banu, R.: Internet of Things for neophytes: a survey. In: 2017 International Conference on Electrical, Electronics, Communication, Computer, and Optimization Techniques (ICEECCOT), pp. 234–242. IEEE (2017)
3. Novo, O., Beijar, N., Ocak, M., Kjällman, J., Komu, M., Kauppinen, T.: Capillary networks-bridging the cellular and IoT worlds. In: 2015 IEEE 2nd World Forum on Internet of Things (WF-IoT), pp. 571–578. IEEE (2015)
4. Fouladlou, M., Khademzadeh, A.: An energy efficient clustering algorithm for wireless sensor devices in Internet of Things. In: Artificial Intelligence and Robotics (IRANOPEN), pp. 39–44. IEEE (2017)
5. Chen, Z., Ma, M., Liu, X., Liu, A., Zhao, M.: Reliability improved cooperative communication over wireless sensor networks. Symmetry **9**(10), 209 (2017)
6. Liu, X., Liu, A., Li, Z., Tian, S., Choi, Y.j., Sekiya, H., Li, J.: Distributed cooperative communication nodes control and optimization reliability for resource-constrained WSNs. Neurocomputing **270**, 122–136 (2017)
7. Himsoon, T., Siriwongpairat, W.P., Han, Z., Liu, K.R.: Lifetime maximization via cooperative nodes and relay deployment in wireless networks. IEEE J. Sel. Areas Commun. **25**(2), 306–317 (2007)
8. Kennedy, J.: Particle swarm optimization. In: Encyclopedia of Machine Learning, pp. 760–766. Springer, New York (2011)
9. Wu, D., Cai, Y., Wang, J.: A coalition formation framework for transmission scheme selection in wireless sensor networks. IEEE Trans. Veh. Technol. **60**(6), 2620–2630 (2011)
10. Heinzelman, W.R., Chandrakasan, A., Balakrishnan, H.: Energy-efficient communication protocol for wireless microsensor networks. In: Proceedings of the 33rd Annual Hawaii International Conference on System Sciences, 10 pp. IEEE (2000)
11. Gao, H., Cao, J.l., Diao, M.: A simple quantum-inspired particle swarm optimization and its application. Inf. Technol. J. **10**(12), 2315–2321 (2011)
12. Rodriguez, A., Ordóñez, A., Ordoñez, H., Segovia, R.: Adapting NSGA-II for hierarchical sensor networks in the IoT. Procedia Comput. Sci. **61**, 355–360 (2015)
13. Li, Y., Chai, K.K., Chen, Y., Loo, J.: Duty cycle control with joint optimisation of delay and energy efficiency for capillary machine-to-machine networks in 5G communication system. Trans. Emerg. Telecommun. Technol. **26**(1), 56–69 (2015)

14. Srinivasa Rao P., C., Banka, H., Jana, P.K.: PSO-based multiple-sink placement algorithm for protracting the lifetime of wireless sensor networks. In: Satapathy, S.C., Raju, K.S., Mandal, J.K., Bhateja, V. (eds.) Proceedings of the Second International Conference on Computer and Communication Technologies. AISC, vol. 379, pp. 605–616. Springer, New Delhi (2016). https://doi.org/10.1007/978-81-322-2517-1_58

15. Park, S.H., Cho, S., Lee, J.R.: Energy-efficient probabilistic routing algorithm for Internet of Things. J. Appl. Math. **2014** (2014)

16. Kumar, R., Kumar, D.: Multi-objective fractional artificial bee colony algorithm to energy aware routing protocol in wireless sensor network. Wireless Netw. **22**(5), 1461–1474 (2016)

Data Integration and Management in Indian Poultry Sector

Susmitha Shankar and S. Thangam[(⊠)]

Amrita School of Engineering, Amrita Vishwa Vidyapeetham, Bengaluru, India
S_thangam@blr.amrita.edu

Abstract. Poultry sector- both commercial and smallholder- contribute significantly to both the financial stability of the poor and the economy of the nation. Record keeping in this sector not only ensures tight financial check of inventories but also helps in analyzing the factors affecting the quality and well-being of poultry. It is estimated that the world poultry production will increase many folds in the coming future, and so would the associated poultry health care analysis, inventory and infrastructure, climate analysis and other associated sectors. With the rise in population and growing demand for poultry product, manual record keeping and manual analysis of such huge, varied and dynamic data would turn out to be tedious and time-consuming task, causing out-of-time delivery of necessary decision. Thus, this sector is in need of software managed data analysis and data integration to ensure timely delivery of necessary action and most accurate prediction to help with the decision. We present a framework for data integration and analysis of poultry data to help in easy prediction, analysis and decision making in this sector, thus increasing the profits earned.

Keywords: Data integration · Poultry · Concatenation-based approach

1 Introduction

The transformation of Indian poultry from an unorganized and non-scientific sector to a commercial system by amalgamating scientific approaches has led to the growth in scientific discoveries in terms of poultry equipment and nutrients. Poultry data tracking can help with efficient tracking of the health of eggs and broilers. The advent of advanced and modern scientific equipment, methods and strategies in poultry industry brought about a lot of data processing and analysis for better poultry product production in terms of both quality and quantity. The global rise in egg production and consumption has been increasing. The enormous data would help in better decision-making faster and effectively.

Data analysis in poultry using computational techniques has shown remarkable results, indicating which factors largely affect the eggs and broilers and how much. Apart from the phenotypic and environmental factors that affect the poultry health, studies on the genetic structure of the poultry have also been made, thus helping in selection while breeding. The extensive use of mathematical and statistical approaches coupled with recent next-generation sequencing technology in the domain has helped in a detailed study of epidemiology [1]. Using the machine learning technique for

N. Kumar and R. Venkatesha Prasad (Eds.): UBICNET 2019, LNICST 276, pp. 96–102, 2019.
https://doi.org/10.1007/978-3-030-20615-4_7

automating the decision making on various aspects of poultry production cycle has been a keen research aspect for a decade. With highly efficient techniques such as SVM, regression models, HMMs, early prediction on the quality of the eggs and broilers could be made with higher accuracy and confidence [2].

With the advent of new technologies, the poultry data has grown enormous. Thus, the traditional manual method of record keeping is no longer suitable for decision making. Understanding the poultry to a maximum extent would require the comprehensive sight of all factors, including environmental factors such as the amount of ammonia in air, chlorine in water, number of flocks in unit kilometers as well as genetic factors. Although work on automated prediction of health and drops in egg production has been done, no work on the integration of poultry data has been found to the best of our knowledge. Processed data from multiple sources integrated into one platform could significantly increase the predictive analysis. An efficient platform for dynamic integration of the poultry data coupled with the visualization tool could help the poultry farmers to yield better decisions. Thus, this work aims at the creation of a framework for integration and visualization of poultry data.

The understanding of the domain for the work is taken from various articles and published materials as presented in Sect. 2. Followed by Sect. 2, the proposed architecture is presented in Sect. 3 and Sect. 4 deals with the implementation. Section 5 concludes the work.

2 State of Art

The appropriate synchronization of the two sectors, namely the commercial sector and the unorganized sector, helps in enhancing the economic conditions of the smallholders. The United State Department of Agriculture (USDA) Global Agricultural Information Network (GAIN) report for 2015 and 2016 estimates per capita consumption of poultry meat to be around 3.1 kg per year and 3.6 kg per year respectively and was forecasted to rise by 7% over 2016. Also, the per capita consumption of eggs in India is reported to be 62 eggs per year. However, both consumption of meat and egg is considerably lower compared to the world average (17 kg per year for meat), which establishes the possibility of the further flourishing market [3]. With the rise in income and demand, the need for healthier products would also increase. Active research and development facility from governmental and private sectors to develop quality and quantity of poultry product would further raise the poultry sector.

The profitability in the poultry sector also depends on the ease of vertical and horizontal integration [4, 5] and the support of governmental agencies for the same. Vertical integration in the poultry sector refers to one company many controls policy, wherein one company owns multiple stages of productions such as feed mills, hatcheries and many more. This leads to independent complete production groups, the better utility of space, enhanced quality control, and comparatively higher productivity and profitability. These are also referred to as "integrators". Horizontal integration helps in rearing different types of dependent livestock rearing such as poultry with fisheries, etc. The interdependencies of various livestock enhance the symbiotic existence, quality and the by-product such as generated wastes, have higher nutritive proportion and are best in quality. Although there is a high scope of profitability in the poultry sector in India, there are also challenges that have to be seriously dealt with.

Diagnosis of the health of poultry at the appropriate time, efficient management and reuse of bio-waste, proper storage, and transport facilities, availability of quality supplements and many more factors. To cope with the challenges listed above, the Government of India has formulated infrastructural regulations as mentioned in Poultry Farm Manual (2014–15) by Department of Animal Husbandry, Dairying and Fisheries, Ministry of Agriculture and Farmers Welfare, Government of India, which includes compliance of location of farm with the State Pollution Control Board, minimum geographical distance of more than 100 m from major water drinking source and 500 m from other poultry enterprise source, proper drainage outlet, dimension of the farm, etc. Strict check and regular follow-ups on these rules must be initiated [6]. Also, there are few international agencies ready to join hands with Indian Poultry sector to yield necessary technical guidance to enhance this field [7].

However, voluntary check by the organizations and small-scale farmers along with motivation by the governmental and non-governmental organization would prove to be much beneficial and effective. The analysis and decision making in this sector involve a lot of factors to be considered. Missing a few factors would reduce the efficiency of the farm product, leave a bad influence on the farm and poultry product and may also affect the health of the poultry. Thus, a software managed check and automated decision analyzer could prove to be a great help.

Various case studies in automated livestock handling have been done, all of which points towards the need for software enhanced study [8]. Studies on the economic condition bought due to the rearing of poultry, a harmful environmental condition due to the emission of ammonia from the pig farm, efficient routing technique for transportation, maintaining inventory management according to the supply-demand chain are studied in detail [9, 10]. Most of the decision made in traditional livestock rearing set-up are sequential and not strategic. The strategic decision could yield more profit. Stable strategies, one which aims at the sustainability of the production system while maximizing the profit, are also emerging research goal [11]. Many integrative methods are used to create multi-model strategic plans including the use of fuzzy logic.

Programming models target efficient supply-chain decision making in seasonal and non-seasonal supply chain products [12]. The use of a Bayesian network to analyze the supply chain demand, thereby deciding whether to enter the market on the basis of available resources has been studied by Laper et al. [13]. Machine learning approaches such as SVM, are used to analyze the factors while making the decision on commercial egg production and broiler management [14, 15].

Mathematical and statistical approaches are discussed in detail to analyze various aspects of egg production, broiler feeding, accurate cut while extracting meat, inventory management and other aspects of poultry rearing [16]. Many artificial intelligence tools can also be made use of to enhance high-quality poultry product.

3 Proposed System

The framework aims at creating a data integration platform for unified and complete analysis of poultry data to extract valuable inferences. It is composed of 2 layers: the presentation layer and the processing layer. The presentation layer deals with taking inputs from the consumers, who could be poultry farmers, researchers, government agencies, etc., form queries to extract result and also to display those results. This could also be used by the producers of the information to put the data into the processing unit. The processing unit deals with the data integration platform. The data integration platform extracts the time-series and high-dimensional poultry information from the producer, make quality check on the basis of the error rate for the data, prepares the data by cleaning and processing for redundant and inconsistent data, choosing appropriate data integration technique on the basis of the data to be integrated, applying the integration technique and finally checking the quality of the integrated system.

The consumer enters the keyword related to which the inference is to be extracted. These keywords are converted to query, which is then run under the corresponding database to extract information. The integrated database would be formed when the producers or suppliers of the data gives the data to the platform which goes through correction, preparation and integration process, and is stored in the database. Figure 1 shows the diagrammatic representation of the proposed architecture.

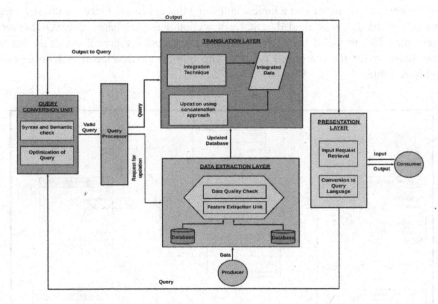

Fig. 1. Diagrammatic illustration of the proposed architecture.

4 Implementation

The data were extracted one by one from the data repository in raw format, mostly in json and xlsx. The data sources used in the integration was the open source poultry data from data.gov.in [17] and indiastats.com [18]. The first step involved the analysis of the data and the interpretation of different features associated. The statistical analysis such as correlation among the data, was conducted using R. The data represented longitudinal aspects, that is country wise or region wise studies, statistics of backyard desi and improved poultry for 2016–17, statistics of the actual the estimated production of poultry from 1993 to 2014, per-capita egg production from 1950 to 2018 for the state of Tamil Nadu and the total production of eggs for all Indian States. The challenge of missing values, due to unavailability of information for various time range, were fixed by referring to multiple sources for creating a consistent model. Once the data was extracted from their respective sources, the first step was to standardize the data.

These data were then segregated into different classes based on their interpretation, significance and the relation between them to multiple classes, programmatically using C# in .Net Core environment. Since the data separated into logical chunk involved a large amount of data operations, the code was run in an asynchronous parallel fashion. The segregation was done in such a way that the inconsistency is reduced. This was achieved by normalizing the data to 3NF. Concatenation based approach was used as the integration technique for this model. The data from multiple sources in varied format were concatenated into a logical unit using this approach. Once the classes were created and the data was divided, a SQL connection was established with SQL Server, where the tables reside, using Microsoft Azure Data Studio. Figure 2 shows the entity class diagram for the integrated poultry. The framework developed is feasible and highly scalable.

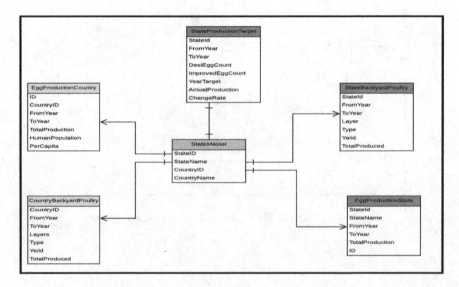

Fig. 2. Entity-class diagram for integrated poultry database

5 Conclusion and Future Work

The Poultry farming is one of the important means by which the rural community can be uplifted. The data from poultry is rich, dynamic, large and from varied sources. For proper analysis, the integration of this data is the need of the hour. Effective integration could be made after ensuring the quality of each of the source of the data and pre-processing. Automation of the task of integration would be helpful in making logical and efficient decision to the utmost level of confidence, even in the absence of a human. The choice of implementation of a machine learning algorithm for the integration of this multi-sourced varied data would show a promising result.

The proposed architecture deals with the creation of an integrated system for poultry data from multiple sources coupled with the visualization tool. The system so integrated is present in the Relational Database Management System. Although the system is implemented for the data of Tamil Nadu, the study can be extended to multiple regions, providing better longitudinal studies and analysis. This data could be made public for the researchers to analyze the state of art for poultry for a particular region. The creation of better model requires the availability of open source data in poultry. The availability of a larger amount of data could pose a big-data challenge. This would create a strong load on the system. Thus, the future scope involved in the project is the use of distributed big-data technology such as Hadoop Distributed System, to ensure efficient model even if the data in the integrated system explodes.

References

1. Kao, R.R., Haydon, D.T., Lycett, S.J., Murcia, P.R.: Surprise me: how whole-genome sequencing and big data are transforming epidemology. Trends Microbiol. **22**, 282–291 (2014)
2. Hepworth, P.J., Nefedov, A.V., Muchnik, I.B., Morgan, K.L.: Broiler chickens can benefit from machine learning: support vector machine analysis of observational epidemiological data. J. R. Soc. Interface **9**, 1934–1942 (2012)
3. Intodia, V.: Poultry And Poultry Products Annual 2016, Usda Gain Report, New Delhi (2016)
4. Olasunkanmi, M.B., Dayo, O.A., Philips, S.M.: Vertical integration and technical efficiency in poultry (egg) industry in Ogun and Oyo states, Nigeria. Int. J. Poult. Sci. **5**, 1164–1171 (2006)
5. Moses, B.O., Olanrewaju, O.A., Olubanjo, I.A.: Economics of horizontal integration in poultry industry in South-West Nigeria. Int. J. Poult. Sci. **11**, 39–46 (2012)
6. Viaene, J., Verbeke, W.: Traceability as a key instrument towards supply chain and quality management in the belgian poultry meat chain. Supply Chain. Manag. Int. J. **3**, 139–141 (1998)
7. Our Bureau. Good Scope for FDI in Poultry Sector, Says Assocham @Businessline (2018). https://www.Thehindubusinessline.Com/Economy/Agri-business/Good-scope-for-fdi-in-poultry-sector-says-assocham/Article20348014.Ece1. Accessed 25 Aug 2018
8. Rebolledo, B., Gil, A., Pallarés, J.: A spatial ammonia emission inventory for pig farming. Atmos. Environ. **64**, 125–131 (2013)

9. Song, Q., Gao, X., Santos, E.T.: A food chain algorithm for capacitated vehicle routing problem with recycling in reverse logistics. Int. J. Bifurcat. Chaos **25**, 1540031 (2015)

10. Ten Napel, J., Van Der Veen, A.A., Oosting, S.J., Groot, P.W.: A conceptual approach to design livestock production systems for robustness to enhance sustainability. Livest. Sci. **139**, 150–160 (2011)

11. Teimoury, E., Jabbarzadeh, A., Babaei, M.: Integrating strategic and tactical decisions in livestock supply chain using bi-level programming, case study: iran poultry supply chain. PLoS ONE **12**, E0185743 (2017)

12. Baky, I.A.: Solving multi-level multi-objective linear programming problems through fuzzy goal programming approach. Appl. Math. Model. **34**, 2377–2387 (2010)

13. Sauian, M.S., Othman, N.C.: Optimizing livestock rearing using MCDM. In: 2012 International Conference on Statistics in Science, Business and Engineering (ICSSBE) (2012). https://doi.org/10.1109/icssbe.2012.6396584

14. Morales, I.R., Cebrián, D.R., Blanco, E.F., Sierra, A.P.: Early warning in egg production curves from commercial hens: a SVM approach. Comput. Electron. Agric. **121**, 169–179 (2016)

15. Fialho, F.B., Ledur, M.C.: Segmented polynomial model for estimation of egg production curves in laying hens. Br. Poult. Sci. **38**, 66–73 (1997)

16. Barge, P., Gay, P., Merlino, V., Tortia, C.: Radio frequency identification technologies for livestock management and meat supply chain traceability. Can. J. Anim. Sci. **93**, 23–33 (2013)

17. data.gov.in. (Internet). https://data.gov.in/. Accessed 14 Jan 2019

18. Socio Economic Statistical Data & Facts About India - e-Resource Library for Research | Indiastat (Internet). https://www.indiastat.com/. Accessed 14 Jan 2019

CA-RPL: A Clustered Additive Approach in RPL for IoT Based Scalable Networks

Soumya Nandan Mishra[✉] and Suchismita Chinara

National Institute of Technology Rourkela, Rourkela, India
{617cs3001,suchismita}@nitrkl.ac.in

Abstract. Applications of the Internet of Things (IoT) span from the industrial field to the agriculture field and from the smart city to the smart city healthcare. The wireless sensors play a major role in making these applications work as they are desired. These tiny, light-weight and low battery-powered sensors make the smallest of the smallest device communicate in an IoT environment. All of these applications require hundred to thousands of nodes to solve a purpose. Routing in such energy constrained network becomes a challenging task, so scalability in IoT is one of the major challenges that need to be solved. Routing protocol for low power and lossy networks (RPL) is one of the protocols developed by the Routing Over Low Power And Lossy Networks (ROLL) group to meet the QoS requirements for various IoT based applications. However, the existing versions of RPL fail to provide better results when the number of nodes in the network is increased. Our proposed protocol Clustered Additive RPL (CA-RPL) uses a weight based clustering technique to meet the efficiency of a scalable network. In addition to that, the path selection for data transmission is done by considering three parameters namely Expected transmission count (ETX), hop count and available energy. It is observed that the proposed approach outperforms other approaches in terms of packet delivery ratio, end to end delay and energy consumption in the network.

Keywords: IoT · RPL · Cluster · Additive

1 Introduction

IoT [1] is basically the communication between everyday objects that are connected through the Internet, capable of collecting and analyzing data from the surroundings and then transferring the obtained information to the required destination for further processing. If we talk about the layered architecture of IoT, it consists of four layers starting from the bottom as follows: the sensors layer, network layer, the management service layer and the topmost application layer.

The network layer mainly consists of the routing protocols which are designed for efficient communication between the devices or routers and sending the resulted useful information to the destination for further processing. Several IoT

© ICST Institute for Computer Sciences, Social Informatics and Telecommunications Engineering 2019
Published by Springer Nature Switzerland AG 2019. All Rights Reserved
N. Kumar and R. Venkatesha Prasad (Eds.): UBICNET 2019, LNICST 276, pp. 103–114, 2019.
https://doi.org/10.1007/978-3-030-20615-4_8

applications like healthcare, agriculture sectors, military and non-military applications use a large number of nodes to form a networking environment, which opens the issue of scalability in an IoT network. The routing protocol must be designed in such a way that it performs well in environments where the number of nodes may range from hundreds to thousands. Performing clustering in such an environment can be one of the solutions to achieve network scalability. In the clustering approach, there is cluster formation and from each cluster, a cluster head is selected. The task of the cluster head is to aggregate the data from its cluster members and forward it to the sink for further processing.

Some of the cluster head selection parameters that need to be considered while using clustering on routing protocols for a scalable network are:

- As we know, the sensor nodes in an IoT environment have very limited battery power. So battery power can be one of the parameters considered for selection of cluster head.
- The cluster head holds the responsibility to send data to the base station through other cluster heads. So in order to reduce the number of cluster heads, the degree of connectivity can be considered as another parameter for selecting a cluster head. A higher degree of connectivity means large sized clusters are formed, thereby reducing the number of cluster heads.

By allowing the protocol to operate in a clustered environment, we can reduce the energy consumption, minimize routing overheads, thereby, increasing the lifetime of the network. There are several routing protocols developed for IoT based scenario that work on reliable data transmission from source to destination. RPL [2] is one of the IoT based routing protocols which is designed for low power and lossy networks (LLN). It is a distance vector routing protocol where each router updates other neighbours about the network topology periodically. The routing process in RPL starts by forming a Destination Oriented Directed Acyclic Graph (DODAG) topology containing a single root known as DODAG root. Networks can have more than one DODAG's, each identified by a unique DODAG ID. At each RPL node, a rank is calculated based on some objective function. Using the rank information, the node tries to select the best parent through which it forwards the data packet to the root. RPL uses four control messages to construct the DODAG topology, they are DODAG Information Solicitation (DIS), DODAG Information Object (DIO), DODAG Destination Advertisement Object (DAO) and DAO-ACK. RPL uses trickle algorithm which decides how often the node sends these control messages to update the network.

The rest of the paper is organized as follows: In Sect. 2 all the related works are mentioned. In Sect. 3, the proposed work is described in detail with example diagrams. In Sect. 4, the performance of the proposed approach is compared with the existing approaches. Finally, the paper is concluded in Sect. 5.

2   Related Work

There are several works in the literature where authors have proposed different methods to calculate the rank of a node in RPL, and select parent based on that rank. Mohamed et al. [3] proposed an objective function which chooses a path having a high transition probability. The transition probability is calculated by taking two metrics into account i.e. transmission delay and residual energy. However, it did not consider the ETX metric for detecting lossy links. So, it may result in choosing inefficient routes.

The authors in [4] have combined four routing metrics namely ETX of the link, REC of the link, RANK of a node and minimized delay metric, to select the most optimal path for data transmission. However, energy consumption of the node has not been taken into account for studying the network lifetime of nodes.

Iova et al. [5] have proposed an Expected Lifetime metric which evaluates the residual time of each node i.e. the time before which the first node runs out of energy. It aims to maximize the lifetime of each node. The authors have compared their proposed approach with several other routing metrics and found their method to be better in terms of longevity of the network. However, the performance metrics like packet delivery ratio and end-to-end delay does not offer good performance.

Kamgueu et al. [6] have proposed an energy-based routing metric to be used by the objective function in RPL. Although the protocol performs better in terms of energy. consumption, there is no consideration of link quality metrics for path selection, which may result in choosing lossy and inefficient routes.

Sanmartin et al. [7] have proposed a sigma-ETX metric to solve long hop problem. The standard deviation of ETX value for each path is calculated, and the path having the lowest standard deviation is selected as the best path. However, energy metric is not taken into consideration for selecting the path, which can result in faster energy depletion of some nodes.

However, the concept of clustering is not applied anywhere in the above approaches. The clustering technique can solve the issue of scalability in a large network. In clustering mechanism, only the cluster heads are responsible for forwarding the data packets to the required destination, thus reducing the amount of traffic in the network. As a whole, the energy consumption is reduced which increases the network lifetime. Clustering can be one-hop or multi-hop. In one-hop clustering, the cluster members are at one-hop distance from the cluster head, so the distance between any two clustered members in a cluster is at most two. Whereas in multi-hop clustering the members can be at multi-hop distance from its cluster head.

Chinara et al. [8] have done a simulation survey for one hop clustering algorithms in mobile ad hoc networks and have proved that consideration of multiple parameters for clustering ensures a better result in terms of the number of clusters, network lifetime and the number of members per cluster. Another weight based clustering algorithm (WBCA) has been proposed by the authors in [9] that considers the degree of connectivity and available battery power of a node to calculate the weight of each node to be considered for cluster head. Few other one-hop weight based clustering algorithms have been proposed in [10–12].

The proposed protocol Clustered Additive - RPL (CA-RPL) uses a weight based clustering to select cluster heads. In addition to it, our method calculates rank of a node by combining three metrics additively, the metrics are Expected transmission count (ETX), hop count (HC) and available energy (AE). The result shows that our approach outperforms the traditional approaches in terms of packet delivery ratio, end to end delay and energy consumption. Thus, in a network consisting of large number of nodes, CA-RPL proves to be well fitted for a scalable network.

3   Proposed Work

In our proposed work CA-RPL, we have applied a weight based clustering algorithm to form clusters and select cluster heads. Only the cluster heads trigger the objective function, where the rank of the cluster head is calculated by combining three routing metrics (ETX, HC, AE) additively. Using the rank information, the cluster head selects its parent cluster head through which it forwards the data to the destination.

The proposed protocol CA-RPL works as follows. Initially, the DODAG root broadcast DIO packets to all reachable nodes with information about rank, objective function, ETX and residual energy of the node. Upon reception of DIO packets, the cluster formation process starts. The algorithm for cluster head selection is called. For each node within the transmission range of the receiver, the weights are calculated as given in Eq. 1:

$$W_d = a_1 * D_d + a_2 * E_{residual} \tag{1}$$

Where D_d is the degree difference of a node d and $E_{residual}$ is the residual energy of a node d. The degree difference [9] is can be calculated as given in Eq. 2:

$$D_d = | C_d - K_d | \tag{2}$$

Here C_d is the degree of node d and K_d is the mean connectivity degree of node d. The mean connectivity-degree can be calculated as:

$$K_d = \sum_{j=1}^{C_d} \frac{C_{dj} + C_d}{C_d + 1} \tag{3}$$

where C_d, C_{dj} denotes degree of connectivity of node d and degree of connectivity of jth neighbour of node d respectively. The residual energy E_d is calculated from the power trace module present in Contiki OS.

The node having the highest degree difference and highest remaining energy should be considered as the cluster head. Therefore, after the weights of the node are calculated as given in the Eq. 1, the one having the highest weight is selected as the cluster head. In this way, the clusters are formed and cluster head gets selected. When a cluster head receives a DIO packet, it calculates its rank as given in Algorithm 1, and based on this rank information it chooses its next hop parent to forwards the data packet. But, if the non-cluster head node receives the DIO packet, it chooses the cluster-head node in that cluster as its preferred parent.

In the maintenance phase of CA-RPL, if a new node wants to join the DODAG, the node broadcast DIS message in the network. If a non-cluster-head receives the DIS packet, it discards the packet. And if the cluster head receives the DIS packet within its vicinity, the cluster head sends DIO message to the node that wants to join the DODAG. The transmitter of DIS then sends DAO message to choose that cluster head as the preferred parent. If the DIS message received by the cluster head is not its vicinity, the DIS transmitting node calls Algorithm 1 for parent selection.

Algorithm 1. Rank calculation using additive approach by cluster heads

---

Require: Node ID and rank of parents
Ensure: Select the parent through which path cost is minimum
1: Let P_1, P_2,..., P_n be the parent list for a node X.
2: $Preferred\_Node\_Rank$ = INFINITY
3: **for** $Parent(P) \in$ P_1, P_2, P_3,..., P_n **do**
4:     $Rank(Child) = Rank(P) + c(i, j)$
5:     $c(i, j) = \alpha_1 * c_{\text{ETX}}(p) + \alpha_2 * c_{\text{HC}}(p) + \alpha_3 * c_{\text{AE}}(p)$
6:     **if** $Preferred\_Node\_Rank > Rank(Child)$ **then**
7:         $Preferred\_Node\_Rank = Rank(Child)$
8:         $Select\_Parent = Preferred\_Parent\_Id$
9:     **end if**
10: **end for**
11: RETURN $Select\_Parent$

The routing process can be better understood with the help of an example topology as mentioned in Figs. 1 and 2. In Fig. 1, there are seven clusters and each cluster has a cluster head in it which holds the responsibility to transmit the data to the sink. Figure 2 shows the communication between cluster member and cluster head. CA- RPL follows multi-hop inter-cluster communication between cluster head and sink and single hop intra-cluster communication between cluster members and cluster head. Single-hop intracluster communication shows good performance in terms of consumption of energy than multi- hop [13,14]. For achieving a scalable network, multi-hop inter-cluster communication is better than single-hop [15]. In Fig. 1(a), node I chooses path I→J→K→S, L chooses path L→M→N→S and O chooses O→N→S to forward the packet to the sink S. The path selection strategy can be explained from the Fig. 1(b). The path is selected on basis of three parameters i.e. ETX, Hop count and available energy. These three parameters are combined additively to form our required objective function, and based on the objective function the rank of the node is calculated. Node I can choose node J, M or L as its preferred parent to forward the data. To select the best parent among these, the rank of node I is calculated as given in Algorithm 1. For example, in this case, rank of I through J can be calculated as follows:

$$Rank(I) = Rank(J) + \frac{1}{3} * \frac{ETX_{i \to j} + ETX_{j \to k} + ETX_{k \to s}}{3}$$

$$+ \frac{1}{3} * (HC_{i \to j} + HC_{j \to k} + HC_{k \to s}) \tag{4}$$

$$+ \frac{1}{3} * \frac{(\frac{1}{AE_i} + \frac{1}{AE_j} + \frac{1}{AE_k} + \frac{1}{AE_s})}{4}$$

The ETX value for each link is calculated using the following formula:

$$ETX_i = \frac{s + f}{s} \tag{5}$$

where s denotes the number of packets successfully delivered to the neighbour node and f denotes the number of packets failed to be delivered. As, we can see from the equation that the ETX value is inversely proportional to the number of packets successfully delivered, therefore, the path having minimum average ETX value is preferred for forwarding the packets. The available energy of each node is obtained from the power trace model available in Contiki OS. The average available energy in a path can be calculated using the following equation:

$$AE(p) = \frac{\sum_{i=1}^{n} \frac{1}{AE_i}}{n(p)} \tag{6}$$

In the equation, $AE(p)$ denotes the available energy for a particular path p which is a ratio of two quantities namely available energy of a node (AE_i) and the total number of hops $n(p)$ in that path. Here, we are taking the reciprocal of the energy metric because the metric needs to transform into a minimizable metric for rank calculation.

Similarly, Rank of I is calculated through parent M and parent L. Node I select node J as its next hop instead of node M and L since it finds that through node J it obtains lower rank, which means that the path cost is minimum if node I transmits the data packet through J. Following the similar method, node L and node O selects M and N as its preferred parent for data transmission. Figure 2 shows the communication between cluster members and cluster head within a cluster. In cluster$_i$, node I have the highest value of weight i.e. 20, so that node is chosen as the cluster head, and other nodes act as cluster members. When any cluster member in cluster$_i$ receives DIO message from cluster head I, it transmits DAO packet to select I as the preferred parent. So, as shown in this figure all the cluster members in cluster$_i$ select the node I as their preferred parent. And if the cluster member has more than one option to choose the cluster head, then it sends DAO packet to the cluster head having the lowest rank. As in this case, the cluster member CM has two options, it can send DAO to cluster head I or J. Here, we assume that node J has lower rank value than node I, so it selects node J as preferred parent.

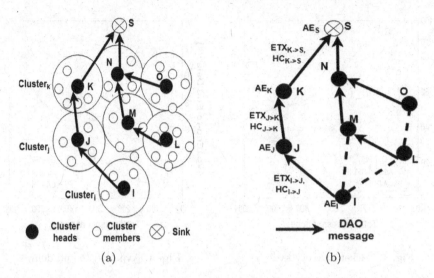

Fig. 1. Custer head selecting another cluster head as its parent for data transmission (Inter-cluster communication)

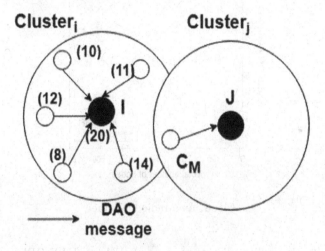

Fig. 2. Cluster members selecting cluster head as the preferred parent for data transmission (Intra-cluster communication)

4   Result and Discussion

The proposed protocol is simulated using cooja simulator in Contiki OS in a 100 * 100 square area with the number of nodes varied from 50 to 600. The simulation parameters are shown in Table 1. Network parameters like packet delivery ratio, average end to end delay and average radio ON time are used to compare the efficiency of CA-RPL in a large network. The result of the proposed work is

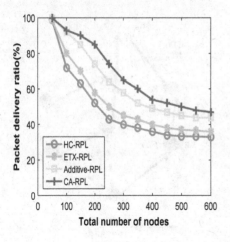

Fig. 3. Packet delivery ratio

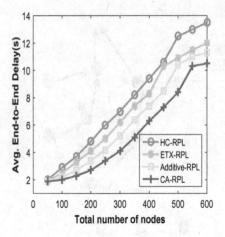

Fig. 4. Avg. end to end delay

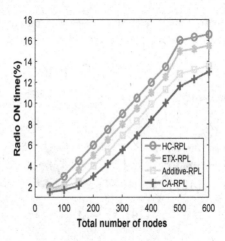

Fig. 5. Avg. radio ON time

compared with the earlier existing versions of RPL i.e. ETX-RPL and HC-RPL that uses objective function MRHOF and OF0 respectively. Our method is also compared with Additive-RPL which calculates the rank as mentioned in proposed work section, but it does not apply clustering technique in it.

Figure 3 shows the packet delivery ratio comparison of four approaches in RPL. The packet delivery ratio can be calculated as the ratio between the total number of packets received by the sink to the total number of packets sent to the sink. We observe that the proposed approach CA-RPL shows higher packet delivery ratio as compared to other approaches. HC-RPL and ETX-RPL use hop count and ETX values respectively to select the best route. In HC-RPL, it chooses path which needs to be traversed with least hop count to reach the sink

Table 1. Simulation parameters

Parameters	Value
Routing metric	ETX, HC, AE
DIO min	12
DIO doublings	8
RDC channel check rate	16 ms
RX ratio	10–100%
TX ratio	100%
TX range	50 m

but it does not consider link metric like ETX, therefore it might happen that the path selected would be congested enough to drop the packet, and hence it shows the least packet delivery ratio as compared to remaining three approaches. In ETX-RPL, although it considers ETX value as its path choosing metric still it does not considers node metrics like residual energy. In Additive-RPL, the path is chosen by combining three metrics additively by giving equal weight to ETX, HC and available energy metrics. And finally, in the case of CA-RPL we apply the method of clustering to increase the packet delivery ratio when the number of nodes is large. Since in CA-RPL only the cluster heads of respective clusters are responsible to forward the packet, the number of nodes taking part in communication is reduced significantly, so the probability of a packet to reach the sink increases.

Figure 4 explains the results obtained for the average end to end delay. The end to end delay is calculated by taking the difference between the time a packet was sent from a node and the time when that packet was received by the sink. The average end to end delay is calculated by taking the average of all delay of packets generated by the whole network of nodes. In the figure, the delay of CA-RPL is less as compared to other approaches. Since only the cluster head holds the responsibility to transmit the data to the sink, the number of intermediate nodes required to send the data from the source node to the sink decreases, thereby reducing the delay.

Figure 5 shows the comparison of radio ON time of all the approaches. Radio ON time considers the radio transmit time, radio listen time, CPU time and the time in which the nodes operate on low power mode i.e. LPM time. Here, the average values of radio ON time of each node in the network is considered. If the radio of a node is kept ON for a lesser amount of time, then less energy will be consumed, hence it will increase the network lifetime. In the case of HC-RPL and ETX-RPL, they do not consider the energy node metric for path selection, so their energy consumption is more as compared to other approaches. In CA-RPL, since only the cluster heads are required to transmit the data packets to the destination, so the non-cluster heads keep their radio OFF most of the time.

Therefore, a significant improvement in the radio ON time is observed in the case of CA-RPL.

In Fig. 6, CA-RPL shows significantly less average power consumption than other approaches in terms of radio transmit, radio listen, CPU and LPM time. So, there is an overall increase in network lifetime in case of CA-RPL. Figure 7 shows the average duty cycle of nodes in the network. In this case, the CA-RPL shows a significant decrease in the duty cycle of the nodes as opposed to the other three approaches.

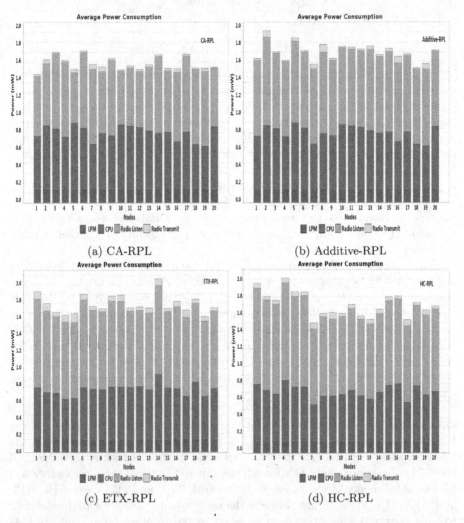

(a) CA-RPL

(b) Additive-RPL

(c) ETX-RPL

(d) HC-RPL

Fig. 6. Comparison of average power consumption of first 20 nodes for all approaches

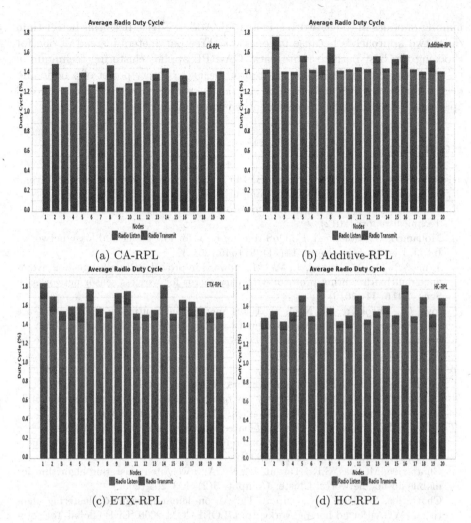

Fig. 7. Comparison of average duty cycle of first 20 nodes for all approaches

5   Conclusion

When it comes to routing data over a large network with energy constrained nodes, scalability is one of the major issues that the network has to face. In a large network, there is more probability that the packets are being collided, thereby giving poor results in terms of network parameters. So the routing protocols developed for IoT based applications must consider necessary parameters to give better results even when the network size is large. The existing approaches ETX-RPL and HC-RPL consider only a single routing metric for path selection, which cannot satisfy all the QoS requirements of the applications for which it is developed. Also, their performance gets degraded when the number of nodes in the network is increased. Additive-RPL performs better than those two approaches because it considers three parameters instead of one for choosing the best path to route data. CA-RPL applies clustering technique in it, where the cluster heads are selected on basis of battery power of a node and degree connectivity of a node. The simulation results show that our proposed approach CA-RPL outperforms the other three approaches.

References

1. Stergiou, C., Psannis, K.E., Kim, B.G., Gupta, B.: Secure integration of IOT and cloud computing. Future Gener. Comput. Syst. **78**, 964–975 (2018)
2. Winter, T., et al.: Rpl: Ipv6 routing protocol for low-power and lossy networks. Technical report (2012)
3. Mohamed, B., Mohamed, F.: QoS routing RPL for low power and lossy networks. Int. J. Distrib. Sens. Netw. **11**(11), 971545 (2015)
4. Tang, W., Ma, X., Huang, J., Wei, J.: Toward improved RPL: a congestion avoidance multipath routing protocol with time factor for wireless sensor networks. J. Sens. **2016**, 11 (2016)
5. Iova, O., Theoleyre, F., Noel, T.: Using multiparent routing in RPL to increase the stability and the lifetime of the network. Ad Hoc Netw. **29**, 45–62 (2015)
6. Kamgueu, P.O., Nataf, E., Ndié, T.D., Festor, O.: Energy-based routing metric for RPL. Ph.D. thesis, INRIA (2013)
7. Sanmartin, P., Rojas, A., Fernandez, L., Avila, K., Jabba, D., Valle, S.: Sigma routing metric for RPL protocol. Sensors **18**(4), 1277 (2018)
8. Chinara, S., Rath, S.K.: A survey on one-hop clustering algorithms in mobile ad hoc networks. J. Netw. Syst. Manage. **17**(1–2), 183–207 (2009)
9. Yang, W.D., Zhang, G.Z.: A weight-based clustering algorithm for mobile ad hoc network. In: Third International Conference on Wireless and Mobile Communications ICWMC 2007, p. 3. IEEE (2007)
10. Chatterjee, M., Das, S.K., Turgut, D.: WCA: a weighted clustering algorithm for mobile ad hoc networks. Cluster Comput. **5**(2), 193–204 (2002)
11. Chatterjee, M., Das, S.K., Turgut, D.: An on-demand weighted clustering algorithm (WCA) for ad hoc networks. In: GLOBECOM 2000 IEEE Global Telecommunications Conference, vol. 3, pp. 1697–1701. IEEE (2000)·
12. Chatterjee, M., Das, S.K., Turgut, D.: A weight based distributed clustering algorithm for mobile ad hoc networks. In: Valero, M., Prasanna, V.K., Vajapeyam, S. (eds.) HiPC 2000. LNCS, vol. 1970, pp. 511–521. Springer, Heidelberg (2000). https://doi.org/10.1007/3-540-44467-X_47
13. Wang, L., Yang, J.Y., Lin, Y.Y., Lin, W.J.: Keeping desired QoS by a partial coverage algorithm for cluster-based wireless sensor networks. JNW **9**(12), 3221–3229 (2014)
14. Quang, P.T.A., Kim, D.S.: Throughput-aware routing for industrial sensor networks: application to ISA100. 11A. IEEE Trans. Ind. Inform. **10**(1), 351–363 (2014)
15. Gupta, S.K., Jain, N., Sinha, P.: Energy efficient clustering protocol for minimizing cluster size and inter cluster communication in heterogeneous wireless sensor network. Int. J. Adv. Res. Comput. Commun. Eng **2**(8), 3295–3304 (2013)

Implementation of Trilateration Based Localization Approach for Tree Monitoring in IoT

Naren Tada$^{(\boxtimes)}$, Tejas Patalia, and Shivam Trivedi

V.V.P. Engineering College, Rajkot, India
naren.tada@gmail.com, pataliatejas@rediffmail.com,
shivtrivedi97@gmail.com

Abstract. The Internet of thing is widely used term as progression in innovation. It is a system of physical devices embedded with electronic motes,
sensors, and software which empower these devices to exchange data through
the internet. Moreover, to localize and monitor environmental conditions on the
real time basis system may use Global Positioning System framework but it
expends more energy as such system compromise resource constrain devices. In
this research paper, we have concentrated to develop Global Positioning System
independent localization algorithm for real-time tree monitoring. Our proposed
algorithm comprises of two sub-algorithms which are Received Signal Strength
Indicator and trilateration. Localization uses routing of data and it consumes
more energy. Hence, we require energy efficient routing protocol. To fulfill the
purpose we used (RPL) Routing Protocol for Low-Power and Lossy Networks
routing protocol which is developed specially for low power and lossy networks.
Simulation of the whole system is carried out In Contiki-OS with the help of
built-in COOJA simulator.

Keywords: IoT · Environment monitoring · Localization · Contiki OS · RPL ·
COOJA · Wireless sensor network · Sensor network

1 Introduction

Trees are playing a crucial role in the ecosystem. Urban street trees has proven benefits
such as providing oxygen, storing carbon dioxide, stabilizing soil, providing shelter
and shades and food and raising property value etc. We think that urban landscape is a
harsh place to thrive and survive. City foresters are trying hard to track and manage
urban forests but almost 60% urban trees are grown on private property. This makes
difficult to track down and manage each and every tree. Keeping in mind the importance of tree in life, Indian judiciary system have decided, once in five years,
mandatory carrying out a tree census program which is also called as tree act 1975.

In April 2016, Pune Municipal Corporation started a high-tech tree census program to
track the location, type and other details of every tree in the city area. In their high-tech
project they are using GPS (Global Positioning System) & GIS (Geographic Information
System) [1]. GPS is using 1.5 GHz high frequency; those radio waves could not penetrate
through a dense medium. When we talk about the urban area, there are many high rise

N. Kumar and R. Venkatesha Prasad (Eds.): UBICNET 2019, LNICST 276, pp. 115–123, 2019.
https://doi.org/10.1007/978-3-030-20615-4_9

buildings so the sky becomes obscured and sensor barely sees the satellites, then it may be result in inaccurate reading. The goal of this paper is to localize blind nodes using low power routing. People has come up many routing proposal for low power and lossy network such as MEAL (Multi-hop Energy efficient leach) [2], LEACH (Low Energy Adaptive Clustering Hierarchy) etc. For the routing, we have used RPL protocol which was developed by IETF (Internet Engineering Tasks Force) for low power and lossy network [3]. With the best of our knowledge no one has come up with the solution for localizing tree with RPL routing protocol.

For localization three anchor nodes are used, anchor nodes are the nodes whose positions are known. They perform RSSI (received signal strength indicator) based trilateration to estimate the position of blind nodes in the deployed network [4]. In our work we have localize trees without using GPS and GIS system. We have modified RPL in such a manner so that we can calculate RSSI and pass this value through routing to the base station with the help of trilateration method.

Rest of the paper is organized is as follows, proposed work illustrate the overall idea of how system works, simulation of proposed work which illustrate the simulation platform and how proposed method is implemented in the given platform, the result and analysis we have presented result with some of the actual coordinates of estimated coordinates with some simulation error present in the estimated and finally conclude our work with the future scope for the improvements.

2 Proposed System

As trees are the static entity we need a system which gives us real-time data and precise location of the tree. After completion of first phase, sensors start monitoring tree. Sensor stores data and send it to the base station based on the information we get, we need to take action to regulated expected values (Figs. 2, 3 and 4).

A. Received Signal Strength Indicator
The distance estimation includes calculation of RSSI values from the anchor nodes and based on that value, the corresponding distance estimate is calculated by the blind node. The RSSI values are obtained by using CC2420 radio transceiver that is fitted in all the motes. The mathematical formulation is given as follows:

$$RSS = RSS_VAL + RSS_OFFSET [dBm] \tag{1}$$

Where RSS OFFSET is roughly −45[4] and RSS VAL is the power received by the C2420 radio transceiver. Utilizing RSSI value, the distance estimation is done as follows. Expecting that the transmission power Ptx, the path loss model, and the path loss coefficient are known, the receiver can use the received signal strength Prcvd to solve for the distance d in a path loss equation like;

$$d = \frac{(C * Ptx)}{Prcvd} * \alpha \tag{2}$$

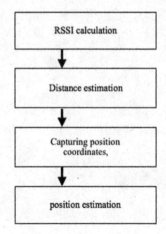

Fig. 1. Proposed system

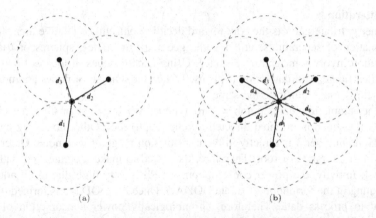

Fig. 2. Distance measurements and multilateration (Ranging circles). (a) Trilateration. (b) Multilateration.

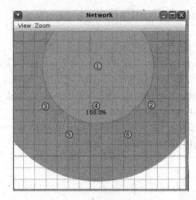

Fig. 3. Small scale implementation of RPL in COOJA

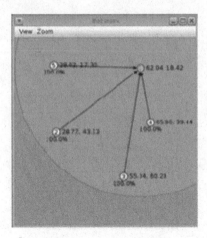

Fig. 4. Simulation of RSSI

B. Trilateration

In geometry, trilateration is the way toward deciding outright or relative areas focuses on estimation of separations, utilizing the geometry of circles, spheres or triangles. Trilateration involves measuring distance. Using anchor nodes, it locates blind nodes within their range. Multilateration [5] is used when the number of nodes are more than three. Below image illustrate the same.

In the simulation node number 1 root node which is responsible for creating DODAG (Destination oriented directed acyclic graph) root. Other nodes are neighbor nodes. Node number 4 is directly in the transmission range of root node. Other nodes are not in direct range of root. Therefore, they need to make a connection with node number 4. Initially, the power consumption in RPL is very high due to all nodes are participating in the formation of stable DODAG. Once the DODAG is formed, there is no need to process data. Therefore, chronologically power consumption of entire topology will decrease. RPL topology is stable topology until any new node is added or any present node is removed from the topology.

3   Implementation and Simulation

All the simulations were performed using Contiki-OS v-2.7 and emulated sky motes [6]. The environment is set to unit disk graph medium (UDGM): distance loss for the deployment of sky motes in the network. Up to four nodes were deployed for the purpose of simulation that includes a blind node (also called as sink node) and three anchor nodes. The transmission range and interference range is set to 50 and 100 m respectively. The deployed anchor nodes should be within the transmission range of the blind node in order to send the packets.

A. RSSI Contiki Implementation

To estimate precise location using Trilateration method, we first calculate RSS value of each node. The distance estimation involves calculation of RSSI values from the anchor nodes and based on that value, the corresponding distance estimate is calculated by the blind node. The RSSI values are obtained by using CC2420 radio transceiver that is fitted in all the nodes (Fig 7).

Time	Mote	Message
05:16.921	ID:1	Sink got message from 2.0, seqno 221, hops 1: len 9 'Fight On'
05:16.923	ID:1	RSSI of 2.0 is -80
05:16.944	ID:3	Sending
05:17.016	ID:2	Sending
05:17.046	ID:1	Sink got message from 4.0, seqno 252, hops 1: len 9 'Fight On'
05:17.048	ID:1	RSSI of 4.0 is -46
05:17.049	ID:5	Sending
05:17.187	ID:3	Sending
05:17.378	ID:5	Sending
05:17.422	ID:1	Sink got message from 3.0, seqno 211, hops 1: len 9 'Fight On'
05:17.424	ID:1	RSSI of 3.0 is -81

Fig. 5. Mote output of RSSI

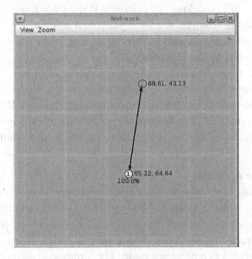

Fig. 6. Network topology of two nodes

Figure 5 shows the network of RSSI simulation. Node 1 is a root node and other nodes are neighbor nodes. RSSI is a line of sight communication; therefore, we cannot get the RSSI value of that particular node if any node is outside of the transmission range of root node. Here, in Fig. 5, all nodes are in the transmission range of root node so that we are able to get RSSI of each node.

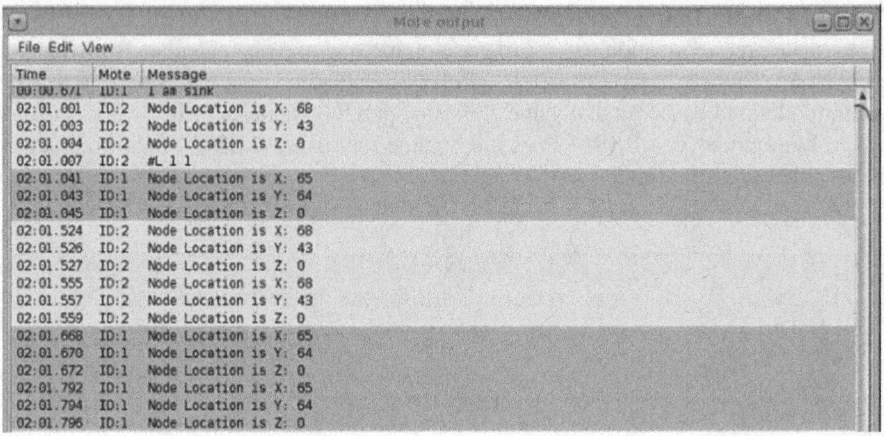

Time	Mote	Message
00:00.671	ID:1	I am sink
02:01.001	ID:2	Node Location is X: 68
02:01.003	ID:2	Node Location is Y: 43
02:01.004	ID:2	Node Location is Z: 0
02:01.007	ID:2	#L 1 1
02:01.041	ID:1	Node Location is X: 65
02:01.043	ID:1	Node Location is Y: 64
02:01.045	ID:1	Node Location is Z: 0
02:01.524	ID:2	Node Location is X: 68
02:01.526	ID:2	Node Location is Y: 43
02:01.527	ID:2	Node Location is Z: 0
02:01.555	ID:2	Node Location is X: 68
02:01.557	ID:2	Node Location is Y: 43
02:01.559	ID:2	Node Location is Z: 0
02:01.668	ID:1	Node Location is X: 65
02:01.670	ID:1	Node Location is Y: 64
02:01.672	ID:1	Node Location is Z: 0
02:01.792	ID:1	Node Location is X: 65
02:01.794	ID:1	Node Location is Y: 64
02:01.796	ID:1	Node Location is Z: 0

Fig. 7. Mote output for node position

RSSI refers to the transmitter power output as received by a reference antenna (receiver). Transmitter continuously sends packets to the receiver and receiver nodes continuously receive those packets. To calculate RSSI from those received packets we need proper function. In Contiki, We have packetbuf attr() which is used to create an outbound packet to store an inbound packet. When the driver reads out received frame, the RSSI observed during the reception will get copied to the packetbuf. Figure 5 shows the output of the RSSI value of the created network in Fig. 6. Root node which id node number 1 is getting output from the other nodes. Node number 2 and 3 are located far from the root node, therefore, we are getting high RSSI value for them which is −80 dbm and −81 dbm respectively. Node number 4 is located near to the root node; therefore, its RSSI value is high as compared to node number 2 and 3 which is −46 dbm

B. Getting Position of Nodes

We have created interfaces which can communicate between Contiki and COOJA. After adding mote interface selected C source file which calculates the position of nodes. Figure 6 shows the network topology of 2 nodes whose position is going to estimate. For the simplicity, we have chosen only 2 nodes. Node number 1 is a root node and node number 2 is a neighbor node. The simulation environment is 2D hence only X and Y coordinate will be computed. After hitting start in the simulator the script will run in the background and started getting the position of nodes. But as the compiler used in Contiki does not support floating point value we are unable to get exact floating value. The next thing is we are running a simulation in a 2D environment but the code is able to work in a 3D environment. That means the source code is designed to work in real time environment which captures all X, Y & Z coordinates. Due to simulation environment restrictions, we are only getting a value of X and Y.

C. Trilateration Algorithm

The term coordinate matrix stores the X & Y axis in an array, as we are using 2D environment for the simulation. Estimated distance matrix store the X & Y coordinates of a blind node [6].

The simulation was conducted at a specific 8 positions coordinates of the anchor nodes and resulting in actual and estimated coordinates of blind nodes. After estimating all position coordinates, the localization calculated as follows.

$$\text{Localization Error} = \sqrt{(X2 - X1)^2 + (Y2 - Y1)^2} \qquad (3)$$

In the above equation (x1, y1) is actual position coordinates of a blind node and (x2, y2) is the estimated position coordinates of the blind node. Obtain values are finalize after the simulation was repeated for more than 50 times. The overall localization error was obtained by finding the average of all the obtained localization error during the simulation. For the simulation of trilateration algorithm, we have created a simulation using 8 sky motes in COOJA simulator. In Fig. 8, 8 sky motes [7] are shown using 10-m boundary grid. In the deployed network we require to define 3 anchor nodes to start the trilateration process, hence node 1(85.31, 41.94), node 6 (64.24, 37.49), and node 8 (89.54, 15.23) are anchor node and will try to estimate the position of remaining blind nodes.

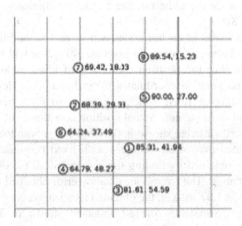

Fig. 8. Network topology for proposed system

Time	Mote	Message
00:05.681	ID:5	!----Calculating RSSI and Distance of nodes----!
00:05.685	ID:5	RSSI and Distance of last received mote is -44 and 50m.
00:05.688	ID:5	Current position of mote 5 at X-axis:90
00:05.691	ID:5	Current position of mote 5 at Y-axis:27
00:05.693	ID:5	Current position of mote 5 at Z-axis:0
00:05.698	ID:5	!----Node position estimation using Trilateration algorithm----!
00:05.701	ID:5	Estimated position of mote 5 at X-axis:91
00:05.704	ID:5	Estimated position of mote 5 at Y-axis:29
00:05.706	ID:5	Estimated position of mote 5 at Z-axis:0

Fig. 9. Mote output of proposed algorithm

Table 1. Simulation Results and Localization Error

Mote No.	Actual Coordinates	Estimated Coordinates	Localization Error (m)
1	(85.31, 41.94)	(85.31, 41.94)	0.00
2	(68.39, 29.33)	(67.39, 28.33)	1.4142
3	(81.61, 54.59)	(80.61, 55.59)	1.4142
4	(64.79, 48.27)	(66.79, 46.27)	2.2828
5	(90.00, 27.00)	(91.00, 29.00)	2.236
6	(64.24, 37.49)	(64.24, 37.49)	0.00
7	(69.42, 18.33)	(70.42, 19.33)	3.6055
8	(89.54, 15.23)	(89.54, 15.23)	0.00

4 Result and Analysis

The steps involved in the proposed system are shown in Fig. 1. The very first step is to calculate the RSSI value of every node. After this, algorithm calculates the distance of the deployed nodes. For that 3 pre-defined anchor nodes send the packets to the blind nodes, and based on the received power RSSI value will be calculated. Based on the calculated RSSI value blind node estimates its distance from the anchor node. In Fig. 9, entire output is shown for the mote number 5. Energy efficiency consider as per the author has stated in [8].

The position coordinates of anchor nodes will be sent to the blind nodes. Utilizing the anchor nodes coordinates, blind nodes position estimation will be performing using trilateration algorithm. For the position estimation of blind nodes, we must require estimated distance and position coordinates of anchor nodes. Here, for the distance estimation, we are utilizing RSSI which are prone to error because of multipath propagation in the real environment. Actual position coordinates of the blind nodes and estimated position coordinates are shown in the table below with localization error. The simulation was repeated more than 10 times with fixed coordinates and the overall localization error was obtained by finding the average of all the obtained localization error during the simulation. The overall localization error obtained after performing all the simulation rounds is 1.37 m. Yet, the obtained localization error is acceptable in the real-time environment. Simulation of last round is shown in Table 1 for all the 8 deployed nodes.

5 Conclusion and Future Work

This proposed work is built for the purpose GPS independent localization scheme. By utilizing this scheme we can determine position coordinates of a blind node on the based on the distance estimation and position coordinates of the anchor nodes deployed in the network. For the simulation, we have utilized Contiki-OS with the help of COOJA simulator. After getting final simulation result the overall localization error obtained is about 1.37 m. In the localization field, this margin is not accurate enough.

Yet, it is acceptable in the environment in which this system will be going to use. This work can be additionally reached out later on by enhancing the positional accuracy of a blind node by considering distance estimations from more than 3 nodes; this is about utilizing multilateration strategy. The positional accuracy of a sensor node is relying upon the precision of the distance estimation based on the RSSI value.

References

1. P. M. Corporation, Tree census: Pune municipal corporation (2018). https://pmc.gov.in/en/tree-census-1. Accessed 15 Mar 2018
2. Patalia, T., Tada, N., Patel, C.: MEAL based routing in WSN. In: Satapathy, S.C., Das, S. (eds.) Proceedings of First International Conference on Information and Communication Technology for Intelligent Systems: Volume 2. SIST, vol. 51, pp. 109–114. Springer, Cham (2016). https://doi.org/10.1007/978-3-319-30927-9_11
3. Winter, T., et al.: RPL: IPv6 routing protocol for low power and lossy networks. Roll Working Group (2011)
4. Chen, C.Z., Xia, F., Huang, T., et al.: A localization method for the Internet of Things. J. Supercomput. **63**, 657 (2013). https://doi.org/10.1007/s11227-011-0693-2
5. Asmaa, L., Hatim, K.A., Abdelaaziz, M.: Localization algorithms research in wireless sensor network based on multilateration and trilateration techniques. In: 2014 Third IEEE International Colloquium in Information Science and Technology (CIST), pp. 415–419. Tetouan (2014)
6. Contiki: The open source operating system for the internet of things (2018). http://www.contiki-os.org/. Accessed 2 Feb 2018
7. Chipcon products from texas instruments (2018). http://web.stanford.edu/class/cs244e/papers/cc2420.pdf. Accessed 10 Feb 2018
8. Naren, T., Dishita, B.: TVAKSHAS - an energy consumption and utilization measuring system for green computing environment. In: Kumar, N., Thakre, A. (eds.) UBICNET 2017. LNICST, vol. 218, pp. 37–45. Springer, Cham (2018). https://doi.org/10.1007/978-3-319-73423-1_4

Expert System Design for Automated Prediction of Difficulties in Securing Airway in ICU and OT

D. K. Sreekantha[1]([✉]) [iD], H. K. Rachana[1], Sripada G. Mehandale[2],
Mohammed Javed[3], and K. V. S. S. S. S. Sairam[4]

[1] Department of CSE, NMAM Institute of Technology,
Nitte, Karnataka, India
sreekantha@nitte.edu.in
[2] Anaesthesiology and Critical Care Unit,
KSHEMA, Mangalore, Karnataka, India
[3] Department of IT, Indian Institute of Information Technology,
Allahabad, India
[4] Department of E&CE, NMAM Institute of Technology,
Nitte, Karnataka, India

Abstract. The maintenance of uninterrupted patient respiratory passage (airway) and unhindered breathing is the primary duty of an anesthesiologist or other physicians involved in patient care under emergency trauma or surgical procedures in ICU (Intensive Care Unit) and Operation Theatre (OT). Anesthesiologist should ensure the full control over the patient airway management either bypassing an endotracheal tube or any other similar devices. The unanticipated difficulties in airway management are the most important contributors to airway related mishaps, if these are not managed effectively may lead to death or permanent bodily harm to the patient due to inadequate oxygenation. The recent survey reports revealed that 53% of anaesthetic deaths are either airway or respiratory related. Incidence of difficult airway among patients has been predicted to be in the range of 1.1 to 3.8%. This paper aims at identifying all the critical risk parameters contributing to difficult airway and subsequently developing a framework to automate the prediction of difficult airways well in advance. Authors have designed an expert system prototype for predicting the difficulties in airway management and suggesting appropriate remedies using machine learning algorithms.

Keywords: Difficult airway · Endotracheal intubation · Anaesthesia · Laryngoscopy · Prediction · Intensive Care Unit (ICU) · Decision tree · Machine learning · Expert system and knowledge base

1 Introduction

The term airway [1] is defined as the passage for air from external nares (nostrils) or lips to alveoli in the lungs, upper airway and extra-pulmonary portion of this passage consisting of the nasal and oral cavities, pharynx, larynx, trachea and large bronchi.

© ICST Institute for Computer Sciences, Social Informatics and Telecommunications Engineering 2019
Published by Springer Nature Switzerland AG 2019. All Rights Reserved
N. Kumar and R. Venkatesha Prasad (Eds.): UBICNET 2019, LNICST 276, pp. 124–141, 2019.
https://doi.org/10.1007/978-3-030-20615-4_10

The term difficult airway is defined by American Society of Anaesthesiologists (ASA) as a clinical condition in which generally trained anesthesiologists have a skill to analyse the difficulty with the mask ventilation or with the tracheal intubation or both. Competence in airway management is an important medical specialty.

The primary objective of anesthesiologist should be to make every possible effort to ensure secure airway in the very the first intubation attempt successfully with good confidence. It is very important to assess patients for both difficult mask ventilation as well as intubation. Airway management is ensuring safe anesthetic routine and in most of the cases it is uncomplicated [2]. It has been acknowledged for lot many years that, the occurrence of difficulty in airway management can result in serious consequences [3]. Difficult airway management has two vital ways mask ventilation or providing air or oxygen to lungs using a bag filled with breathing gases, mask fitting over nose and mouth [4]. The process of passing tube into trachea (endotracheal tube) is called endotracheal intubation. Endotracheal intubation is very often performed for a period of mask ventilation with 100% oxygen before undertaking any definitive airway management. This helps in overcoming preexisting oxygen deficiency or increase oxygen stores to tide over the duration of laryngoscopy and intubation during which patients are not able to breath. The passing of an endotracheal tube is to convey respiratory gases from outside in to lungs of patients with depressed consciousness, victims of physical trauma, infection, or cancerous growth in the upper airway. This passing of tube is required to support the breathing (respiratory failure mandating ventilator support) and for those undergoing surgery under general anaesthesia. This endotracheal intubation requires a clear view of larynx (sound box), which is generally by direct vision using a device called laryngoscope. This clear vision of larynx demands aligning oral, pharyngeal and laryngeal axes, which is not straight forward affair in majority of patients. The difficult airway occurs in some individuals for various reasons ranging from facial skeletal anomalies, infections leading to swellings in and around the face, decreased mouth opening, growth around the airway, decreased neck mobility and obesity. In such cases the airway management may become difficult or sometimes impossible [5].

The recent survey [6] reported that 53% of anesthetic deaths are either airway or respiratory related. A study by anaesthesia residents in 2012 discovered that first-pass success rates did not stabilize until they perform more than 150 intubations [7]. The general anesthesia may lead to direct or indirect airway damage. Direct damage is caused by necessary or excessive force applied on airway instrumentation or injury during airway device insertion or removal. Indirect damages are inadequate oxygenation, ventilation and such injuries may overlap with respiratory problems [7]. The difficult tracheal intubation elucidate 17% of the respiratory related injuries with the consequences in notable morbidity and mortality [3]. Any delay in resumption of oxygenation during an attempt to secure the airway (failed mask ventilation or failed intubation or both) can result in severe damage from temporary to permanent brain damage or death. In fact, about 28% of all anesthesia related deaths are subordinate to the inability to mask ventilate or intubate [15]. The mask ventilation is the fundamental component of airway management and in case of difficult intubation, it serves a major role [11]. American Society of Anesthesiologists (ASA) data suggested that one third of most common respiratory problems lead to brain damage and patient death [19]. In United Kingdom in the year 2011, 4th National Audit Project (NAP4) inspected anesthesia related primary airway complications and discovered 50 obstructed airway cases [24].

This inspection revealed that one of the most important causes of airway related mishaps were poor assessment of airway, prior to airway intervention. Acute airway obstruction is considered as medical emergency which potentially resulting in serious morbidity and mortality. The difficult airway being multifactorial, several assessment tools were studied, but none of them were found fully satisfactory till date. The two most commonly employed tools for airway difficulty prediction are Mallampati and Wilson score correlating with Cormack Lehane grading [16]. These methods considered the various parameters associated with difficult tracheal intubation, extubation and mask ventilation. Some of difficult airway parameters are mouth opening, head and neck movement (atlantoocipital joint assessment), Mallampati classification and receding mandible, protruding maxillary incisors (buck teeth), thyromental distance, sternomental distance, obesity, history of difficult intubation, extubation and mask ventilation [4].

Authors have carried out an extensive study of literature and identified critical risk parameters leading to difficult airway management. These risk parameters are organized in a hierarchical frame work for prediction of difficulties. These risk parameters are assigned the weights based on their impact in prediction of difficulty in decision making. The set of rules governing the decisions are studied from doctors and incorporated in to rule base. The actual representative sample data from patients is gathered by doctors in KSHEMA and given to us for study. Authors have simulated large data set using these samples. This data set processed using algorithms in Intel distributed Python toolbox.

Rest of this paper is organized in to sections. Section 2 focuses on Recent related work is dealing with discussion on work carried out by earlier researchers in this area. Section 3 discusses on Proposed Expert system methodology adopted by the authors. Section 4 has description on Data preparation and Implementation of various machine learning algorithms using Intel Distributed Python tools. Section 5 deals with Results discussion. Authors have given their Conclusions on their study in the last section of the article.

2   Recent Related Work

The summary of literature review carried out by the authors is presented in this section. The expert system is software that imitates the decision making competency of a human expert. A special framework of risk parameters was designed to predict the hepatitis contamination [8]. An information based expert framework with an objective to provide the restorative exhortation to the patients and the essential information about the diabetes was also designed [9]. This framework incorporates a new learning experience about the sustenance, exercise, medicine and how to deal with the glucose levels. The identification of difficult airway parameters related to intubation and extubation in adults was studied [7]. This paper explored the issues related to surgical operation tubes and tube displacement. The critical care physicians are required to be conversant with difficult airway algorithms and pertinent airway adjuncts. The nursing expert system fundamentally served the general population living with diabetes particularly in provincial territories [10].

This system educates the patient about the background for appropriate diagnosis and treatment. This expert system utilizes a rule-based reasoning technique through easy querying of symptoms, signs and examination carried out on the patient. The expert system is used for diagnosing heart diseases in patients to facilitate treatment. The applications of decision support systems are explored in medicine, anaesthesia, critical care and intensive care medicine [11]. Airway management can be divided into three regions i.e. the upper, middle and lower regions. These regions can be correlated with difficult laryngoscopy, intubation and mask ventilation consequently [12]. The main objective of laryngoscopy is to produce an eminent perspective of vocal cards to easily perform the intubation. The airway difficulties can lead to morbidity and mortality. The doctors during clinical examination of the airway can observe several distinguishing features such as tempero mandibular joint mobility, decreased neck mobility (Delilkan test).

The respiratory events are the most basic reasons for the anesthetic related injuries such as dental damage. The main causes for the respiratory related injuries are inadequate ventilation, oesophageal intubation and difficult tracheal intubation [13]. The doctor conducts general physical and regional examination such as mouth opening, neck extension, Mallampati test, Patil's thyromental distance, neck circumference. LEMON method of airway assessment is looking for congenital anomalies, radiographic assessment, quick airway assessment, for the prediction of difficult airway. Cormack Lehane grading of laryngoscope view conveys the difficulty in having proper vision of larynx and feasibility of endotracheal intubation. One single test cannot provide a prediction of high sensitivity and specificity, as a result it should be a composition of multiple tests. In the event of an unanticipated difficult airway, anesthesiologists must be well prepared with a combination of practical and pre-formulated methods for the airway management. The tracheal re intubation in patients is found to be more complex, because it includes several parameters associated with hypoxia, haemodynamic problems, hypercarbia, agitation and airway obstruction [14]. The different parametric concepts correlated with the mechanism of tracheal intubation mainly in children was also studied [15]. This study on the problems involved in the pediatric airway management difficulties with unsuccessful endotracheal intubation or the mask ventilation, and the immediate causes of mortality and perioperative morbidity was carried out [16]. This study attempts to predict the difficulty in tracheal intubation and direct laryngoscopy among the newborn. The authors followed one of the most generally used algorithm mainly from the American society of Anesthesiology (ASA) in 2013 which mainly helps to describe the difficult airways. Most of the difficult airway problems in children can be easily predicted. The definite mechanism to preserve the airway patency and ventilation control, is intubation laryngoscopy and trachea mechanism that helps to identify the difficult airway. The observational study to determine the prediction, incidence and outcomes leading to impossible mask ventilation was carried out on the adult patients over a period of four years [17]. The primary outcome of this study was to classify impossible mask ventilation and secondary outcome was direct laryngoscopic views and the difficult airway management techniques.

The cross-sectional study to correlate a preanesthetic evaluation to predict a difficult intubation with the certain conditions are met at laryngoscopy and endotracheal intubation were also carried out [18]. The data of eighty one patients submitted to general anesthesia was examined at a preanesthetic consultation in accordance with modified Mallampati classification, Wilson score and American society of anesthesiologists (ASA) difficult airway algorithm. The advantages of applying Mallampati and Wilson's grading for the prediction of difficult laryngoscopy and intubation were studied [19]. The goal of this study is to estimate the accuracy of the modified mallampati test and the Wilson score for predicting difficult tracheal intubation. The comparative study of Wilson score, modified mallampati and Cormack Lehane grading was carriedout. The association and accuracy of CLT (cuff-leak-test) only or associated with another laryngeal parameter with PES has been primarily determined [20]. In a medical surgical intensive care unit 51 mechanically ventilated adult patients were tested.

The observations from extubation using CLT, laryngeal ultrasound and indirect laryngoscopy recorded the parameters of biometric, laryngeal and endotracheal tube (ETT). No single form of the CLT or PES have accurately predicted the combination with laryngeal parameters. The applications of different airway devices for emergency airway management in endotracheal intubation reported complications occurred [21]. The authors suggested to airway passage consultants (non-physician and physician providers) to plan out the successful intubation in very first pass intubation attempt. The prehospital airway management using supraglottic airway devices and procedural experiences, success rates of intubation are analyzed [15]. Author's main goal was to find the relation between the system-wide initiation of king LT and ETI success rates. The retrospective observational study from 37 Emergency Medical Service (EMS) agencies within a country division of south western Pennsylvania was carried out. The orotracheal intubation [10] is mainly received by fewer patients with advanced airway management by introduction of knowledge based expert system. The authors stated that this system helps the patients by educating them about diabetes and also provides the medical advice. This system is highly useful because doctors don't have a time to explain about the symptoms and risk factors to the diabetic patients and it educates them about food, exercise, medication and how to manage the blood sugar levels [15]. Authors have compared the advantages Mallampati and Wilson's grading for the prediction of difficult in laryngoscopy and intubation. Researchers have discussed systematically airway prediction of difficulties in mask ventilation. They have compared the accuracy of the modified Mallampati test, Wilson score for predicting difficult tracheal intubation [22]. Authors have studied Cormack Lehane grading and presented an efficient heart disease prediction system using data mining. This paper discussed cardiovascular disorder which is a considerable reason for mortality and in the current living style. The main objective of this study is to help a non-specialized doctors to make correct decision about the risk level in heart diseases. Authors proposed to use KEEL (Knowledge Extraction Based on Evolutionary Learning). KEEL is an open source (GPLV3) Java programming apparatus mainly used to implement developmental process for data mining issues.

The literature study enabled authors have discover that many researchers have worked to identify, classify the various risk parameters in predicting difficult airway in children and adults. Researchers have studied the difficult mask ventilation, intubation cases. The comparative study of Mallampati and Wilson's grading and AAS algorithms was carried out. The expert systems solutions developed for diabetics and heart diseases were studied. This study has enriched the knowledge of authors and given the insight in to the identification, classification of difficult airway risk parameters and conception of expert system for prediction of difficult airway, well in advance by novice doctors.

3 Proposed Methodology

3.1 Proposed Expert System Approach

Authors have discovered the urgent need for the facility to retrieve and correlate similar cases from a centralized airway patient database. This facilitate to predict and enable self learning/training in assessment of difficult airway before the actual surgical procedure. This capability would help the novice doctors for managing airway in a professional way. The survey reveals the main reason for unanticipated difficult airway is the lack of systematic study of patient's physical parameters and the lack of technology support. So authors aimed at designing the prototype expert system. This proposed expert system has user friendly interface thorough which user enters input the physical risk parameters. The inference engine processes these input parameters and determines the difficult airway risk levels. This expert system has knowledge base that facilitates the users to retrieve and relate similar cases from a centralized knowledge base to predict difficult airway. The expert system has self learning capability to update the new cases. A novice anesthesiologists are advised to take the help of this expert system for assessing the difficult airway, before the actual surgical procedure. In summary from techno medical point-of-care project this paper's first objective is to save the patient from complications (like damage of lungs, breathing problems) and inadequate oxygenation that arise because of shortcomings in managing difficult airway. Second objectives is to design an expert system to support the novice anesthesiologist to perform like expert anesthesiologist using this expert system tool. This expert system boosts the confidence of the novice doctors to manage the eventuality by helping them to understand the situation in advance and accordingly enabling them to manage the surgical complications.

3.2 Architecture of Proposed Expert System Design

Authors have discussed with doctors from the department of Anaesthesia and Critical care of K.S. Hegde Medical Academy, Mangalore and understood the manual process of airway management. At present in manual system anaesthesian diagnoses the patient's physical parameters and applies the sequence of airway techniques with increasing order of difficulties or risk in airway management. Anaesthesian first checks if mask ventilation is possible, then carries out mask ventilation. Only when mask ventilation is not possible, then doctor proceeds checking for Supraglottic airway, Laryngoscopy and Intubation, Extubation one after the other in increasing order of difficult airway risk. These interactions with doctors and visit to hospital has enriched the authors to conceive the design of an expert system prototype for airway management. The architecture of proposed expert system is shown in Fig. 1.

Anaesthesian examines the patient who has to undergo airway management treatment and records the patient physical parameters to assess whether there is any symptoms for difficulty airway. In the case of unpredictability in difficult airway, doctors calls for the support from expert systems. The physical airway parameters of the patient are feed in to the expert system through user interface. The inference engine processes this physical parameter data and predicts the difficulties in airway management. The expert system advises doctors through SMS and mails along with the detailed assessment report. This report contains the information about which airway technique to apply and gives justification as to why doctor has to apply that particular technique to that patient. This system is designed to help novice doctors to take better airway related decisions because there is an acute shortage of expert anaesthesian nationally (Fig. 2).

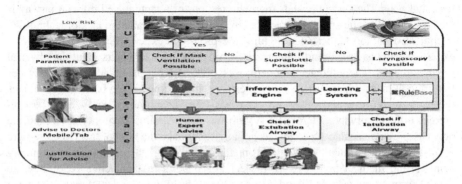

Fig. 1. Architecture of airway management expert system

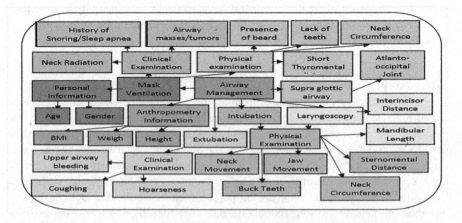

Fig. 2. Architecture of airway management physical parameters

3.3   Architecture of Airway Management Physical Parameters

Authors have discussed with expert anaesthesian and identified all the parameters associated with difficult airway. These parameters are organized based on their significance and features as shown Table 1.

3.4   Patients Physical Airway Parameters Associated with Difficult Mask Ventilation

The difficult airway risk parameters for different airway techniques such as mask ventilation, laryngoscopy, supraglottic airway, intubation and extubation have been studied and classified by the researchers. The following Tables 1 and 2 shows the parameters, descriptions and corresponding standard values. The difficult airway parameters for Mask Ventilation and their description are listed in the Table 1.

Table 1.   Physical airway parameters of difficult mask ventilation

Sl. no	Parameter	Grades	Predictive value	Prediction level	Difficulty decision
1.	BMI (Body Mass Index)	Grade 0	<18.5	Normal	Easy
		Grade 1	18.5–24.9	Mild	Slightly difficult
		Grade 2	25–29.9	Moderate	Difficult
		Grade 3	30 or 50	Significant	Very difficult
		Grade 4	Greater	Severe	Impossible
2.	Mallampati Grade (It was performed with the patient in the sitting position, the neck held in the neutral position and the tongue fully protruded without phonation)	Grade 0	Tip of the Epiglottis is seen, Tonsils, Pillars and Soft palate are clearly visible.	Normal	Easy
		Grade 1		Mild	Easy
		Grade 2	The uvula, pillars & upper pole are visible	Moderate	Slightly difficult
		Grade 3	Only part of the soft palate is visible	Significant	Difficult
		Grade 4	Only the hard palate is visible	Severe	Impossible
3.	Weight (Weight of patient) is the main parameter of the intubation?	Minimum	<1–90 kg	Normal	Easy
		Standard	90–110 kg	Moderate	Difficult
		Maximum	>110 kg	Severe	Impossible
4.	Neck Circumference (Measured using a flexible tape at the level of the cricoid cartilage while patient is in the sitting position with the head and neck in the neutral posture)	Grade 0	<=44 cm	Normal	Easy
		Grade 1	>44 cm	Moderate	Slightly difficult

(continued)

Table 1. (*continued*)

Sl. no	Parameter	Grades	Predictive value	Prediction level	Difficulty decision
5.	Mandibular length	Grade 1	>9 cm	Normal	Easy
		Grade 2	<=9 cm	Moderate	Slightly difficult
6.	Interincisor Distance (The patient is asked to open his/her mouth as wide as possible, the distance between the upper and lower incisors was measured)	Grade 1	>4 cm	Normal	Easy
		Grade 2	<=4 cm	Moderate	Slightly difficult
7.	Thyromental distance (Measured by a small cricket ruler with the head fully extended and the mouth closed)	Grade 1	>6.5 cm	Normal	Easy
		Grade 2	<=6.5 cm	Moderate	Slightly difficult
8.	Sternomental distance	Grade 1	>13.5 cm	Normal	Easy
		Grade 2	<=13.5 cm	Moderate	Slightly difficult

Table 2. Parameters for difficult mask ventilation and their standard values

Sl. no	Risk parameters	Description
1	Increased Body Mass Index (BMI)	Over weight of the body
2	Presence of beard	Creates problem for mask seal to fit correctly
3	Lack of teeth	No teeth
4	Age (Greater than 55 years)	Advanced age (age > 55) is also associated with difficulty for mask ventilation
5	Male gender	This problem is mainly found in male
6	Airway masses/tumors	This problem is mainly causes difficulty in mask ventilation
7	Mask seal	Mask seal is important, so any feature that may interfere with this component of mask ventilation such as beard are important to note
8	Obesity/A history of airway obstruction	Obesity or history of airway obstruction such as obstructive sleep apnea
9	Shrinking of corners of mouth	One of the reasons for difficult mask ventilation is ill fitting of mask due to slagging of cheek and shrinking of corners of mouth in edentulous patients

(*continued*)

Table 2. (*continued*)

Sl. no	Risk parameters	Description
10	History of snoring, sleep apnea or stiff lungs	Edentulous patients due to poor mask seal and those with stiff lungs (such as smokers or those with COPD) will also find it difficult to ventilate. A history of snoring is related to obesity & OSA obstruction with the muscles of the Orthodox are relaxed, during the sleep & likely during sedation/Anesthetists

The Table 2 above shows the identified risk parameters and their standard description. These values are used in designing the rule base and data set validation.

3.5 Rulebase Design

Researchers have studied from expert anaesthesian/doctors, the risk parameters and designed the set of rules that are to be followed by while managing the difficult airway. This organized set of rules are called a rule base. Expert systems are using this rule base for processing the input and interpreting output. Authors have designed the rule base by considering five different hierarchical categories of airway management from minimum to maximum risk levels. The minimum risk is associated with mask ventilation, next risk is supraglottic airway, next is laryngoscopy, highest risk is intubation and extubation. If first method is not successful, then we move on to the next higher risk methods.

Table 3. Sample Fuzzy Logic rule base for mask ventilation

Rule no.	Antecedent- IF	Consequent- THEN
1.	Patient is Elder AND Gender is Male AND BMI is higher side	Patient is in a mild condition, Mask ventilation is difficult
2.	Patient is Elder AND Gender is Male AND Beard is Present	Patient is in a mild condition, Mask ventilation is difficult
3.	Patient is Elder AND Gender is Male AND Mallampati III or IV grade is visualized	Patient is in a mild condition, Mask ventilation is difficult
4.	Patient is Elder AND Gender is Male AND Neck radiation is high	Patient is in a severe condition, Mask ventilation is impossible
5.	Patient is Elder AND Gender is Male AND Lack of teeth factor have been observed	Patient is in a mild condition, Mask ventilation is difficult
6.	Patient is Elder AND Gender is Male AND Airway masses/tumors have been seen	Patient is in a mild condition, Mask ventilation is difficult
7.	Patient is Elder AND Gender is Male AND BMI is increased AND Airway masses/tumors have been observed	Patient is in a moderate condition, Mask ventilation is difficult

(*continued*)

Table 3. (*continued*)

Rule no.	Antecedent- IF	Consequent- THEN
8.	Patient is Elder AND Gender is Male AND BMI is increased AND Obesity have been increased	Patient is in a moderate condition, Mask ventilation is difficult
9.	Patient is Adult AND Gender is Male AND BMI (Grade 0) is low	Patient is in a normal condition, Laryngoscopy is easy
10.	Patient is Adult AND Gender is Male AND Neck Circumference is very low AND Mandibular length is very low AND Interincisor Distance is very low AND Thyromental Distance is very low AND Sternomental Distance is very low	Patient is in a moderate condition, Laryngoscopy is difficult
11.	Patient is Adult AND Gender is Male AND Neck Circumference is very low	Patient is in a moderate condition, Laryngoscopy is difficult
12.	Patient is Adult AND Gender is Male AND Mandibular length is very high	Patient is in a severe condition, Laryngoscopy is impossible
13.	Patient is Adult AND Gender is Male AND Mandibular length is very high	Patient is in a severe condition, Laryngoscopy is impossible
14.	Patient is Adult AND Gender is Male AND Interincisor Distance is very high	Patient is in a severe condition, Laryngoscopy is impossible

Table 4. Patient age classification

Sl. no.	Age linguistic value	Range of age in years
1.	Child	1–12
2.	Teenager	13–19
3.	Adult	20–39
4.	Middle aged	40–50
5.	Elder	51–69
6.	Old aged	70 Onwards

Table 5. Summary of airway safety rules

Sl. no	Safe level	Hierarchical order	No. of rules
1.	1st safe level	Mask ventilation	111
2.	2nd safe level	Supra glottic airway	5
3.	3rd safe level	Laryngoscopy	47
4.	4th safe level	Intubation	94
5.	5th safe level	Extubation	23

3.6   Rulebase for Mask Ventilation

Authors have designed few hundred rules for various techniques of airway management using Fuzzy Logic. The sample rules for mask ventilation are shown in Table 3. These rules are based patients age, gender and other physical parameters such as neck circumference etc. for predicting the difficulty in mask ventilation and laryngoscopy. The patient's current age is also one of the risk factor which is fuzzified and shown in Table 4. Authors have designed rules for each airway management technique. Table 5 shows the number of rules designed for each airway management.

4 Expert System Implementation

4.1 Software Tools Used

Authors have used Intel distributed python tools for building the prediction of airway difficulties. Intel distributed python tools are easy to learn, use, have an extensive library support that enables users to perform complex analysis. Anaconda tools provides iPython Notebook that supports us to code in Python. iPython notebook contains many cells where user can readily write code and add comments (in Markdown) to a cell. The notebook is displayed right into your web browser.

4.2 Patient Data Processing

The difficult airway parameter data is classified in to five stages like Mask ventilation, intubation and Laryngoscopy, Extubation, and Supraglottic airway. The patient data about these five difficult parameters are collected. The units for measuring these parameters are represented as numerical values. These parameter values are used as features for classification. The doctors from KSHEMA have provided actual patients data collected from their database for training and testing of the expert system model. The range of parameter data values varies from Indian patients and other country patients. The collected data set is in Comma Separated Values (CSV) format file.

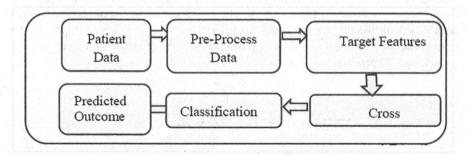

Fig. 3. System flow showing steps in prediction of difficult airway Intel Distributed Python package

The Steps in Data Experimentation

The patient data is cleaned, checked for categorical values (if any) and converted to numerical data. This process is performed using a technique called One Hot Encoding, which is important step because a few classifiers in scikit-learn work only with numerical values. Authors have conducted experiments to predict the difficulty associated with intubation airway management. The step by step followed in conducting experiment and outcome of each step is described below in Fig. 3.

```
In [8]: df1['Prediction'] = df1['Prediction'].map({'E':0,'D':1})
        df1.head()
```

Out[8]:

	Sl.No	Age at initial pathologic diagnosis	Weight	C-L (Grade 3 or 4)	Mallampati score	Interincisor gap	Retrognathia	Buck teeth	Prediction	Thyromental distance	Cervical joint rigidity
0	1	40	110	High	Low	Low	Moderate	Absent	1	6.5	High
1	2	41	90	High	Low	Low	Moderate	Absent	1	6	High
2	3	42	75	Low	High	High	Absent	Absent	0	7	Low
3	4	43	65	Low	High	High	Absent	Absent	0	8.5	Low
4	5	18	85	High	High	High	Moderate	Absent	1	3.7	High

Fig. 4. Load the pre-processed patient parameters data

Target Feature Identification

After pre-processing, all the parameter columns except prediction field is considered as the features. Prediction column is taken as the target.

Step-1 Load the libraries and patient parameters data

Step-2 Reading input parameter data

This input CSV file is read into python using the Jupyter integrated development environment. As shown in Figs. 4 and 5. The Fig. 5 shows the list of parameters data such as patient weight, age, cl grade, buck teeth, mallampati score are inputs to the system and prediction column shows prediction outcome of airway is difficult or easy for selected 20 patients.

```
In [4]: df1
```

Out[4]:

	Sl.No	Patient id	Age at initial pathologic diagnosis	Weight	C-L (Grade 3 or 4)	Mallampati score	Interincisor gap	Retrognathia	Buck teeth	Prediction	Thyromental distance	Cervical joint rigidity
0	1	IMM01	40	110	High	Low	Low	Moderate	Absent	D	6.5	High
1	2	IFM02	41	90	High	Low	Low	Moderate	Absent	D	6	High
2	3	IMM03	42	75	Low	High	High	Absent	Absent	E	7	Low
3	4	IFM04	43	65	Low	High	High	Absent	Absent	E	8.5	Low
4	5	IMT05	18	85	High	High	High	Moderate	Absent	D	3.7	High
5	6	IFT06	19	75	High	High	High	Moderate	Absent	D	5.3	High
6	7	IMT07	16	55	Low	Low	High	Absent	Moderate	D	8	High
7	8	IFT08	14	57	High	Low	High	Moderate	Severe	D	3.9	Low
8	9	IMM09	45	90	Low	Low	Low	Moderate	Absent	E	7.1	Low
9	10	IFM10	47	95	Low	Low	Low	Moderate	Absent	E	6.8	Low
10	11	IME11	52	106	Low	High	Low	Absent	Moderate	D	2.9	Low
11	12	IFE12	51	94	Low	High	High	Absent	Absent	E	6.6	Low
12	13	IME13	55	85	NT	NT	NT	NT	Absent	E	NT	NT
13	14	IFE14	53	70	NT	NT	NT	NT	NT	E	NT	NT
14	15	IME15	61	81	High	NT	NT	NT	NT	D	NT	NT
15	16	IFE16	63	74	High	NT	NT	NT	NT	D	NT	NT
16	17	IME17	60	69	Low	NT	NT	NT	Absent	E	NT	NT
17	18	IFE18	59	87	Low	NT	NT	NT	Moderate	E	NT	Low
18	19	IMM19	45	116	NT	NT	NT	NT	Absent	D	NT	Low
19	20	IFM20	47	112	NT	NT	NT	NT	Absent	D	NT	Low
20	21	IMM21	48	100	Low	Low	Low	Severe	Absent	D	7.3	Low

Fig. 5. Input Patient Data set loaded

Step-3 Cross validation split

The data set is split into two subsets. 70% of the data is used for training and 30% is used for testing. This split is done using the Stratified Shuffle Split function from cross validation module of Scikit-Learn

Step-4 Classification

The Scikit-Learn python tool provides a wide variety of machine learning algorithms for the classification. Ten classifiers from the package were used for the study: Decision Tree classifier, Gaussian NB, SGD Classifier, SVC, K Neighbors Classifier, One Vs Rest Classifier, Quadratic Discriminant Analysis (QDA), Random Forest Classifier, MLP Classifier, and AdaBoost Classifier. Keeping the default environment intact the accuracy of each classifier is recorded using the scikit-learn package of python.

Setp-5 Prediction outcome

After processing data with prediction rules by the inference engine. The predictions classified as easy or difficult airway. The conclusions are drawn based on the risk parameter values of those five stages.

5 Results Analysis

The final results after experimentation with this prototype are shown in Fig. 6. The difficult airway outcome is encoded with symbol 0 as easy and symbol 1 as difficult. The numerical airway parameters values are converted into fuzzy linguistic values ranging from LOW, Moderate and High. Age and weight of the patient pathologic diagnosis, Weight and C-L grade are shown in Fig. 6. Three patients with serial number 1, 12 and 45 are predicted as having difficult airway rest are having easy airway passage.

```
In [8]: df1['Prediction'] = df1['Prediction'].map({'E':0,'D':1})
        df1.head()
```

Out[8]:

SLNo	Age at initial pathologic diagnosis	Weight	C-L (Grade 3 or 4)	Mallampati score	Interincisor gap	Retrognathia	Buck teeth	Prediction	Thyromental distance	Cervical joint rigidity
0	1	40	110	High	Low	Low	Moderate	Absent	1	6.5	High
1	2	41	90	High	Low	Low	Moderate	Absent	1	6	High
2	3	42	75	Low	High	High	Absent	Absent	0	7	Low
3	4	43	65	Low	High	High	Absent	Absent	0	8.5	Low
4	5	18	85	High	High	High	Moderate	Absent	1	3.7	High

Fig. 6. Airway difficulty prediction based on input data

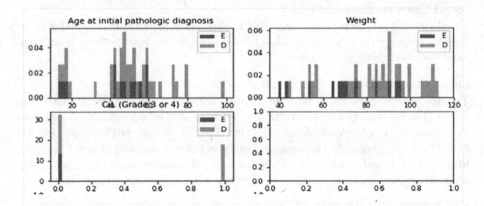

Fig. 7. Histogram showing the Age and Weight relationships

Mean values of age at initial pathologic diagnosis, weight and C-L grade are used in the classification of the intubation airway technique is shown in Fig. 6. Higher values of these parameters tend to show a correlation with difficult airway surgery. Mean values of thyromental distance, Mallampati scores and buckteeth does not show a particular preference of one technique over the other. In any of the histograms there are no noticeable large outliers that warrants further cleanup as shown in Fig. 7.

Logistic Regression Model

Logistic regression is widely used for classification of discrete data. This algorithm uses only binary (1, 0) for classification. Based on the observations in the histogram plots in Fig. 7, Authors have reasonably hypothesized that the airway problem prediction depends on the mean age at initial pathologic diagnosis, mean weight, mean thyromental distance, mean C-L grades and mean neck circumference. Authors then performed a logistic regression analysis using those features as follows, the prediction accuracy is 89.444% which is reasonable. The accuracy of the predictions is good but not great. The cross validation scores are reasonable.

```
predictor_var = features_mean
model = RandomForestClassifier(n_estimators=100,min_samples_splits=20, max_depth=7, max_features=2)
classification_model(model,traindf1,predictor_var,outcome_var)

------------------------------------------------------------------

NameError                           Traceback (most recent call last)
<ipython-input-3-e1f7f67a384d> in <module>()
----> 1 predictor_var = features_mean
      2 model = randomForestClassifier(n_estimators=100,min_samples_splits=20, max_depth=7, max_features=2)
      3 classification_model(model,traindf1,predictor_var,outcome_var)
```

Fig. 8. Screen shot of Random Forest algorithm experiment

Accuracy from Random Forest algorithm is: 95.72

Random Forest Model

This algorithm uses all the features and improves the prediction accuracy to 95.729% and the cross-validation score is great. An advantage with Random Forest model is that it returns a feature importance matrix which can be used to select features as shown in Fig. 8.

The authors have experimented with four different algorithms and discovered that Random Forest prediction algorithm works best with 95.72% prediction accuracy compared to other three algorithms as shown Table 6.

Table 6. Comparison of accuracy by different algorithms for the prediction

Sl. no	Classifier algorithm	Accuracy %
1.	Logistic regression model (Training data)	89.44
2.	Random forest (Training data)	95.72
3.	Decision tree (Training data)	96.98
4.	Random forest (Test data)	95.72

6 Conclusions

Authors have studied the literature on airway management from articles from reputed high impact factor journals from IEEE, Springer and Elsevier publishers. The data was collected from K.S. Hegde Medical Academy, Mangalore. Researchers have built an expert system prototype model to predict the difficulty in airway management. This paper discussed the implementation of fuzzy rule base model using Intel Distributed Python package.

Authors have experimented with four algorithms and would like to experiment with more algorithms to fine tune the rule base, data to get better results and accuracy.

Limitations and Future Work

Authors are collaborating with doctors in KS Hegde Medical Academy to collect more real data on day to basis from patients and implement this prototype in this hospital on day to day basis. Authors are designing a website, apps for doctors and hospital to share patient's data to build standard database for airway management. In future this website will facilitate doctors to share airway management experiences with each other case by case to enhance the skill of novice doctors.

References

1. Tu, J.: Computational Fluid and Particle Dynamics in the Human Respiratory System, Biological and Medical Physics, Biomedical Engineering. Springer Science + Business Media Dordrecht, Netherlands (2013). https://doi.org/10.1007/978-94-007-4488-2_2
2. Rudra, A., Chatterjee, S., Das, T., Sengupta, S., Maitra, G., Kumar, P.: Obstructive sleep apnoea and anaesthesia. Indian J. Crit. Care Med. **12**(3), 116–123 (2018). http://www.ijccm.org/text.asp?2008/. 43680

3. Cook, T.M., Woodall, N., Frerk, C.: Major Complications of Airway Management in the UK: Results of the Fourth National Audit Project of the Royal College of Anaesthetists and the difficult airway society, pp. 617–631 (2011). https://doi.org/10.1093/bja/aer058, https://www.ncbi.nlm.nih.gov/pubmed/21447488

4. Qureshi, M.J., Kumar, M.: Laryngeal mask airway versus bag-mask ventilation or endotracheal intubation for neonatal resuscitation. Cochrane Database Syst. Rev. **3**, Art. CD003314 (2008). https://doi.org/10.1002/14651858.cd003314.pub3

5. Becker, D.E., Rosenberg, M.B., Phero, J.C.: Essentials of airway management, oxygenation, and ventilation: part 1: basic equipment and devices. Anesth. Prog. **61**(2), 78–83 (2014). https://doi.org/10.2344/0003-3006-61.2.78leandro

6. Braz, L.G., Braz, D.G., Cruz, D.S.D., Fernandes, L.A., Módolo, N.S.P., Braz, J.R.C.: Mortality in anesthesia: a systematic review. Clinics **64**(10), 999–1006 (2009). https://doi.org/10.1590/s1807-59322009001000011

7. Dushianthan, A., Grocott, M.P.W., Postle, A.D., Cusack, R.: Acute respiratory distress syndrome and acute lung injury. Postgrad. Med. J. **87**, 612–622 (2011). https://doi.org/10.1136/pgmj.2011.118398

8. Lavery, G.G.: The difficult airway in adult critical care. Crit. Care Med. **36**(7), 2163–2173 (2008). https://doi.org/10.1097/ccm.0b013e31817d7ae1

9. Dragulescu, D., Adriana, A.: Medical prediction system. Acta Polytechnica Hungarica **4**(3) (2007). http://www.aut.upt.ro/~adrianaa/publications.html

10. Makhubele, K., Audrey, M.: A Knowledge based expert system for medical advice provision. kulanithesis (2012). http://pubs.cs.uct.ac.za/honsproj/cgi-bin/view/2012/makhubele/files/

11. Soltan, R.A., Rashad, M.Z., El-Desouky, B.: Diagnosis of some diseases in medicine via computerized experts system. Int. J. Comput. Sci. Inf. Technol. (IJCSIT) **5**(5), 79 (2013). https://doi.org/10.5121/ijcsit.2013.5505, http://airccse.org/journal/jcsit/5513ijcsit05

12. Hemmerling, T.M., Cirillo, F., Cyr, S.: Decision Support Systems in Medicine - Anesthesia, Critical Care and Intensive Care Medicine. http://dx.doi.org/10.5772/51756

13. Vaughan, R.S.: Predicting difficult airways. Br. J. Anaesth. CEPD Rev. **1**(2), 45–47 (2001)

14. Gupta, S., Sharma, R., Jain, D.: Airway assessment: predictors of difficult airway. Indian J. Anaesth. **49**(4), 257–262 (2005). https://www.medind.nic.in/iad/t05/i4/iadt05i4p257

15. Matsumoto, T., de Carvalho, W.B.: Tracheal intubation. J. de Pediatria **83**(2) (Suppl) (2007). https://doi.org/10.2223/jped.1626

16. Hernández-Cortez, E., Martinez-Bernal, G.F.: Airway in the newborn patient. J. Anesth. Crit. Care **5**(1), 00172 (2016)

17. Kheterpal, S., Martin, L., Shanks, A.M., Tremper, K.K.: Prediction and outcomes of impossible mask ventilation: a review of 50,000 anesthetics. Anesthesiology **110**(4), 891–897 (2009). https://doi.org/10.1097/aln.0b013e31819b5b87

18. Wanderley, G.H.S., Lima, L.C., de Menezes, T.C., Silva, W.V., Coelho, R.Q.G.: Clinical criteria for airway assessment: correlations with laryngoscopy and endotracheal intubation conditions. Open J. Anesth. **3**(7), 320–325 (2013). https://doi.org/10.4236/ojanes.2013.37070

19. Shelgaonkar, V.C., Sonowal, J., Badwaik, M.K., Manjrekar, S.P., Pawar, M.: A study of prediction of difficult intubation using mallampati and wilson score correlating with cormack lehane grading. J. Evid. Med. Healthc. **2**(23), 3458–3466 (2015). https://doi.org/10.18410/jebmh/499

20. Patel, A.B., Ani, C., Feeney, C.: Cuff leak test and laryngeal survey for predicting post-extubation stridor. Indian J. Anaesth. **59**(2), 96–102 (2015). https://doi.org/10.4103/0019-5049.151371

21. Norskov, A.K., et al.: Prediction of difficult mask ventilation using a systematic assessment of risk factors vs. existing practice-a cluster randomised clinical trial in 94,006 patient. Anaesthesia **72**(3), 296–308 (2016). https://doi.org/10.1111/anae.13701, https://www.ncbi.nlm.nih.gov/pubmed/27882541
22. Purushottam, Saxena, K., Sharma, R.: Efficient heart disease prediction system. Procedia Comput. Sci. **85**, 962–969 (2016). www.sciencedirect.com

A Comparative Study on Load Balancing Algorithms in Software Defined Networking

Neha Joshi and Deepak Gupta[✉]

Computer Science and Engineering, NIT Arunachal Pradesh, Yupia, India
nehajoshi4321@gmail.com, deepakjnu85@gmail.com

Abstract. Advent of big data, cloud computing and IOTs resulted into significant increase in traffic on servers used in traditional networks as these networks are normally non-programmable, complex in management, highly expensive in nature, and have tightly coupled control plane with data plane. To overcome these traditional network-based issues a newly emerging technology software defined networking (SDN) has been introduced which decouples the data plane and control plane and makes the network fully programmable. SDN controllers are programmable so an efficient load balancing algorithms must ensure the effective management of resources as per client's request. Based on these parameters i.e. throughput, transaction rate, & response time the qualitative comparison between the load balancing algorithms of SDN is done to generate the best results.

Keywords: Software defined networking (SDN) · SDN controller · Mininet emulator tool · Sniper tool · Siege tool · Open flow

1 Introduction

SDN is rapidly emerging technology in the networking field, by using SDN architecture we can easily manage different network applications and services. SDN separates the network logic control plane and the forwarding element data plane (e.g. Router, switch). As a result, the network management information and the network logic are centralized together over the SDN controller (also known as control plane). The lead role in SDN architecture is played by the SDN controller, which controls all the functions of the network by the help of openflow protocol [1, 2].

With SDN, the network is fully programmable, more agile and scalable. It provides the flexibility to switch into the cloud environment, virtualization, private network and public network. Therefore, we can easily add or remove different routers, switches as per the requirement and implements different network application by the help of software based SDN controller in the system. The major applications of SDN are cloud integration, network monitoring, distributed system control, security services, automation, etc. However, in traditional network systems both planes i.e. data, and control plane are securely coupled with each other. Therefore, every network application needs an individual hardware and that hardware's are very expensive, inflexible and vendor-specific. The traditional load balancers are manufacturer based and they set the specific algorithms on it, which we cannot change according to our feasibility.

© ICST Institute for Computer Sciences, Social Informatics and Telecommunications Engineering 2019
Published by Springer Nature Switzerland AG 2019. All Rights Reserved
N. Kumar and R. Venkatesha Prasad (Eds.): UBICNET 2019, LNICST 276, pp. 142–150, 2019.
https://doi.org/10.1007/978-3-030-20615-4_11

To solve these issues in conventional load balancing method, we develop the load balancing algorithm and implement it over the control plane which convert the simple Openflow device into an effective load balancer [3, 4].

The enhancement in network technology introduces so many challenges. One of the major issues in network architecture is delay in providing the response to end users. Usually delay occurs when the system device is overloaded and creates a bottleneck situation in the system. To distribute the load among the different servers and to prevent the bottleneck situation we require the load balancers. In existing network system load balancer device uses various types of load balancing algorithms, so to distribute the large amount of client traffic into several servers it takes too much time to process and make the system inconsistent. One of the major applications of network is load balancer so that we implemented the load balancing application over the SDN controller and then controller is act as a load balancer. Thus, an SDN load balancer distributes traffic more easily in less amount of time and in efficient manner [5, 6].

To investigate the network load balancer performance of SDN, we compare different load balancing algorithms to evaluate the best performance among different scheduled algorithms. We implemented load balancing application over the SDN controller (i.e. POX Controller). To perform the task, POX controller is used which supports the Python language and mininet emulator tool is used to create the network topology, which provides the same virtual hardware setup as in realistic environment.

In this paper, we compare four different load balancing algorithms of SDN on the basis of following parameters as: response time, transaction rate, and throughput. The following four algorithms are as:

- Round-Robin Strategy [7, 8]
- Implementation of server load balancing algorithm [9]
- Flow statistics load balancing algorithm [10]
- Least time based weighted load balancing algorithm [11]

The main tasks performed in this experiment are:

- Tested the comparison on Mininet emulator tool [12, 13].
- Compared above mentioned algorithms by the help of various parameters namely throughput, response time, and transaction rate.
- Tested the result by the help of Load Balancer Sniper and Siege Tool.

This paper consists of five sections. Section 2 represents the background and related work of the load balancing and related algorithm using SDN and also displays the SDN architecture consisting of all the layer i.e. application layer, control layer, and infrastructure layer. Section 3 describes the load balancer architecture related to our topology used in the simulation process. Section 4 consists all experimental result, network setup, load testing tool, and emulator tool description. Overall this section shows the graphical representation of all the result. Section 5 represents the conclusion and future work of the paper.

2 Background and Related Work

The enhancement in network technology leads to increase in network traffic. Therefore, it is hard to handle the large amount of requests by the single server. The main aim of load balancer is to disburse the load among various servers and help us to increase the network performance by efficient use of all available resources in the network systems.

Silva et al. [6] explained that SDN load balancers are real, flexible, agile, and cost-effective over the conventional load balancers. They evaluated the performance of SDN load balancers with different scheduled algorithms. Kaur et al. [8] executed the Round Robin strategy. The demerit of this paper is that it does not include the load of the server & time delay. This method supposed that all the servers present in that particular network system have equal number of request and every link possess same speed. However, in real world the scenario is quite different. Practically all the link has different bandwidth and speed. Kaur et al. [11] implemented the least time based load Balancing strategy. In that case, the load balancer sends the client request to that server which has least time delay instead of any other servers having more delay. Koerner et al. [14] discussed one or more load balancing concepts in which one of the load balancer is taken care of balancing web servers whereas another load balancer is needed for balancing e-mail servers.

2.1 SDN Architecture

The SDN Architecture as shown in Fig. 1 consists mainly three components:

- **Application Layer**: It is the topmost layer of the SDN architecture. The SDN application layer consists of many network applications which create an abstract view from the internal network and to build the communication with SDN controller the API (Application Program Interface) used by the programmer is called Northbound API.
- **Control Layer:** It is also known as the control plane of the SDN architecture. All the routing decisions, management of the network is done by control layer. It is also called as the network operating system (NOS) that control all the operations of the SDN. To communicate with various network devices like routers, switches, etc. the SDN controller uses southbound API. The load balancer application is run on top of the SDN controller and the load balancing algorithms is installed on load balancer application.
- **Infrastructure Layer:** The bottom layer of SDN architecture also known as data layer. This layer helps to forward the packets by some set of rules given by the SDN controller. The infrastructure layer is the connection of various physical devices or virtual devices such as routers, switches, etc. The SDN controller defines and installs rules on the flow tables of Openflow switches.

The decoupled data plane and control plane are communicated by the help of Openflow protocol. This protocol helps us to exchange the information between these two planes. A secure channel is used to carry the information from the Openflow switch and the control plane by the help of Openflow protocol [2].

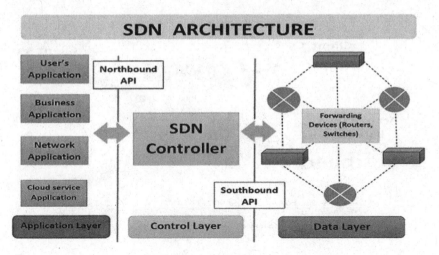

Fig. 1. SDN architecture

This architecture of SDN supports all the legacy network applications and provides the more enhanced features of the network system such as scalability, feasibility, adaptability, flexibility etc. So, this is only being happened due to its programmable nature. As we all know SDN controller is programmable so now it is easy to implement any kind of application over it and make the network more agile and programmer dependent [15].

3 Load Balancing Architecture

It consists the SDN controller, which is fully programmable and behaves like a Load Balancer after installing the load balancing algorithms over it and represents number of servers where load is distributed according to the load balancing algorithms as shown in Fig. 2.

The load balancer application consists an algorithm by which it takes the decision to select one server from the pool of servers and distributed the load simultaneously as per client's request [4]. In this architecture of load balancing first client sent the request to the server which is controlled by the SDN controller (act as a load balancer) then load balancer sent their request to the one server according to their scheduled algorithm. Server processes the client requests and gives the response back to the client. In this scenario, the controller communicates with openflow switch via openflow protocol using southbound API. In our experiment, we use four types of load balancing algorithms, which are described below:

Round-Robin Strategy: This algorithm is defined as the requests are sent to each server available in the queue one by one in a circular manner. When any packet is arriving, the next chosen server is available on the queue of all present servers in the

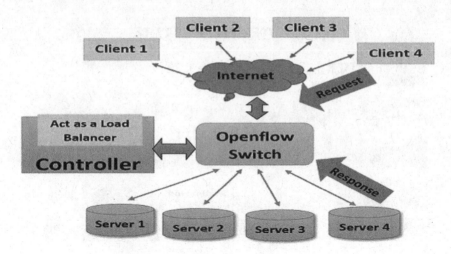

Fig. 2. Load balancing architecture of software defined networking.

network system. So, that all the servers in the list is in the same order and handles the equal number of load, excluding the load present on each server [8].

Server Load Balancing: This algorithm is explained as the load is served to that server where the server has the lowest CPU load value and the server, which has the minimum load value, is chosen. The server determines their current load value by the help of mpstat command [9].

Flow Statistics Load Balancing: It is defined as the server, which has minimum number of flow connection, is selected for processing the next request. After every 5 s the Openflow switch receives the flow-statistics request message from the load balancer. The total no. of requests that were sends to each server is counted by the load balancer. Then after the server with least active connection handles the next upcoming packet for processing which is send by the load balancer [10].

Least Time Based Weighted Load Balancing: It depends on the time delay of the server. Server with less delay can deal with the more no. of requests. At first, we assigned various delay on every link between the Openflow switch and the servers. Secondly, we assigned unique weight to the server based on delay on each server. Then we set more weight to that server which has least delay and that server is connected to Openflow switch [11].

4 Result and Discussion

There are various tools available by which we can test and compare our SDN load balancer application. We used the mininet emulator tool which helps us to create the network topology containing the number of hosts, forwarding element switches and the controllers [12, 13]. In our framework we implement the python based POX controller as load balancer and one device act as an Openflow switch (forwarding element) and other systems act as a host and remaining systems works as a server where load is distributed by the help of load balancer [16]. We also use load balancer Sniper testing tool on host computer to generate the readings of different parameters to find the least active connection in the server, mpstat and netstat command is used.

For experimental estimation, we compare the above mentioned load balancing algorithm with each other by the help of the attributes like throughput, response time, and transaction rate.

Mathematically the throughput can be calculated as the number of bits processed in per unit time. It is denoted as:

$$throughput = \frac{\#bits}{second}$$

Response time is defined as the total processing time for all the users and is divided by the number of users. Response time usually gives the total time taken by the request response process. It is the amount of time to process the request by the servers when it is received the request by the client. We calculate the response time by the given formulae:

$$response\ time = \frac{total\ processing\ time}{total\ number\ of\ users}$$

Transaction rate can be calculated as the number of http request-response pair is processed in per unit time. It is usually an amount of information or request-response pair is exchanged from the server in a given amount of time. So, the maximum transaction rate shows the faster and better response. It can be denoted as:

$$transaction\ rate = \frac{\#\ http\ request\ response\ pair}{second}$$

We simply send the different number of requests as per clients to the load balancer tool (i.e. siege tool and sniper tool) according to the scheduled algorithms and it displayed the output readings of different attributes. Based on these above mathematical equations the parameters like throughput, response time and transaction rate gave their value. By running this whole setup by the help of mininet emulator tool we get the results and on the basis of those output readings graph is plotted.

The graphical representation of all the parameter results is shown as below:

Figure 3 represents the throughput result. Horizontal axis represents the concurrent users and vertical axis represents the throughput (mb/sec). On behalf of this parameter, server load balancing shows the better result than any other given algorithms. Throughput means the number of requests in bits is processed in a given amount of time.

Figure 4 presents the response time result. Horizontal axis denotes the no. of users and vertical axis shows the response time in sec. Based on this parameter, flow-statistics algorithm has the least response time among all other given algorithms. By the way, both server load balancing and flow statistics load balancing algorithms shows the similar kinds of results. However, flow statistics based application gives the better response time.

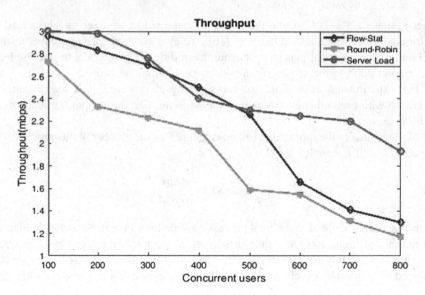

Fig. 3. The throughput comparison of three algorithms i.e. round-robin, flow statistics, server load algorithm.

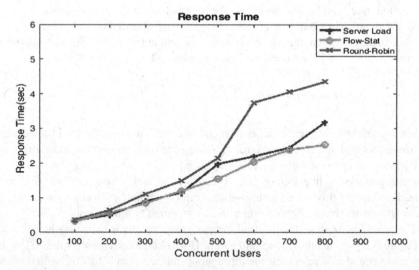

Fig. 4. The response time result of three algorithms as round-robin, flow statistics, server load

Figure 5 shows the transaction rate of the server. In that case server load balancing is compared to the round-robin strategy and it gives better results than round-robin method. Server load balancing algorithm has the higher transaction rate that means it processes the request faster than the round-robin algorithm. The X-axis of the graph shows the total number of users sends the requests and the Y-axis represents the transaction rate of the server.

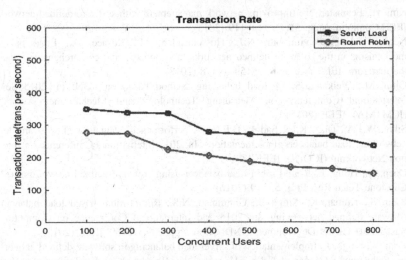

Fig. 5. The transaction rate of server load and round-robin algorithm.

5 Conclusion and Future Work

SDN load balancer deals with lots of issues of conventional load balancer in an efficient and cost-effective way. By the help of above experiment and comparison, the result is that among these four types of algorithms "Implementation of server load balancing" is the best load balancing algorithm in software defined networking with respect to these parameters as throughput, transaction rate, and response time.

However, the flow statistics based algorithms shows the better response time in comparison to the server load balancing algorithms. The main challenge of this experiment is that it is not tested in the real time hardware system, it is based on the mininet emulator tool, which provides the real time simulation of the experiment but not in the actual hardware.

To get the better results we can use RYU controller instead of using POX controller and can use more than one controllers in place of using single controller. So, that if any failure is occurring in the single controller we can easily recover it by using another controller [17].

Acknowledgment. We thank Mr. Sunit Kumar Nandi of NIT Arunachal Pradesh for helping us to understand the RYU controller functionalities and to learn the mininet emulator tool concepts.

References

1. Kreutz, D., Ramos, F.M.V., Verissimo, P.E., Rothenberg, C.E., Azodolmolky, S., Uhlig, S.: Software-defined networking: a comprehensive survey. Proc. IEEE **103**(1), 14–76 (2015)
2. Xia, W., Wen, Y., Foh, C.H., Niyato, D., Xie, H.: A survey on software-defined networking. IEEE Commun. Surv. Tutorials **17**(1), 27–51 (2015)

3. Kim, H., Feamster, N.: Improving network management with software defined networking. IEEE Commun. Mag. **51**(2), 114–119 (2013)
4. Neghabi, A.A., Navimipour, N.J., Hosseinzadeh, M., Rezaee, A.: Load balancing mechanisms in the software defined networks: a systematic and comprehensive review of the literature. IEEE Access **6**, 14159–14178 (2018)
5. Qilin, M., Weikang, S.: A load balancing method based on SDN. In: 2015 Seventh International Conference on Measuring Technology and Mechatronics Automation (ICMTMA). IEEE (2015)
6. Silva, W.J.A., Dias, K.L., Sadok, D.F.H.: A performance evaluation of software defined networking load balancers implementations. In: 2017 International Conference on Information Networking (ICOIN). IEEE (2017)
7. Deep, G., Hong, J.: Round robin load balancer using software defined networking (SDN). Capstone Team Res. Proj. **5**, 1–9 (2016)
8. Kaur, S., Kumar, K., Singh, J., Ghumman, N.S.: Round-robin based load balancing in software defined networking. In: 2015 2nd International Conference on Computing for Sustainable Global Development (INDIACom), pp. 2136–2139. IEEE (2015)
9. Kaur, S., Singh, J.: Implementation of server load balancing in software defined networking. In: Satapathy, S.C., Mandal, J.K., Udgata, S.K., Bhateja, V. (eds.) Information Systems Design and Intelligent Applications. AISC, vol. 434, pp. 147–157. Springer, New Delhi (2016). https://doi.org/10.1007/978-81-322-2752-6_14
10. Kaur, K., Kaur, S., Gupta, V.: Flow statistics based load balancing in OpenFlow. In: 2016 International Conference on Advances in Computing, Communications and Informatics (ICACCI). IEEE (2016)
11. Kaur, K., Kaur, S., Gupta, V.: Least time based weighted load balancing using software defined networking. In: Singh, M., Gupta, P.K., Tyagi, V., Sharma, A., Ören, T., Grosky, W. (eds.) ICACDS 2016. CCIS, vol. 721, pp. 309–314. Springer, Singapore (2017). https://doi.org/10.1007/978-981-10-5427-3_33
12. Mininet: "Mininet - An Instant Virtual Network on your Laptop (orother PC)" (2016). http://mininet.org/
13. De Oliveira, R.L.S., Schweitzer, C.M., Shinoda, A.A., Prete, L.R.: Using mininet for emulation and prototyping software-defined networks. In: 2014 IEEE Colombian Conference on Communications and Computing (COLCOM), pp. 1–6. IEEE (2014)
14. Koerner, M., Kao, O.: Multiple service load-balancing with OpenFlow. In: 2012 IEEE 13th International Conference on High Performance Switching and Routing (HPSR). IEEE (2012)
15. Salman, O., Elhajj, I.H., Kayssi, A., Chehab, A.: SDN controllers: a comparative study. In: 2016 18th Mediterranean Electrotechnical Conference (MELECON), pp. 1–6. IEEE (2016)
16. Kaur, S., Singh, J., Ghumman, N.S.: Network programmability using POX controller. In: ICCCS International Conference on Communication, Computing & Systems, vol. 138. IEEE (2014)
17. De Oliveira, B.T., Gabriel, L.B., Margi, C.B.: TinySDN: enabling multiple controllers for software-defined wireless sensor networks. IEEE Latin Am. Trans. **13**(11), 3690–3696 (2015)

CloudSDN: Enabling SDN Framework for Security and Threat Analytics in Cloud Networks

Prabhakar Krishnan[(⊠)] and Krishnashree Achuthan

Amrita Center for Cybersecurity Systems and Networks,
Amrita Vishwa Vidyapeetham, Amrita University, Amritapuri, Kerala, India
kprabhakar@am.amrita.edu

Abstract. The "Software-Defined Networking (SDN), Network Function Virtualization (NFV)" are recent network paradigms and "OpenStack", a widely deployed Cloud management platform. The goal of this presented research work is to integrate the SDN, NFV into OpenStack based Cloud platform, draw practical insights in their inter-play, to solve the problems in the Cloud network orchestration and applications security. We review key prior works in this intersection of SDN, NFV and Cloud computing domain. The OpenStack based Cloud deployment integrates SDN through its Neutron module, which has major practical limitations with respect to scalability, security and resiliency. Aiming at some critical problems and overall Cloud security, we postulate certain SDN scheme that can distribute its own Network Function (NF) agents across the dataplane and deploy applications across the control plane that centralizes the network management and orchestration. A novel security scheme for Cloud Networks "CloudSDN", enabling SDN framework for Cloud security is proposed and implemented, addressing some well-known security issues in Cloud networks. We demonstrate the efficacy of the attack detection and mitigation system, under Distributed Denial of Service (DDoS) attacks on the Cloud infrastructure and on to downstream servers as well. We also present a comparative study with legacy security approaches and with classical SDN implementations. We also share our future perspectives on exploiting the myriad of features of SDN such as global view, distributed control, network abstractions, programmability and mitigating its security issues.

Keywords: SDN · NFV · DDoS · Intrusion Detection Systems (IDS) · Intrusion Prevention Systems (IPS) · Cloud · OpenStack · Network security

1 Introduction

Cloud Computing is a paradigm that aims at enabling ubiquitous, on-demand access to a shared pool of configurable computing and infrastructure resources. The modern Cloud data centers are designed for enterprise needs, distributed computations and data intensive applications, composing computational servers, data-storage systems internetworked with routers and Internet facing gateway devices. In large Data Center Networks (DCN), the prevalent security systems are usually connected in series mode

© ICST Institute for Computer Sciences, Social Informatics and Telecommunications Engineering 2019
Published by Springer Nature Switzerland AG 2019. All Rights Reserved
N. Kumar and R. Venkatesha Prasad (Eds.): UBICNET 2019, LNICST 276, pp. 151–172, 2019.
https://doi.org/10.1007/978-3-030-20615-4_12

causing network congestion and these mechanisms themselves become bottlenecks and offer limited protection in specific static network paths. The computing resources which include both hardware/software and networks, are usually geographically distributed across the globe, thus imposing challenges to the interconnecting network & operations. To solve this very issue of traffic orchestration and engineering, the emerging paradigms such as SDN/NFV are crucial to meet the user demands. The SDN enabled networking architectures, offer features such as programmability, flexible reconfigurations, dynamic policy enforcement and global views.

Security and privacy are of critical concern to cyber security and data center administrators and for Cloud service providers. For legacy network environment, SDN can be a value-add-on, whereas for today's Cloud data centers, in Clouds, virtual network implementation it is essential. In the networking domain, "Software-Defined Networking (SDN)" [1] is emerging as the most disruptive paradigm, redefining network architectures, topologies, orchestration and complex policies [2] of large applications, data centers and Cloud infrastructures. Network Function Virtualization (NFV) [3] is one of the rapidly adopted paradigms in the modern data centers, that offer virtualized networking services & functions as "Virtualized Network Functions (VNFs)".

Current day networking applications demand advanced services with varying policy-processes, so in data centers need to: "line up a sequence of NFs, various types of state changes by NFs: changing the packet contents (e.g., Network Address Translation-NAT changes addresses/ports), dropping packets (e.g., firewall), or absorbing packets and generating new ones (e.g., L7 load balancer terminates client's TCP session and establishes new session with the appropriate server)". In virtualized SDNFV data centers, the SDN controller can't track the packet-streams/flow, as it doesn't have full view of the NF processing functions that are either embedded in monolithic kernel or implemented as hardware chip in middlebox appliances. Therefore, limitations in SDN's global view of the network states of sessions, problems in optimal NF service chaining, have not been solved yet in these researches.

Further, to address open problems in Cloud security [4–6], "SDNFV enabled architectures help to bring in easy solutions and mechanisms for these cyber-threats. SDN defines the decoupling of the control plane and the data plane that share the traditional network equipment. On one hand, such decoupling is beneficial as it enables centralized decisions about data traffic in networks. This way, policies can be enforced quickly in response to emerging network requirements, as well as to network threats. On the other hand, SDN Security issues [7], such as fraudulent rule insertion, controller-switch communication flood, unauthorized controller access, and controller hijacking, could be exploited in Cloud environments to harm client applications and network performance. From the security point of view, it is relevant to investigate whether SDN constitutes a solution or a problem for Cloud Computing environments, since the answers to this question are important indicators of the trust that a Cloud customer can place in SDN and SDN based Cloud computing services. There are several proposals in the literature that address SDN security. Some position SDN as an additional defense measure to tackle security threats, IDS/IPS and DPI solutions and other proposals address SDN architectural vulnerabilities". Although many proposals are available in the literature, to solve legacy/traditional networking problems, there is a dearth of concrete feasible design, that addresses the applicability of SDN in securing Cloud networks.

Our work begins by arguing "that the current SDN match-and-action model is rich enough to implement a collection of anti-spoofing methods. Secondly, we develop and utilize advance methods for dynamic resource sharing to distribute the required mitigation resources over a network of switches. None of the earlier works attempted to implement security/defense mechanisms in the SDN switch directly and exploited the match-action power of the switch data plane. They just implemented applications on top of the match-and-action controller model and these control programs monitored the flows to enforce security policies. Our method builds on the premise that the SDN data plane switches are reasonably fast and efficient to perform low level primitive operations at wire speed. As such solutions require a number of flow-table rules and switch-controller messages proportional to the legitimate traffic, in order to scale when protecting multiple large servers, the flow tables of multiple switches are harnessed in a distributed and dynamic network-based solution".

Through this research work, we propose a security framework *CloudSDN*, and implemented a security scheme with attack detection mechanism in data-plane and mitigation control in the SDN control plane. Our experiments prove that only a marginal change in processing costs for this co-operative security scheme in SDN (controller/switch). Further, this scheme give protection to the SDN infrastructure from getting into control-plane saturation, flow-table/miss attacks and surely defends downstream servers, middlebox appliances in the network. As data plane is where packets are processed, switches should be enabled with new packets processing functions for DDoS coarse-grained attack detection and mitigation action. We implemented a SDN Integrated Cloud Management system that consists of security monitoring data plane and threat analyzing control plane. We introduced new mechanisms in the SDN stack and run-time library for defense applications. Our evaluations have proved that the extensible stateful SDN data plane within the framework, with NF service chaining, provides superior security compared to traditional firewall/perimeter solutions. The framework also offers developers a set of API & library to implement their custom network functions (NFs) policy and deploy NFVs in CloudSDN framework. We have embraced the OpenStack Cloud [8] and "Open Virtual Network (OVN)" technologies [9] to build the SDN-NFV enabled Cloud computing environment. Our framework is deployed as an active defense mechanism against DDoS Amplification and flooding attacks in Cloud environments and the efficiency is evaluated under various scenarios and comparative analysis with legacy/other SDN approaches.

The rest of the paper is structured as follows: Sect. 2, presents the background for SDN/NFV enabled Cloud computing and articulate our understanding and outline related works in Cloud security. In Sect. 3 we present our proposed SDN-enabled framework for Cloud security called *CloudSDN*, in Sect. 4 we will have a design & implementation discussion and in Sect. 5 we share the results of our preliminary experimentation. The Sect. 6 concludes this paper with summary highlights and an outlook on using SDN for future virtualized modern data centers.

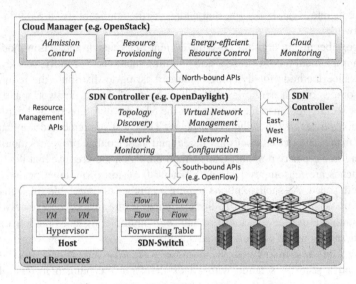

Fig. 1. SDN-centric cloud architecture [10]

2 Background and Motivation

We present here, the necessary background discussion of relevant technologies to build
SDN-enabled Cloud networks and related works.

2.1 SDN-Enabled Cloud Computing

The Cloud computing applications dynamically demand new provisioning, traffic QoS
and swift response to changing events/incidents. With SDN emerging as a reference
architecture (Fig. 1) for Clouds, many modern data centers have embraced this paradigm
shift for SDN-enabled Cloud Computing [10], such as Software-Defined Wide Area
Network (SD-WAN), SD-Clouds. IBM proposed one of the first SDN enabled Cloud
architecture called Meridian [11] with "OpenStack and IBM's Smart Cloud Provisioning
technologies". They adopted programming model of SDN for provisioning and network
management. PDSDN [12] project proposed a scheme/policy layer for "SDN controller-
to-Cloud Manager" to improve the interactions with Cloud users/tenant. They implemented on "SDN Open Floodlight and OpenStack Cloud". Mayoral et al. [13] introduced
SDN OpenDaylight controller into OpenStack Cloud platform and proved an improved
network orchestration service in this integrated Cloud infrastructure.

2.2 SDNFV Converged Architecture

Deploying SDN in legacy IT data centers, require a series of changes in terms of
redefining architecture, topologies, security policies, access-control mechanisms and so
on. The networking appliances and routing equipment are substituted with virtual
software switches (data plane).

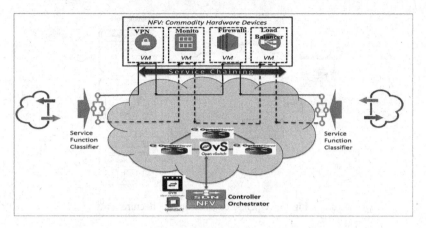

Fig. 2. The emerging SDNFV cloud computing paradigm

The Service Function Chaining (SFC) concept has emerged as a critical operation for IT networking and large-data center Clouds service providers, to establish a sequence of services and NFs (e.g. Firewalls, DPI, Load Balancing). This sequence of services is ordered in a "service list or chain", that is depicted in Fig. 2, namely SDNFV-enabled Cloud computing. The SFC traffic then is forwarded through this service chain by network components. The convergence of SDN and NFV "SDNFV-enabled Cloud computing" will unravel new paradigms, architectures and research problems/solutions for both academia and industry, as they complement and bring cost savings in terms of Capital Expenditure/Operational Expenditure (CAPEX/OPEX) and operational agility, energy saving, elastic provisioning, dynamic security for Cloud computing.

2.3 SDN - OpenStack Interaction Model

In our systematic research of SDN and OpenStack Cloud platform, we postulate that both these technologies can together deploy efficient solutions to enterprise data centric Cloud computing scenarios. Given in Fig. 3, Neutron subsystem is the OpenStack SDN component responsible for ensuring that virtual machines (VMs) have a functioning network. Neutron acts as an abstraction layer with its own plugin mechanism, which gives it the flexibility to incorporate SDN data plane components. OpenStack integrates SDN services through Neutron module. The Neutron server is a RESTful-based API in typical OpenStack style. The Neutron API is the point of contact for any request relating to the SDN configuration in an OpenStack Cloud. The Neutron Server, now extended to include an SDN plugin, acts as a central source of knowledge for all SDN-related information in OpenStack. Virtually all SDN approaches stipulate that flows of traffic from or to the Internet use a separate gateway, which is configured directly from the Cloud.

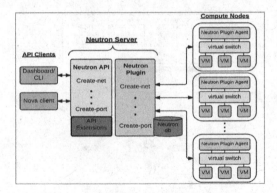

Fig. 3. OpenStack neutron architecture

But the OpenStack Neutron has major practical limitations with respect to scalability, security and resiliency. The reason is that "Neutron does not have its own Layer 3(L3) routing capability, but it uses the Linux kernel bridging and routing mechanisms instead. In a large Cloud environment with a lot of virtual networks, tenants, and applications, all traffic requiring routing and floating IP services need to be handled by the same Neutron L3 agent. Therefore, the agent becomes the choke point. SDN solutions can distribute their own L2/L3 agents among OpenStack nodes to help eliminate Neutron L3 agent bottleneck issue. And SDN controllers centralize the management of physical and virtual networks, so it helps simplify managing and monitoring tasks. OpenStack supports RESTful APIs for every component".

2.4   New Opportunities and Challenges in Cloud Security

SDN offers programmable networking infrastructure and NFV is capable of virtualizing network functions and both independently/combined offer new ways to monitor and secure Cloud networks. The two big questions for SDN in the networking field are: 1. Can SDN centric architecture secure Cloud networks? and 2. How Can SDN architectural vulnerabilities be protected? (Table 1).

2.5   Related Work

The authors of [14], propose an extension to controller for detecting DoS attack based on forwarding flow-tables on switches. In [15] Kumar et al. combine IDS and virtual switches, but the fine-grained latency & forwarding delay measurements were not presented. A "Moving-Target-Defense" scheme which modifies VM's identity is proposed by this paper [16], but the authors don't address insider threats in Cloud. In [17], the authors embed IDS into the control plane function and security is enforced based on dynamic changes to flow-table, but this adds overhead to controller process and choke point. The authors of [18], implemented IPS into controller process, but limited to POX controller. The authors proposed a Cloud-IPS with SDN in [19] and they leveraged the flow-table match-action/miss & sendto_controller as part of the

Table 1. SDN for cloud computing

Cloud networking issues	Advantages	Disadvantages
Proper installation of network firewalls	Central control logic and global topological view help to identify threats efficiently and accurately. Also, quick response to incidents and dynamically pushing the policies/rules	Unauthorized Access could compromise the firewall rules and policies of the network
Network security configurations	Legacy network architecture use appliances and vendor specific tools to orchestrate and manage configuration. SDN use standard interface/API to controller and OF protocol to switches for programming specific configurations	The operation of SDN paradigm revolves around the control protocol standard OpenFlow, which enables the data exchange between the controller and switches and applications. This opens up a critical attack vector for adversaries to saturate the control plane or MITM attacks disrupting the topology & policies. So the security and availability of SDN operations are critical
Internet protocol vulnerabilities	Legacy network protocols are designed based on packet-level decisions or policies on switches or routers. But this leads to congestion & bottlenecks. In SDN, flow-based traffic engineering and orchestrations are done by central control plane with global view, leading to enforcement of consistent policies	Legacy network architecture involves a series of network functions/protocols executed by separate entities. But in SDN, as the network is virtualized into programs and software applications are prone to design flaw or implementation vulnerability
QoS ("Quality of Service")	As SDN offers a programmable network architecture, it's easy to implement QoS policies and run time enforcement using dynamic mapping functions	The SDN based network and data centers incur higher communication overhead and provisioning of network bandwidth, compared to legacy network
Multi-tenant architecture	As SDN architecture is more software centric, its easily programmable for dynamic elastic provisioning models in a large complex multi-tenant data center	The operation of SDN paradigm revolves around the control protocol standard OpenFlow, which establishes flow-tables (equivalent to routing table in legacy network) in the series of switches in the data plane. It might be a challenge to enforce complex tenant SLAs/QoS, priorities and co-existing security/privacy boundaries just by using these flow-table pipeline. It may require sophisticated application software which again opens up bugs and vulnerabilities

OpenFlow protocol. In [20], authors presented a framework "CloudWatcher", using a scripting interface – the specific suspicious flows in the network may be program-matically diverted to scrubbing nodes for further security screening. Yan et al. [21] did a systematic-review on DDoS mitigation with SDN capabilities, at the same time the architecture of SDN paradigm comes with critical vulnerabilities such as control-plane saturation, single-point-of-attack and other side-channel attacks. Chowdhary et al. recommended [22] a novel framework for DDoS mitigation based on game theoretical approach and they demonstrated their solution with OpenDaylight Controller in Mininet simulated SDN environment. Foresta et al. [23] presented the advancements in using SDN OpenvSwitch data plane mechanism as a firewall in OpenStack and compared various performance metrics with the native Linux bridge. The authors in paper [24] proposed an scalable SDN/NFV monitoring framework, by integrating in OpenStack Neutron subsystem and they evaluated in real time traffic monitoring use cases. The authors of [25] proposed a comprehensive analysis of enabling SDN for security in IoT networks and discussed design choices. They further demonstrated the efficacy and feasibility of a SDN Framework for fine grained security monitoring in the data plane, with exemplar applications for defending DDoS/Botnet Attacks.

3   Proposed Architecture

3.1   Architecture Overview

SDN Integrated Cloud Management Framework (Fig. 4) 'CloudSDN' consists of security monitoring in data plane and threat analyzing in control plane. We introduce the major Components of the *CloudSDN* Framework below:

- *Infrastructure*: This layer consists of virtual machines, physical hosts and Cloud infrastructure devices (IoT, mobiles, hubs, modems, services, applications). This resource layer is managed by the 'OpenStack Nova' directly.
- *Switches:* This layer consists of OpenFlow (OF) switches, Core switches, hybrid OF-enabled Edge switches. This layer is managed by the Controller, through OF protocols for data switching, security monitoring and policy enforcement. Probes/Sensors monitor flows/packet-stream, if any anomaly is detected, that flow is flagged (i.e., "DDoS attack"), that specific switch sends in-band message (enclosing the flow-metadata, alerts, extracted feature-digest, synopsis) to Trigger Core Switch or Controller. The corresponding defense-action & cleanup command (NF) will be executed by Mitigator, on that specific Edge switch by Actuators in the data plane.
- *Control Plane:* This layer consists of SDN Controller (OpenDaylight) modified with extensions for the new security monitoring, defense and attack mitigation functions. It leverages uploaded in-band message, feature-digest, synopsis to clas-sify attack type and its global view of the network topology & attack sources. It then calls the defense-action library to implement specific defense-action in the switches that are in the path or closest to attack source.
- *Cloud Admin:* This layer implements Cloud management technologies such as OpenStack, with plug-ins and extensions to Neutron Layer for the SDN based

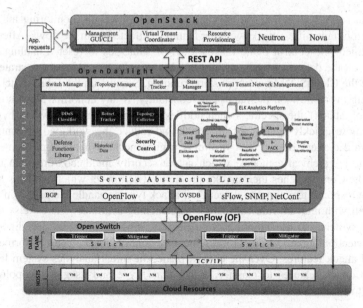

Fig. 4. CloudSDN - SDN integrated cloud management framework

security schemes. The Cloud users interact for services through REST API and Nova Layer establishes a "Virtual Network" for the new tenant.

- *Data Plane*: The following are the major steps in the network packet workflow on the data plane switches – (i) "new flow" in the switch (data plane) will be directed through the IDS/IPS embedded in the switch, chain of NFs following the "match-action" semantics of OpenFlow pipeline. (ii) As IDS/Trigger (NF) detects an Intrusion/Attack (through a 'challenge-response' method), controller will be notified through special OF message (in-band), defense actions will be distributed through flow-table actions (diversion or drop or filter or throttle), executed by IPS/Mitigator in the switch(es) in the path of the attack packets all the way back to the source.

3.2   Multi-plane Collaborative Defense

Our design goal is to architect a holistic monitoring and automated defense framework with fast attack detection. As the single-point of defense (centralized) cannot fully eliminate the threats in large network, hence the case of a multi-plane approach, that has distributed security monitor/enforcement with central control mechanisms deployed at key vantage points of the network. We further argue in SDN architecture, the control layer should do attack analysis on flows and control functions (e.g., attack classification and traffic trace-back). The controller should be responsible for conducting fine-grained attack detection and making high level defense strategies, leveraging its global view of the whole network, abundant computational and storage resources for historical data analysis. As data plane is where packets are processed, switches should be enabled with new packets processing functions for DDoS coarse-grained attack detection and mitigation action. Therefore, on the data plane, a lightweight monitoring mechanism (sensor/probe) identifies attacks with the features extracted from the flows. After attacks are identified, the control plane makes a set of strategies to react. Enabling defense actuators on the data plane dynamically is a key step for executing these strategies.

Once the CloudSDN framework starts running, Sensors on the Edge switches keep monitoring every flow on the data plane constantly. If any abnormal flow is captured (i.e., DDoS attack), the specific switch notifies an appropriate Core switch. In order to respond more quickly against DDoS attack and reduce the workload of controller, a coarse-grained attack detection algorithm & trigger mechanism are implemented in the data plane hierarchical switches, which acts a security middlebox/proxy to the controller. The Core switches then invoke pre-defined action-set which includes a proxy-challenge/response technique to detect DoS attack type or handle the packet in the data plane itself with relevant rules. If there is no matching action-set, the Core switch asks the Edge-switches to do sampling of suspicious flows and triggers new fine-grained attack detection/classification process in the control plane, with information of extracted attack features. Over the control plane, the threat analytics system leverages uploaded attack features to classify DDoS-attack type and its global topology perspective to locate the attack sources.

3.3   Security Service Function Chaining

We implemented dynamic Virtualized Network Function (VNF) service chaining through loadable modules/NFs/applications on the data plane switches. The policies for optimal chaining and placement of these NFs are determined by the Controller. To this end, we extend the classic Open vSwitch (OvS) stack to add stateful-functionalities and security-awareness. So, this translates to eliminating the middleboxes or standalone NFV machines (VMs) out of the data center. Some example NFs that can be deployed as dynamically loadable modules are: "Firewall, load-balancer, Proxy, NAT". We may argue that additional CPU resource is required to execute the VNFs either in VMs or in Switches. Our experience revealed that there is only a marginal difference in network overhead between two approaches. So, for IDS either at Wire-speed solution, NF' service chaining in OvS switch OpenFlow pipeline seems to be the trade-off.

3.4   Operation of CloudSDN

The operation of CloudSDN at run time is given in (Fig. 5), The security scheme in the SDN stack is divided into two phases: detection phase and reaction phase.

In the detection phase, which is spread across both data plane and control plane: a lightweight anomaly detection Statistical/Feature-based flow monitoring algorithm is proposed to serve the data plane as DDoS-attack sensor. The DDoS-attack traffic manifests higher volume and asymmetry in the network and we will monitor these features for our detection. On the control plane, a machine learning DDoS-attack classifier and applications are utilized to locate a DDoS attack in finer granularity (for e.g. attack type, malware, botnet origin location). Specifically, features extracted from attack traffic and holistic information of the network are fed into DDoS-attack classifier and botnet tracker.

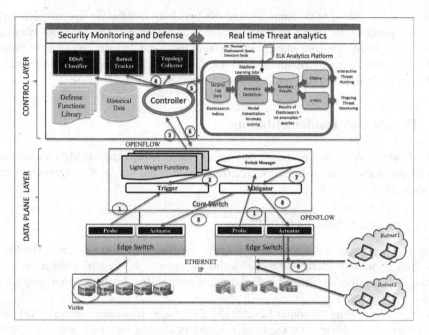

Fig. 5. Operation of CloudSDN framework

In the reaction phase, first level reactive functions executed in data-plane and second level reaction occurs later in control plane, based on the results obtained from the detection phase. A novel defense strategy offloading mechanism is proposed to enable DDoS attack defense actuators to be executed on the SDN Core/Edge switches

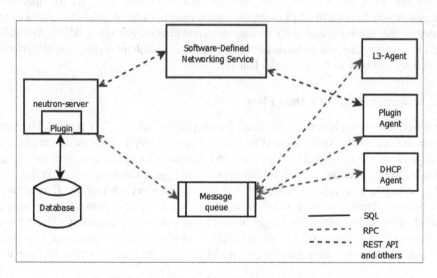

Fig. 6. OpenStack neutron and SDN services

automatically. Thus, SDN controller can be free from conducting specific defensive actions, resulting in attack reaction efficiency and overall traffic load optimization. More specifically, we concentrate on exploiting the computational resources of switch CPUs and the flexibility of southbound interface, in order to deploy defense actuator NFs on the switches which are closest to the botnet.

4 Design and Implementation

The design strategy is to propose extensions to the existing classical SDN architecture and OpenStack Neutron layers, to realize a multi-plane cooperative DDoS security framework.

4.1 OpenStack Neutron SDN Layers

The Fig. 6 depicts the interconnection between the SDN services and OpenStack Neutron layer. The interaction model within Neutron is shown with different colored lines. SDN services are defined as Python class and Neutron invokes them through API calls.

Neutron Plugin: The "Modular Layer 2 (ML2)" plugin, implements generic API, as a "plug-and-play" driver. We used the mechanism drivers for Open vSwitch (OVS), OpenDaylight (ODL). The plugin does all networking services ("creation, updation and deletion of networks, subnets and port resources, port binding") and provides connection between VM's and Cloud controller, also to outside networks.

Neutron Agent: Every plugin comes with an agent module on compute nodes and connect to the virtual switch (OVS) on the node. We designed new plugin using the ML2 core backend and opensource OF Agent to run on virtual switch itself (by extending the OpenvSwitch). The workflow inside Neutron is - "(i) An operation request is sent through the API to the Neutron server. (ii) The Neutron server makes an entry in the database and invokes the corresponding plugin via a REST API call. (iii) Upon receiving this request, the plugin calls the southbound protocols to perform necessary changes to the network elements".

4.2 OpenvSwitch SDN Data Plane

Our baseline implementation is derived from OpenvSwitch of OVN project. The data plane in CloudSDN Architecture (Fig. 7) is not just a group of forwarding entities but consist of a group of software sensors and actuators to detect and react to DDoS attacks. We have added another authoritative-layer/aggregation/core switch in the data plane acting as a main security firewall in the dataplane level, with attack '*Trigger*' and '*Mitigator*'. These can be a subset of existing switches in the network or dedicated switches or routers that have larger memory and processing capability. These Core switches run the complex NFs (service-chain or proxy or security challenge-response) for attack detection, coarse grained flow/packet inspection. These switches will execute

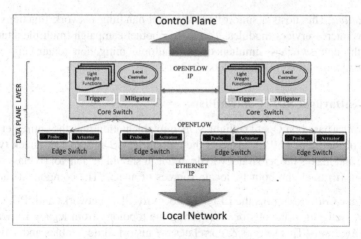

Fig. 7. Data plane operation in CloudSDN

some of the offloaded stateful functions (cached flow-rules/action set) instructed by the controller, on the Edge-switches which have '*probes*' and '*actuators*'.

This leads to our three key functionalities to enhance the existing switches in the data plane. (i) Capture key signatures/features of attacks. (ii) Load mitigation functional modules as instructed by controller and (iii) Execute the mitigation functions to handle the attack traffic. Unlike many other monitoring methods, the monitoring NFs that run as threads on switch software, extract key features of DoS-attacks by polling stat counters of OpenFlow (OF) switches. For non-OF switches the monitoring is done by querying through standard protocols such as SNMP, IPFIX, sFlow.

The functional components of the data plane layer include:

- *Attack probe/sensor:* smart components embedded into Edge switch, that runs a lightweight monitoring logic to detect attacks from hardware/port and changes in flow patterns/characteristics, by exploiting advanced match/actions in OpenFlow 1.5.1 Flow table. For non-OpenFlow switches, we enable the switch management protocols such as SNMP, sFlow, IPFIX.
- *Connection-state:* consists of flow-table analyzer, well-known attack signature database, learning-engine that correlates traffic patterns. dissects packet's headers, creates connection endpoint-profiles from metadata, geo-location, time-stamp and creates profile-synopsis for threat analysis.
- *Feature Extraction:* traffic matching specific rules are captured for attack signature/feature extraction. The *features-digest* includes volume and asymmetry.
- *Attack Detection Trigger:* Active smart probes/sensors deployed in key defensive points in the network (SDN, Legacy, IoT) which may indicate DDoS attacks (suspicious or abnormal traffic pattern, statistical thresholds, matching-flows, stateful filters, rate/velocity of key protocol messages) sends out alerts or trigger commands to controller.

- *Mitigation:* This hosts a suite of Flow/packet-handling network functions virtualized as micro-services/modules. To tackle a botnet campaign (multiple attacks may pass through switches simultaneously) multiple mitigation (chain) has to work independently on single/multiple switches.

4.3 OpenDaylight SDN Control Plane

The controller based on OpenDaylight SDN implementation runs the entire network, as the brain of the framework. It inspects the current DDoS attack (e.g., attack types and its traces) and makes proper strategy to defend it. It should be able to: (i) classify DDoS attacks and (ii) track the botnets, locate sources of attack. The components are:

- *Topology Collection*: runs the LLDP protocol for SDN networks and IPFIX,SNMP, sFlow, NetConf protocols for discovering the topology from legacy-IP networks.
- *Flow Analyser*– This sweeps & correlates the historical flow-tables and active flow-tables deployed by controller-to-switches. This augments the coarse-grained analysis done at data plane, by working on historical larger-data set and anomaly detection, fine-grained correlations between flow-tables from all over the network.
- *Attack Classifier/Detection:* Main Classifier/Detector of any attack type, leveraging the extracted attack-synapses (a small table of extracted features from attack packets) received from switches and trained with dataset samples from known sources.
- *Analytics Engine:* with the help of synopsis-object and features-digest, runs through a suite of classifiers workflow based on machine learning, rate-limiting, entropy based, behavioral correlation and anomaly-based algorithms.
- *Botnet Tracking and Attack Traceback*: It retraces the attack path, identifying the switches in the path from the victim to source network. Starting from point of attack detection (victim's network) moving backwards in the opposite trajectory of attack traffic, the traceback engine, queries the devices (switches/middleboxes) for attack-synapses (small auxiliary table consisting of device profile, metadata and specific features from flows, flow-table entries for the adjacent, neighborhood switches). Using SDN controller's global network topology view, A co-operative traceback analytics algorithm is run across all the participating switches (using our customized OvS switch NF) to trace plausible paths to the source of attack. On analyzing the attack synapses data set, the malicious flow path, the attack source and the affected switches are identified.
- *Attack Mitigation/Response:* When attack-type/botnet-pivots and affected switches in the attack path, source network, are determined, this module sends instructions to those switches with "mitigation cleanup" action through OpenFlow/other standard dataplane protocols. This will block the attack traffic upstream and by purging malicious flows off the switch tables it also prevents ternary content-addressable memory(TCAM)bloating and packet drops issues in the network path.
- *OVSDB:* OpenvSwitch Database records all the flow information; flow rules are installed on to OpenFlow enabled Core Aggregating and Edge switches.

4.4   Implementation

OpenStack has already adopted some of the networking functions of SDN implementations. To optimize and also to secure the OpenStack Cloud deployments we have developed our native SDN components and interfacing modules for general legacy switches. As OpenvSwitch(OvS) based Virtual switches are used in more than 60% of the SDN/NFV enabled data centers, we used it as baseline and implemented extensions. The Fig. 8 shows the implementation of our SDN stack with stateful layers and the packet flow. It consists of two stages processing of application-logic/stateful tables within the switch, spread across User/Kernel spaces and the stateful/application control within the controller.

We illustrate the workflow of the typical Cloud computing use case in Fig. 9. A tenant requests for resources to OpenStack, then Nova module provisions required VM instances in the cloud. Then the SDN OpenDaylight (OD) controller schedules a virtual network (VN) through a RESTful call. The OD calls OpenFlow(OF), OpenvSwitch database (OVSDB) to configure VNs and send the Flow rules to OF switches. The Topology manager stores the VN configurations and topologies. Depending on the operational conditions, this pool of resources in the Cloud may be provisioned or reconfigured. We integrated the SDN and OpenStack in an experimental network, with a suite of anti-DDoS applications built into the package. The OVS switch on top of each cluster of compute nodes will monitor, detect attacks and execute mitigatory Network Functions (NFs) to restrict the attacks to the data plane itself and constantly communicating the statistics to SDN controller through the Neutron Plugins.

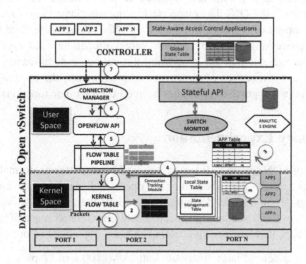

Fig. 8. Modified SDN stack in CloudSDN

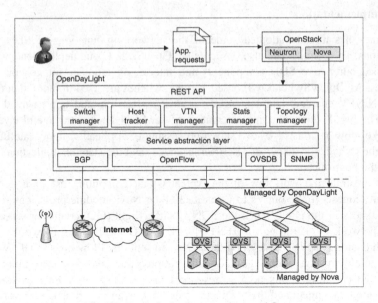

Fig. 9. Typical cloud computing workflow

We improved over the state-of-the-art works, in these aspects: (i) we have implemented a stateful/security-aware SDN dataplane and hence some light-weight detection/computation functions are offloaded to the switches for in-line processing (ii) We implemented the OvS data plane stack using the "Data Plane Development Kit (DPDK)" that consist of Network Interface Card (NIC) drivers/libraries/APIs for high-speed packet processing. Due to fastpath kernel processing and acceleration with DPDK, the flow-analysis pipeline processing throughput is significantly higher in the switch (iii) As a consequence of above two improvements, the processing power & throughput of network-ports of controller is freed up for other functions.

5   Preliminary Experimentation

In this domain of SDN-OpenStack Integration for Cloud platforms, formal specification or benchmarks aren't published in the open and vendors haven't published performance/validation. Hence, deriving from various literature study, we designed an evaluation strategy with security perspective and enumerated a set of network characteristics and Key Performance Indicators. The key objectives of our evaluation are:

- Can detect and defend large distributed attacks ("100 s of Gbps")
- Responsiveness, with acceptable performance hit for the legit users or applications
- To cope with rapidly changing dynamic attack patterns and scale with the network

A Cloud computing cluster (Fig. 10) with 4 machines - controller, network & 3 compute nodes. For evaluation and comparative study each compute node is loaded with different network hypervisor switch – 1. legacy Linux Bridge Firewall (LB FW), 2. native OvS Firewall module and 3. CloudSDN OvS Security modules. We used TCP background traffic, as the majority of traffic (99.1%) in data centers is TCP and about "64% DDoS attacks includes TCP-SYN, DNS and NTP amplification traffic".

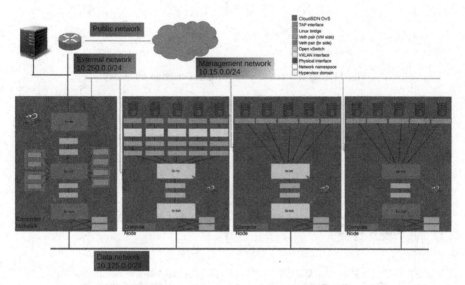

Fig. 10. SDN enabled OpenStack testbed

5.1 Comparison with Traditional Snort-Iptables IDS/IPS

- *IPS Efficiency:* Fig. 11(a) "total-packets processed/sec" varying attack rates. Traditional IPS drops packets and efficiency decreases as rate increases (12K pps to 0 at 37K pps). CloudSDN IPS sustains the packet processing under the same attack.
- *IDS efficiency*: Fig. 11(b) As the attack rate increases the Traditional IDS efficiency drops as the DoS attack floods the network, fills up the "Iptables Queue", saturates and eventually all packets are dropped. In CloudSDN IDS withstands large attack.
- To observe the impact on throughput of normal traffic, in the same network, we setup DoS attack generators towards a Server/VM inside the cluster and target to saturate the gateway switch. CloudSDN maintains throughput of benign traffic while dropping the attack traffic at the switch. With the traditional IPS, the normal traffic throughput is significantly impacted to a point of complete shutdown (Fig. 12a).

(a)   **(b)**

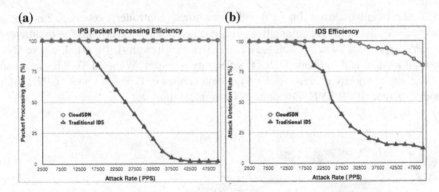

Fig. 11. (a) IPS processing (b) IDS detection efficiency

(a)   **(b)**

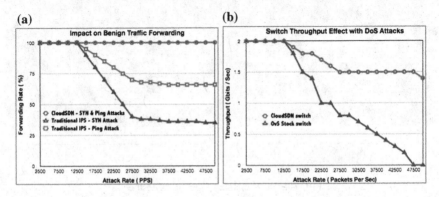

Fig. 12. (a) Impact on benign traffic (b) Switch throughput

5.2   Comparison with Classic OpenFlow SDN

- *Throughput Effect:* Fig. 12(b) Using various 'burst-intervals', UDP attacks (NTP amplification) is fired towards VMs in the cluster passing through switch. We ran normal FTP on another pair of VM's in the cluster. The results show that CloudSDN throughput is sustained at around 2 Gbps at high attack rates, Classic SDN switch degrades as the attack rate is increased to drop down to zero.
- *Mitigating DNS Amplification attacks:* Fig. 13(a), DNS server database/"zone file" and "Scapy as DNS query generator" are setup. DNS tool spoofs 'victim's IP address and floods the targeted DNS server(VM) with 80-byte length QUERY and DNS server responds for each query with REPLY of 4 kb to victim. Thus, the victim is flooded with unsolicited DNS responses saturating the network & CPU on that VM. We evaluated the detection of DNS attack under various scenarios. In 100 iterations, CloudSDN detects & blocks the DNS flooding attack in 4–12 s).
- *Attack Response:* Fig. 13(b) Shows attack-traffic saturating the link and consequently disrupting the legitimate normal traffic. CloudSDN detects in less than 3 s and mitigates (dropping the attack packets) in the data plane itself.

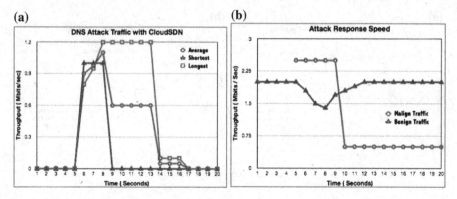

Fig. 13. (a) DNS amplification attack (b) Attack response

Table 2. Latency and packet loss

Metric	Flow table entries duration			
	50 s	100 s	500 s	1200 s
RTT	110.67 ms	56.34 ms	5.28 ms	3.91 ms
Packet loss	3%	1%	0%	0%

Table 3. Memory utilization

Instances/Node	Linux BR FW	OvS classic FW	CloudSDN FW
1	9.2%	22.6%	24.4%
4	14.8%	26.1%	32.2%
8	26.2%	34%	36.2%
16	40%	48.4%	56.8%

- *Latency/Packet-loss:* From Table 2 tests, (a) When DDoS attack begins, number of PACKET_IN events on SDN OpenFlow channel varies between 200 and 2000. Under DDoS attack (i) without security-scheme, Ave. RTT is >100 s and packet loss 100% (ii) With security scheme (a) small duration-the RTT gets affected. (b) longer-duration-the RTT is normal and 0% packet loss. Benign traffic is impacted by attack traffic, but it recovers under longer duration.

5.3   Comparison of Linux Bridge/Classic OpenStack/CloudSDN

To evaluate software nature adopted by CloudSDN, we evaluated the Key Performance Indicators (KPI) computation at various load conditions and networking at various traffic conditions. We set up 5 VM instances/compute-node and sufficient number of CPU cores and memory. We ran "30 tests of netperf TCP STREAM. per node", with one VM instance of server and other clients.

- *CPU, Memory Usage:* Fig. 14(a) shows all three mechanisms (legacy LB, native OvS, CloudSDN) consume similar CPU/memory resources. However, in Table 3, we see that SDN OvS mechanisms consume more memory compared with legacy LB, because of SDN/OvS OpenFlow pipeline tables. As the VMs/node increase, the memory utilization of all 3 mechanisms normalized to a level equal to or even lower than that is used by legacy LB.

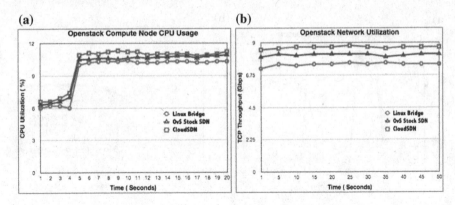

Fig. 14. (a) CPU usage (b) TCP throughput

- *TCP Throughput, Latency:* By varying the number of clients/node and external clients flooding a single server, higher sustained TCP throughput is seen with OvS based firewall than with Linux Bridge approach. This proves that OvS is optimal in the OpenStack Cloud applications. In the long run, the total aggregate throughput for all TCP flows gets closer to the maximum available bandwidth in the network interface. In Fig. 14(b) 4 clients send traffic to 1 server, total TCP throughput is almost 8.4 Gbps. When the number of clients increase, the total aggregated flows utilize the full bandwidth.

6   Conclusions and Future Work

Our work shows potential for software defined networking in achieving one of the paradigm visions i.e. "to provide a programmable capability for global view of the security incidents and respond rapidly", especially in large spatially distributed Cloud networks. In this paper, we presented the integrated view of Cloud computing and SDN under various scenarios especially in the presence of network attacks and DDoS/Botnet attacks. We proposed the CloudSDN Framework, that has the notion of multi-plane collaborative security monitoring, threat analytics, attack detection/mitigation in the emerging SDNFV enabled Cloud computing large-scale applications. We have also contributed key extensions and plugins to OpenStack/SDN based Cloud platform, especially the network architecture, to solve some of the open issues in reliability and security. We demonstrated the feasibility with DDoS/botnet defense applications using novel anomaly detection methods in the control plane and co-operative light weight monitoring/trigger/mitigatory NF mechanisms in the data plane. Our framework is one of the early works to combine the NFV and SDN-enabled Cloud platform, NF service chaining within in the SDN data plane, leading to speed-up and agility, security-awareness in the Cloud networks. CloudSDN design is platform agnostic, extensible to heterogenous network models for any large Cloud applications in IoT, 5G, Industry 4.0.

References

1. Rubio-Loyola, J., et al.: Scalable service deployment on software-defined networks. IEEE Commun. Mag. **49**(12), 84–93 (2011)
2. Hu, F., Hao, Q., Bao, K.: A survey on software defined networking (SDN) and openflow: from concept to implementation. IEEE Commun. Surv. Tutorials **16**(4), 2181–2206 (2014). vol. PP, no. 99, p. 1
3. Han, B., et al.: Network function virtualization: challenges and opportunities for innovations. IEEE Commun. Mag. **53**(2), 90–97 (2015)
4. Singh, A., Chatterjee, K.: Cloud security issues and challenges: a survey. J. Netw. Comput. Appl. **79**, 88–115 (2017). https://doi.org/10.1016/j.jnca.2016.11.027
5. Singh, S., et al.: A survey on cloud computing security: issues, threats, and solutions. J. Netw. Comput. Appl. **75**, 200–222 (2016)
6. Kanagasabapathi, K., Deepak, S., Prakash, P.: A study on security issues in cloud computing. In: Suresh, L.P., Panigrahi, B.K. (eds.) Proceedings of the International Conference on Soft Computing Systems. AISC, vol. 398, pp. 167–175. Springer, New Delhi (2016). https://doi.org/10.1007/978-81-322-2674-1_17
7. Scott-Hayward, S., O'Callaghan, G., Sezer, S.: SDN security: a survey. In: 2013 IEEE SDN for Future Networks and Services (SDN4FNS), pp. 1–7, November 2013
8. OpenStack. https://www.openstack.org/
9. Open Virtual Network Project. https://www.openvswitch.org/
10. Son, J., Buyya, R.: A taxonomy of Software-Defined Networking (SDN)-enabled cloud computing. ACM Comput. Surv. (CSUR) **51**(3) (2017). Article. 59, 36 Pages. https://doi.org/10.1145/3190617
11. Banikazemi, M., et al.: Meridian: an SDN platform for cloud network services. IEEE Commun. Mag. **51**(2), 120–127 (2013)
12. Du, X., Lv, Z., Wu, J., Wu, C., Chen, S.: PDSDN: a policy-driven SDN controller improving scheme for multi-tenant cloud datacenter environments. In: IEEE International Conference on Services Computing, pp. 387–394 (2016)
13. Mayoral, A., et al.: SDN orchestration architectures and their integration with Cloud Computing applications. Opt. Switching Netw. **26**, 2–13 (2017)
14. Giotis, K., et al.: Combining OpenFlow and sFlow for an effective and scalable anomaly detection and mitigation mechanism on SDN environments. Comput. Netw. **62**(5), 122–136 (2014)
15. Kumar, S., Kumar, T., Singh, G., Nehra, M.S.: Open flow switch with intrusion detection system. Int. J. Sci. Res. Eng. Technol. **1**(7), 1–4 (2012)
16. Jafarian, J.H., Al-Shaer, E., Duan, Q.: Openflow random host mutation: transparent moving target defense using software defined networking. In: The Workshop on Hot Topics in Software Defined Networks, pp. 127–132. ACM (2012)
17. Zanna, P., O'Neill, B., Radcliffe, P., et al.: Adaptive threat management through the integration of IDS into software defined networks. In: Network of the Future, pp. 1–5. IEEE (2014)
18. Xing, T., Xiong, Z., Huang, D., et al.: SDNIPS: enabling software-defined networking based intrusion prevention system in clouds. In: International Conference on Network and Service Management, pp. 308–311. IEEE (2014)
19. Chi, Y., et al.: Design and implementation of cloud platform intrusion prevention system based on SDN. In: IEEE International Conference on Big Data Analysis, pp. 847–852 (2017)

20. Shin, S., Gu, G.: Cloudwatcher: network security monitoring using openflow in dynamic cloud networks. In: 20th IEEE International Conference on Network Protocols, pp. 1–6 (2012)

21. Yan, Q., et al.: Software-defined networking (SDN) and distributed denial of service (DDoS) attacks in cloud computing environments: a survey, some research issues, and challenges. IEEE Commun. Surv. Tutorials **18**(1), 602–622 (2016)

22. Chowdhary, A., et al.: Dynamic game based security framework in SDN-enabled cloud networking environments. In: ACM International Workshop on Security in Software Defined Networks & Network Function Virtualization (SDN-NFVSec 2017)

23. Foresta, F., et al.: Improving OpenStack networking: advantages and performance of native SDN integration. In: 2018 IEEE International Conference on Communications (ICC) (2018)

24. Yang, C.-T., et al.: Implementation of a real-time network traffic monitoring service with network functions virtualization. Future Gener. Comput. Syst. **93**, 687–701 (2018). https://doi.org/10.1016/j.future.2018.08.050

25. Krishnan, P., Najeem, J.S., Achuthan, K.: SDN framework for securing IoT networks. In: Kumar, N., Thakre, A. (eds.) UBICNET 2017. LNICST, vol. 218, pp. 116–129. Springer, Cham (2018). https://doi.org/10.1007/978-3-319-73423-1_11

NB-FTBM Model for Entity Trust Evaluation in Vehicular Ad Hoc Network Security

S. Sumithra(✉) and R. Vadivel

Department of Information Technology, Bharathiar University, Coimbatore, India
sumiphdit@gmail.com, rvadivelit@buc.edu.in

Abstract. Vehicular Ad hoc network (VANET) is developed for exchanging valuable information among vehicles. Therefore they need to ensure the reliability of the vehicle which is sending data. Trustworthiness could be achieved based on two methods. The first method is creating entity trust and the second one is data trust. This research focuses on evaluating the trustworthiness of the sender entity (vehicle). This paper proposes NB-FTBM: Naive Bayesian Fuzzy Trust Boundary Model to find entity trust. NB-FTBM contains two modules namely Entity Identification (E-ID) and Entity Reputation (E-RP). The proposed model quickly identifies the entity identification score and entity reputation score of an entity. These scores fall under the trust boundary line. Based on this boundary level the entity is allowed to take the necessary decision for the information received. The main advantage of this approach is it takes the benefit of Naive Bayesian classifier along with fuzzy logic. The proposed trust model evaluates the trustworthiness of the metrics accurately.

Keywords: NB-Naive Bayesian · E-ID Entity Identification ·
E-RP Entity Reputation · Trust boundary · Fuzzy inference ·
FTB-Fuzzy Trust Boundary

1 Introduction

Vehicular Ad Hoc Network is a subclass of mobile Ad Hoc Networks (MANET). Participating vehicles, On-board Units (OBU) and Roadside Units (RSUs) are the VANET components. On-Board Units are responsible for the interaction between the vehicles [1]. VANET works on different architectures namely (i) Vehicle-to-Vehicle communication (V2V): In V2V architecture vehicle communicates only with other vehicles on the absence of roadside infrastructure. (ii) Vehicle-to-Infrastructure (V2I): In V2I architecture vehicles have to communicate with RSUs for information. RSUs are pre-build access pointers that provide necessary information [2]. (iii) Combined architecture: In combined architecture VANET nodes (vehicles) could communicate with both RSUs and other vehicles [3]. Even though

© ICST Institute for Computer Sciences, Social Informatics and Telecommunications Engineering 2019
Published by Springer Nature Switzerland AG 2019. All Rights Reserved
N. Kumar and R. Venkatesha Prasad (Eds.): UBICNET 2019, LNICST 276, pp. 173–187, 2019.
https://doi.org/10.1007/978-3-030-20615-4_13

VANET is a rapidly developing technology it is lacking in providing security [4]. How a vehicle could simply trust another vehicle which is sending some data about the traffic environment? Several security attacks are encountered in VANET. Illusion attack is one of the risky attacks. The attacker creates an illusion of a vehicle and pretends as a good vehicle to spread false information [5]. The victim vehicle believes the information without any condition. Thus based on the rumor data the victim vehicle takes a decision. As the result, the attacker's vehicle creates collision [6]. To avoid such an attack, VANET researchers have proposed several methods, but they still face many limitations. VANET scenario is very much complicated that raise several issues like dynamic network change and heterogeneous traffic environment. On considering these issues, reliability among the entities is achieved by creating trust value for each entity [7]. Key management and cryptographer techniques were former mechanisms established to provide security and trust among VANET nodes. Game theory based approaches worked well [8]. But due to the ephemeral nature of VANET, they fail in certain scenarios. Calculating the reputation score of an entity that is established based on the observations of the historical interactions of the vehicles. Trust management: In VANET, trust is defined as the belief of one node having with another node [9]. Trust management is the main method to ensure the trusted relationship between the vehicles in determining whether the traffic event reported by the sender vehicle is really happening or not. This method is also used to prevent false traffic warning message spreading. Comparing to other wireless networks, trust management is more complex in VANET.

The novelty of this research work is making use of two significant methodologies namely Naive Bayesian theorem and fuzzy logic. The Naive Bayesian theorem works with the independence assumptions between predictors. This theorem assumes the effect of the result by the predictor (X) on a given data-set (C) which is independent from the results of other predictors. Naive is also known as a conditional theorem. This is used for finding the trustworthiness of the evidence of an event. This method gives a clear view of how much we should trust a message coming from a strange vehicle [10].

The statistics and measurements of fuzzy based trust model in Vehicular Ad Hoc networks contain critical characteristics such as trustworthiness assessment for decisions given by a vehicle [11]. To overcome these entire issue, trust model developed based on the fuzzy logic mechanisms will be an effective solution. The development process of trust models lies on properties of trust metrics and various trust models [12]. On receiving incoming messages using an antenna which is fixed in RSUs and other vehicles, could gather input to the application system. Fuzzy based trust model uses the terms like low, high and medium. The final result or outcome of the trust model is the relationship between the data input to be gathered and only two possible values are obtained which are yes/no. Fuzzy logic are based on 'IF-Then' reasoning. The final outcome is expanded by considering each and every parameter that depends on application system type. Example: speed and distance between the vehicles.

Contribution of the Research. As the contribution, we propose an NB-FTBM approach which is based on Naive Bayesian classifier and fuzzy logic. This methodology is separated into three phases namely ETM-Entity Trust Model, FTBM-Fuzzy Trust Boundary Model, and Naive Bayesian Decision making model. The novelty of this research work is combing two significant machine learning techniques to achieve accuracy. The proposed method is enhanced from existing method in time and accuracy management. All the existing methodologies do not concentrate on the time constraint in VANET. The fraction of second could cause enormous damage in Vehicular Ad Hoc Network. The proposed method gives an effective solution by using fuzzy logic and Naive Bayesian classifier.

The paper is organized as follows. Section 2 reviews the challenges faced by VANET, security issues, applications and related methodologies for the security of VANET. Entity Trust Model (ETM) module is presented in Sect. 3. Section 4 reveals the Fuzzy Trust Boundary Model (FTBM). In Sect. 5, the decision making of NB-FTBM is presented. Performance Evaluation of the overall simulation is shown in Sect. 6.

2   Related Work

Since vehicular Ad hoc network is a high mobility based network, it is very complicated in nature. VANET nodes (vehicles) are always movable and rarely stable. Due to this complex feature, security is very important for VANET [12]. Network topology changes frequently. Golle et al. present an approach which aims to address the limitation of detecting and correcting malicious data in vehicular Ad Hoc network [13]. The key concept of the model of their approach is in maintaining a model of VANET at every node [14]. This approach contains all the knowledge that a vehicle has about VANET. Receiving message can then be evaluated the agent's model of VANET. When the entire message received and agrees with high probability, then the vehicle accepts the trustworthiness of message [15]. In case of incoming data, that is not convenient with the model, the vehicles rely on an empirical that tries to restore the consistency through finding the easiest possible and different ranks of trustworthiness [16]. The event message that consists with highest trust score is then accepted by the vehicle. The major strength of this mechanism is that provides tight security against unwanted messages. This may spread malicious data and collapse the network [17]. In opposite to the traditional point of view of entity-centric trust, Raya et al. proposed a new method. Trust metrics depend on the attributes associated with the vehicles. Bayesian inference and DSF-Dempster Shafer Theory tells about evaluating the various shreds of evidence regarding an event. Lin et al. [18] have analyzed the benefits obtained by self-interesting vehicles in vehicular network. This model considers the scenario where vehicles can achieve congestion data from other vehicles through gossiping. This way is more appropriated in ephemeral ad hoc networks. Data level trust evaluation deals with establishing the trustworthiness of the message reported by the entities instead of the entity trust [19]. This model defines various trust parameters which categories the trust relationships for vehicles [20]. There are two different behaviors of vehicles. First one is, vehicles want to maximize their own utility and the second one is, vehicles cause disorder in the network. This is one of the main security threat formed in VANET. The authors realized these issues which resulted in highly complexity and potentially more damaging situations that arise in VANET. These authors also identified the importance to establish trust in VANETs through reputation mechanisms [21]. This is the main module in the proposed work. Regarding security issues in VANET, several authors have studied the security challenges [22,23]. Patwardhan et al. The author [9] developed a reputation based system in order to discover the reliability and accuracy of data accumulated in a distributed manner, pushes devices too quickly adapt the changing conditions. The entity trust model focuses on evaluating the trustworthiness of vehicles with the aim of measuring their daily behavior and selfishness or malicious vehicles to make sure the reliable dissemination of messages among the vehicles [24,25]. The existing entity-centric based trust models compute reputation or trust values based on the trust metrics [26]. Trust metrics are the parameters that tell about the reputation and trust score of the vehicle. The recommendation given by another vehicle is also taken into account [27]. This approach sometimes spreads false recommendations. This approach otherwise called direct trust.

3   Entity Trust Model (ETM)

The proposed work mainly focuses on the entity-centric trust. Entity-centric trust models focus on the trustworthiness of the vehicles. To achieve this, the entity trust model needs sufficient information about the vehicle which is sending data. In the proposed work entity trust is obtained by analyzing two submodules. The identity of the vehicle and the reputation of the vehicle and they are represented as E-ID and E-RP respectively. The block of the data received contains the necessary parameters that are used for measuring the entity trust value. NB-FTBM model has stronger robustness because it adapts more than one framework for calculating trust.

3.1   Entity Identification (E-ID) Module

Entity identification is the submodule of the entity trust model. The proposed model focuses on calculating the trustworthiness of the sender vehicle (S_v). When the receiver vehicle (R_v) receives the block of information it starts analyzing for entity identification (E-ID). E-ID contains the following trust parameters.

The Distance Between S_v and R_v. Inter-vehicle distance (D) is the distance between transmitter and receiver vehicles. Each and every vehicle in VANET should compute the distance of it and neighbor vehicle based on velocity and propagation delay. Vehicles are equipped with GPS (Global positioning system) which is a transceiver that obtains positional data (Longitude, and Latitude) and direction. The proposed work makes use of the Haversine formula for obtaining the distance between S_v and R_v. The Haversine formula is used to determine the great circle distance between two points on a sphere providing their longitude and latitude. These values are given by GPS receiver in the form of degrees, minutes and seconds. The Haversine distance formula is given below:

LON_v is the longitude of the vehicle at one point denoted as α.
$\Delta\alpha$ is the difference between $\alpha1$ and $\alpha2$

$$\Delta\alpha = \alpha2 - \alpha1 \tag{1}$$

LAT_v is the latitude of the vehicle at one point denoted as β.
$\Delta\beta$ is the difference between $\beta1$ and $\beta2$

$$\Delta\beta = \beta1 - \beta2 \tag{2}$$

$$A = (sin(\Delta\beta/2)^2 + cos(\beta1).cos(\beta2).sin(\Delta\alpha/2)^2) \tag{3}$$

$$C = 2.atan2(\sqrt{A}, \sqrt{1-A}) \tag{4}$$

$$D = R \times C \tag{5}$$

where R is the radius of the earth and R = 6371 km. For sender vehicle S_v, the latitude and longitude values are given by GPS, whereas for receiver vehicle R_v the latitude and longitude values are sent through the data block to the S_v.

Bearings/Direction of S_v. The direction of the vehicle is the number of degrees east or west of north or south. There are eight major directions that are commonly used. The first four directions are cardinal directions. Another four directions are. Southeast – SE, Northeast – NE, Northwest – NW, Southwest – SW. These are named as primary Inter-Cardinal directions. The combination of Cardinal and Primary Inter-Cardinal Directions are called as Bearings. Finding the bearing is reading the angle between two points.

Let R_e be the radius of the earth to get the bearing of the vehicle.
Lon_v - Longitude of the vehicle at one point and it is denoted as α.
Lat_v - Latitude of the vehicle at one point which is denoted as β.
B_v - Bearing of the vehicle which is denoted as λ.

Due to the participation of two intercommunicating vehicles, both vehicles have longitude and latitude coordinates which are denoted as ($\alpha1$, $\alpha2$, and $\beta1$, $\beta2$) respectively. Similarly Bearings for both intercommunicating vehicles denoted as ($\lambda1$, $\lambda2$). The following equation finds the bearing factor for S_v and R_v.

$$\lambda = atan2(X, Y) \tag{6}$$

$$X = cos\beta2.sin\Delta\alpha \tag{7}$$

where $\Delta\alpha = \alpha2 - \alpha1$

$$Y = cos\beta1.sin\beta2 - sin\beta1.cos\beta2.cos\Delta\alpha \tag{8}$$

Velocity on Which S_v is Traveling. Velocity is the measure of how fast a particular vehicle is moving in a particular direction. Finding the velocity of the vehicles gives more accurate trust results. Even though velocity details are appended along with the event message, it is necessary to find the trustworthiness of the information. Sender vehicle S_v sends the position information appended with the event message as the longitude and latitude coordinates. The receiver vehicle R_v estimates the distance of the sender vehicle S_v at the instance of propagation time. Therefore D_1 and D_2 are obtained at the time interval T_i and T_f respectively. VANET node is frequently moving in nature. Due to this feature, the distance is estimated from one point of time to another point in time. Distance traveled by S_v is denoted as $\Omega 1$.

$$\Omega = D_2 - D_1 \tag{9}$$

Now compute the velocity V_s with respect to distance traveled and propagation time.

$$V_s = \Omega(T_f - T_i) \tag{10}$$

The Average Velocity AVE_v is the speed of the vehicle traveled in a particular elapsed time.

$$AVE_v = \frac{P_f - P_i}{T_f - T_i} \tag{11}$$

where P_i = Initial position, P_f = Final position, T_i = Initial time, T_f = Final time.

3.2   Entity Reputation (E-RP) Module

Entity reputation module contains three sub parts to find the reputation value of the vehicle. Role of the vehicle tells about the type of vehicle. Recommendation of the vehicle is gathered from RSU in order to get more about the reputation. Response from other vehicles gives positive or negative reputation.

Role of the Vehicle. The role of the vehicle is generated automatically during the registration of the vehicle. Regional Transport Office (RTO) takes care of assigning the role of each vehicle and it is stored centrally. RSUs can access the centrally stored role of the vehicle. Each time the vehicle send data to another vehicle, the role detail of the vehicle is sent along with the data. The receiver vehicle should compare the received role and verify the role of the sender vehicle through RSU. There are different roles for a vehicle such as a highway patrol, ambulance, road engineering vehicles, sanitation vehicles, taxi, goods, and personal vehicles.

Recommendation from RSU. The regional transport office could control the RSUs to manage a database containing all the vehicle users with good or malicious statements. RSUs could store current data storage and processing technologies. It is assumed that every vehicle may store and manage hundreds of trust scores and recommendations equipped with a cache memory in the build.

Response from Neighbor Vehicles. To fully evaluate the reputation of the vehicle, the response from other neighbor vehicles is also considered, because the trustworthiness of an entity depends on the neighbor's reaction. The receiver vehicle R_v checks for the set of response from other vehicles.

Response from neighbor = N_R(Event). The degree of the response will be explained during trust evaluation.

4   Fuzzy Trust Boundary Model

The fuzzy mechanism is a universal approximates. Fuzzy systems are isomorphic between two algebras namely abstract algebra and linear algebra. Fuzzy logic is based on fundamental algebraic theorem called STONE-WEIERSTRASS theorem. This theorem states that every continuous function defined on a closed interval [a,b] can be uniformly approximated as closely as desired by a polynomial function. The flow of the proposed NB-FTBM approach is shown (See Fig. 1). The basic aim of this fuzzy trust model is to categorize the boundary level of the trustworthiness of the parameters. These are otherwise called fuzzy membership functions (MF). MF can hold different levels such as high, medium, low, trust or false, very good, better and poor. The fuzzy membership functions have been defined using the experts domain knowledge. To calculate the trust values of the entity parameters considered in this paper, a new mechanism is introduced namely Fuzzy Trust Boundary Model (NB-FTBM). Many degrees of membership is allowed. Membership function can be represented as:

$$MF = \mu_A(x) \tag{12}$$

This is the Membership Function associated with fuzzy set A such that the MF maps every element of the universe of discourse x to the interval [0,1].

$$\mu_A : X \to [0, 1] \tag{13}$$

The proposed NB-FTBM model uses Gaussian membership function. Gaussian MF specifies up to three parameters.

4.1   E-ID Trust Boundary

Trust Boundary for Distance and Bearing (TBDB). Algorithm 1 describes the method to find the distance and bearing of the sender vehicle.

$\mu_A(D_s)$ = Membership function of Distance.

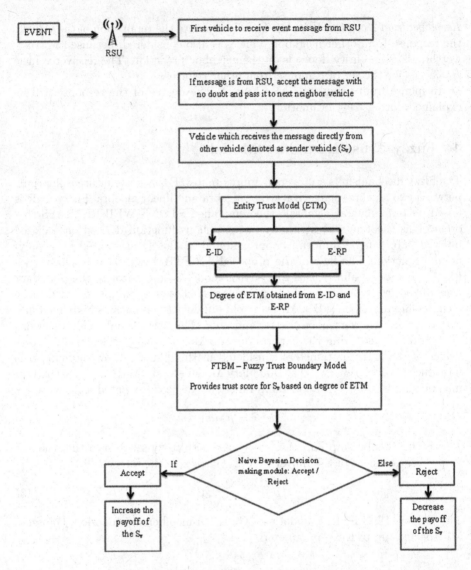

Fig. 1. NB-FTBM diagrammatic representation.

Trust Boundary for Velocity (TBV). Using the value of distance traveled, velocity is measured. By the initial position, final position and initial time, the final time of the vehicle, the average velocity is calculated. Algorithm 2 tells about the velocity of the sender vehicle.

$\mu_A(V_s)$ = Membership function of velocity.

Algorithm 1. Distance and Bearings.

Input: LON, LAT (sender and receiver), radius (earth), a, c
Output: Distance (D) of sender and receiver, Bearing (B) of sender and receiver
dLatitude ← LAT_{v2} - LAT_{v1}
dLatitude ← LON_{v2} - LON_{v1}
a ←(sin (dLatitude/2)^2) + cos(LAT_{v1}).cos (LAT_{v2}).sin(dLatitude/2)^2)
c ← 2 × atan2 ($\sqrt{a}$, $\sqrt{1-a}$)
D ← radius × c
B ← atan2 (X,Y)
X ← cos Lat 2. Sin (dLongitude)
Y ← cost Lat1 . sin Lat2 − sin Lat1 . cos Lon2 . cos (dLatitude)

Algorithm 2. Velocity.

Input: Dis_1 ← distance at initial time, Dis_2 ← distance at final time $Time_i$ ← initial
time, $Time_f$ ← final time
Pos_i ← initial position, Pos_f ← final position
Output: $Velocity_s$ ← velocity of sender vehicle
Ave_v ← Average velocity
Dis_t ← Distance traveled
Dis_t ← Dis_2- Dis_1
$Velocity_s$ ← Dis_t ($Time_f$ - $Time_i$)
Ave_v ← (Pos_f - Pos_i) / ($Time_f$ - $Time_i$)

4.2   E-RP Trust Boundary

Entity reputation module contains the role of the vehicle, recommendation provided by RSU for reputation and the response from the neighbor vehicles for the event message.

The Degree of the Role (DROL). The degree of the role of the vehicle is measured in three types which are High, medium and low. The role of a vehicle is said to be a high degree if it is a highway patrol or an ambulance. The role of a vehicle is said to be a medium degree if it is a road engineering vehicle, sanitation vehicle or goods vehicle. The role of a vehicle is said to be low degree if it is a taxi or personal vehicle.

RL_s → Role of the sender vehicle.
D_R (S_v) → Degree of Role μ_A (RL_s) = Membership function of Role

$$D_R(S_v) \rightarrow \begin{cases} 1, & S_v = High \\ 0.5, & S_v = Medium \end{cases} \tag{14}$$

The Degree of Recommendation (DREC). The degree of recommendation is the reputation grade that is been given by the RSU based on the performance of the vehicle. RTO-Regional Transport Office is responsible for holding this database. To find out the trustworthiness of the vehicle this information is very much useful. During each and every interaction between the vehicles, its payoff will increase or decrease. A good successful interaction provides increment payoff for the vehicle. An unsatisfied and failure interaction provides payoff decrements for the vehicle.

$RSU_R \in [0,1] \to$ Recommendation from RSU,
$\mu_A(RSU_R) \to$ Membership function of Recommendation from RSU.
$Rec_d(S_v) \to$ Degree of Recommendation

$$Rec_d(S_v) \to \begin{cases} 1, & S_v = Reputed \\ 0, & S_v = Non - Reputed \end{cases} \tag{15}$$

The Degree of Neighbor Response (DNR). The receiver vehicle should analyze the response of other vehicles for the same event message. The response from neighbor vehicles will bring out the actual trustworthiness of the vehicle and message. This parameter is also applicable for evaluating the trustworthiness of event data. The degree of response carries two membership function namely accepts or reject.

$N_R(Event) \to$ Response from neighbor
$\mu_A(N_R) \to$ Membership function of neighbor response

$$Res_d(N) \to \frac{Accept - Reject}{Tot_R(Event)} \tag{16}$$

where $Tot_R(Event)$ = Total number of Response for an event, Accept = Number of accepts, Reject = Number of rejects.

5   Decision making in NB-FTBM

The fuzzifier in fuzzy logic transforms the Crisp values (input values) into equal linguistic values. In NB-FTBM model the input parameters are gathered by the receiver vehicle (R_v) using the data message from the sender vehicle (S_v). The input parameters are fuzzified with the use of membership functions. The fuzzy inference engine for E-ID and E-RP is assessed. After calculating the fuzzy inference engine for E-ID and E-RP, they start to evaluate the fuzzy rules for decision making. In the proposed model the membership function of each parameter is obtained. E-ID and E-RP membership functions used to set three fuzzy rules namely high, medium and low. The final fuzzy rules are constructed based on the number of input parameters. The final fuzzy inference engine to make a decision based on the event message (See Table 1).

5.1 Naive Bayesian theorem

Table 2 provides the dataset or class for Naive Bayesian classifier. The novelty of this research work is making use of two significant methodologies namely Naive Bayesian theorem and fuzzy logic. This theorem assumes the effect of the result of the predictor (X) on a given dataset (C) is independent from the results of other predictors. Naive is also known as a conditional theorem. This is used for finding the trustworthiness of the evidence of an event. This method gives a clear view of how much we should trust a message coming from a strange vehicle.

$$P(C \mid X) = \frac{P(C \mid X)P(C)}{P(X)} \qquad (17)$$

where P(Decision) = P(Accept) OR P(Reject)
   According to dataset, P(Accept) = 5/9, P(Reject) = 4/9

Probability of Acceptance	Probability of Rejection
P(E-ID = High | Decision = Accept) = $\frac{3}{5}$	P(E-ID = Low | Decision = Reject) = $\frac{2}{4}$
P(E-RP = High | Decision = Accept) = 3/5	P(E-RP = Low | Decision = Reject) = 2/4
P(X | Decision = Accept) P(Decision = Accept)	P(X | Decision = Reject) P(Decision = Reject)
$\frac{3}{5} \times \frac{3}{5} \times \frac{5}{9} = 0.2$	$\frac{2}{4} \times \frac{2}{4} \times \frac{4}{9} = 0.111$

$$P(X) = P(E\text{-}ID = High) \times P(E\text{-}RP = High)$$
$$P(X) = \tfrac{5}{9} \times \tfrac{5}{9} = 0.30864$$
$$P(Decision = Accept \mid X) = 0.2/0.30864 = 0.648$$
$$P(Decision = Reject \mid X) = 0.111/0.30864 = 0.3596$$
$$0.648 > 0.3596$$

Therefore Acceptance probability is greater than Reject and the decision made is to accept the event message ad reacts.

Table 1. Fuzzy inference engine for decision making using E-ID and E-RP.

S.no	E-ID	E-RP	Decision
1	Low	Low	Reject
2	Low	Medium	Reject
3	Low	High	Accept
4	Medium	Low	Reject
5	Medium	Medium	Reject
6	Medium	High	Accept
7	High	Low	Accept
8	High	Medium	Accept
9	High	High	Accept

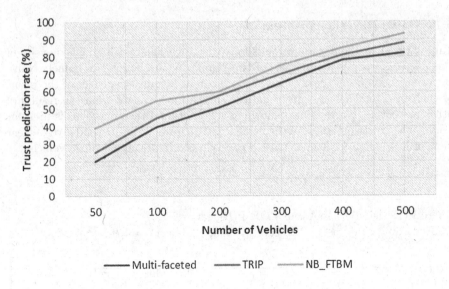

Fig. 2. The accuracy level of trust prediction

6   Performance Evaluation

To demonstrate the performance of NB-FTBM model, the following scenario is used. The proposed algorithms are implemented in network simulator 2 (NS2). The Simulation of Urban Mobility (SUMO) traffic simulator is used along with NS2. The proposed NB-FTBM model concentrates on the highway and urban scenarios. Simulation area is set up to 3 km × 3 km. the maximum speed of a vehicle is set to 100 km/h. Node density of the simulator area is 500 vehicles.

Simulation Results and Discussion. The parameters or trust metrics for evaluating the trust for an entity or vehicle are distance, bearings, velocity, recommendation from RSU, role of the vehicle and response from other vehicles. Time and Accuracy are the performance parameters to calculate the improvisation between the existing methodologies and the proposed NB-FTBM method. In the Simulation of the proposed method, we employ two main constraints. One is elapsed time for predicting trust and other one is accuracy of trust calculation. The existing approaches hardly concentrate on time and accuracy. The proposed NB-FTBM model is compared with Multifaceted and TRIP mechanisms of entity-centric trust evaluation. The simulation time is set up to 300 s. Based on the time intervals the accuracy level of trust prediction is done.

Simulation Assumptions. When a VANET node encounters a malicious node sending false information, the received information is simply discarded. The prevention mechanism is not analyzed in this paper when a node is been attacked. We assume that over 40% of vehicles are set as malicious nodes from total number of vehicles. In the first Simulation at the level of 50 vehicles in during the simulation, the multifaceted approach could reach 20% of accuracy level.

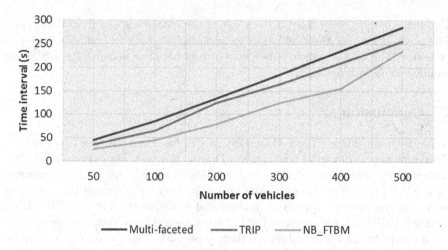

Fig. 3. Elapsed time interval

Table 2. Simulation parameters.

Parameter type	Value
Map scenario	Coimbatore (P N. Puthur to Gandhi park)
Network simulator	NS2 2.34
Traffic simulator	SUMO
Routing protocol	DHRP
Transmission range	250 m
Simulation time	300 s
Traffic density	500 vehicles
Vehicle speed	40 km/hr
Simulation area	3 km × 3 km
Packet size	512 bytes

The TRIP model could achieve 25% of accuracy level. The proposed model achieves 40% of accuracy level of trust prediction. At the end of simulation with 500 vehicles, NB-FTBM model achieves nearly 90% of accuracy level. (see Fig. 2). In the second Simulation, the simulation runs for 300 s. The Simulation shows how fast the trust evaluation approaches predict the trustworthiness of the entities. The x-axis shows the number of vehicles which increase according to the simulation. The y-axis shows the elapsed times which vary by seconds (see Fig. 3). As the simulations time increases, the traffic density is also increased. On comparing the elapsed time used for trust calculation the proposed method consumes less time than other two methods of entity-centric trust evaluation in VANET. The threat is entering only via vehicle to vehicle communication.

The malicious behavior from RSU is out of the research scope from this paper. The assumptions for the simulation scenario are set only for malicious vehicles or nodes. The RSUs malicious behavior rarely happens because the RSUs are handled by Government.

7 Conclusion

Naive Bayesian Fuzzy Trust Boundary Model has been proposed to evaluate the entity trust among VANET nodes. Due to the unstable nature of VANET environment, malicious behavior such as illusion attacks spread false information. NB-FTBM results in providing better security by detecting the malicious node. On comparing with TRIP method and Multifaceted method, NB-FTBM is improvised based on accuracy level of trust prediction with less elapsed time. From this research work we observed that, Vehicle identity and vehicle reputation plays a major role in providing trustworthiness among the vehicles. Trustworthiness is an essential constraint for achieving the full benefits of VANET. In future VANET researchers could use more efficient machine learning concepts for providing security. In this paper the comparison is made between elapsed time and accuracy. We could further add more comparison metrics. Malicious Attack prevention mechanism is not spoken in this paper. In future preventing malicious activity could be taken into account. Other than these thoughts and ideas, we have to ensure that the threat is not entering from RSUs.

References

1. Sharef, B.T., Alsaqour, R.A., Ismail, M.: Vehicular communication ad hoc routing protocols: a survey. J. Netw. Comput. Appl. **40**, 363–396 (2014)
2. Mehdi, M.M., Raza, I., Hussain, S.A.: A game theory based trust model for vehicular ad hoc networks (VANETs). J. Comput. Netw. **121**, 152–172 (2017)
3. Seuwou, P., Patel, D., Ubakanma, G.: Vehicular ad hoc network applications and security: a study into the economic and the legal implications. Int. J. Electr. Secur. Digit. Forensics **6**(2), 115–129 (2014)
4. Hubaux, J.P., Capkun, S.: The security and privacy of smart vehicles. IEEE Secur. Priv. Mag. **2**(3), 49–55 (2004)
5. Sumra, I.A., Hasbullah, H.B.: Trust levels of vehicular ad hoc network (VANET). Int. J. Inf. Technol. Electr. Eng. 3(5) (2014). ISSN: 2306–708X
6. Gerlach, M., Fokus, F.: Trust for vehicular applications. In: Proceedings of the 8th International Symposium on Autonomous Decentralized Systems, pp. 295–304 (2007)
7. Khainar, V.D., Kotecha, K.: Performance of vehicle-to-vehicle communication using IEEE 802.11p in vehicular ad hoc network environment. Int. J. Netw. Secur. Appl. **5**(2), 143–170 (2013)
8. Sharmaa, V., Srinivasan, K., Chaoc, H.-C., Huag, K.-L., Cheng, W.-H.: Intelligent deployment of UAVs in 5G heterogeneous communication environment for improved coverage. J. Netw. Comput. Appl. **85**, 94–105 (2017)
9. Pham, T.N.D., Yeo, C.K.: Adaptive trust and privacy management framework for vehicular networks. Veh. Commun. **13**, 1–12 (2018)

10. Karagiannis, D., Argyriou, A.: Jamming attack detection in a pair of RF communicating vehicles using unsupervised machine learning. Veh. Commun. **13**, 56–63 (2018)
11. Jalalia, M., Aghaee, N.G.: A fuzzy reputation system in vehicular ad hoc networks. Procedia Comput. Sci. **5**, 951–956 (2011)
12. Regan, K., Poupart, P., Cohen, R.: Bayesian reputation modeling in e-marketing places sensitive to subjective, deception and change. In: Proceedings in the 21st Conference. Artificial Intelligence, pp. 1206–1212 (2006)
13. Li, X., Liu, J., Li, X.: RGTE: a reputation based global trust establishment in VANETs. In: IEEE 5th International Conference (2013)
14. Ma, S., Wolfson, O., Lin, J.: A survey on trust management for intelligent transportation system. In: IWCTS', November 2011
15. Raya, M., Papadimitrator, P., Gligor, V., Hubaux, J.: On data-centric trust establishment in ephemeral Adhoc networks. In: IEEE INFOCOM 2008-The 27th Conference on Computer Communications, April 2008
16. Huynh, T., Jennings, N., Shabalt, N.: An integrated trust and reputation model for open multiagent systems. Auton. Agent. Multiagent Syst. **13**, 119–154 (2006)
17. Minhas, U.F., Zhang, J., Trans, T., Cohen, R.: Towards expanded trust management for agents in vehicular ad hoc networks. Int. J. Comput. Intell. Theor. Pract. (IJCITP) **5**(1), 3–15 (2010)
18. Chen, C., Zhang, J., Cohen, R., Ho, P.H.: A trust-based message propagation and evaluation framework in VANETs. In: Proceedings of International Conference on Information Technology Convergence and Services (2010)
19. Li, F., Wang, Y.: Routing in vehicular ad hoc networks: a survey. IEEE Veh. Technol. Mag. **2**(2), 12–22 (2007)
20. Raya, M., Hubaux, J.-P.: Securing vehicular ad hoc networks. J. Comput. Secur. **15**(1), 39–68 (2007)
21. Boukerche, A., Xu, L., El-Khatib, K.: Trust-based security for wireless ad hoc and sensor networks. Comput. Commun. **30**(11–12), 2413–2427 (2007)
22. Nassar, L., Karray, F., Kamel, M.S.: VANET IR-CAS for commercial SA: information retrieval context-aware system for VANET commercial service announcement. Int. J. Intell. Transp. Syst. **13**(1), 37–49 (2015)
23. Wang, S., Yao, N.: LIAP: a local identity-based anonymous message authentication protocol in VANETs. Comput. Commun. **112**, 154–164 (2017)
24. Shaikh, R.A.: Fuzzy risk-based decision method for vehicular ad hoc networks. Int. J. Adv. Comput. Sci. Appl. **7**(9), 54–62 (2016)
25. Liu, Z., Ma, J., Jiang, Z., et al.: LSOT: a lightweight self-organized trust model in VANETs. J. Mob. Inf. Syst. **2016**, 1–15 (2016). Article id 7628231
26. Harika, E., Satyananda Reddy, C.: A trust management scheme for securing transport networks. Int. J. Comput. Appl. **180**(8), 38–42 (2017)
27. Chen, Y.M., Wei, Y.C.: A beacon-based trust management system for enhancing user-centric location privacy in VANETs. J. Commun. Netw. **15**(2), 153–163 (2013)

Threshold Cryptography Based Light Weight Key Management Technique for Hierarchical WSNs

K. Hamsha[(⊠)] and G. S. Nagaraja

R V College of Engineering, Bangalore 560059, Karnataka, India
hamshak@gmail.com, nagarajags@rvce.edu.in

Abstract. Secure communication among sensors is strongly needed to avoid malicious activity. Security is a major issue in self-organized, infrastructure less networks with limited resources such as energy, transmission range, and processing. The amount of network overhead needs to be reduced to improve the network performance. The size of the secret key to be communicated among the sensor nodes is also contributing in network performance. The Proposed Light Weight Threshold Key Management Scheme (LWKMS), reduces the size of the secret key to be communicated. It reduces the network resource utilization, in sharing the secret among the sensor nodes in the network and provides efficient security even when the keys are compromised by an attacker node. Simulation results shows that the proposed light weight scheme provides less overhead along with less energy consumption as compared to existing method namely Group Key Management Scheme (GKMS).

Keywords: Light weight key management · Secure hierarchical networks · Threshold cryptography · WSN

1 Introduction

Wireless Sensor Networks (WSN) [1] are used for a wide variety of applications ranging from target detection to environment modeling. The network performance gain and QOS are important entities for WSNs. WSN are exposed to various attacks and also there is much malicious intent which occurs. Establishing a secure channel of communication is a demanding task [2]. The major challenge is to secure data transmission with more integrity and confidentiality constraints [3]. Data collection cycle performs round transmissions between the Base Station (BS) and other sensor nodes (SN) in the network. In order to reduce the number of control packets for a given data packet gathering is used by BS [4–6]. There are many encryption and decryption schemes which have been suggested by various researchers. Key management layer is responsible for the generation of keys, distribution of keys, revocation of keys among sensing device [7].

Cryptographic methods for WSNs has been proposed by authors [8, 9] which adopts hierarchical architecture for secure communication. In secret sharing scheme proposed by authors [10, 11] employs secret key distribution into nodes, to generate

© ICST Institute for Computer Sciences, Social Informatics and Telecommunications Engineering 2019
Published by Springer Nature Switzerland AG 2019. All Rights Reserved
N. Kumar and R. Venkatesha Prasad (Eds.): UBICNET 2019, LNICST 276, pp. 188–197, 2019.
https://doi.org/10.1007/978-3-030-20615-4_14

and assign keys. However these schemes consume more energy, large memory space and high communication overhead in exchanging messages to establish key system.

LWKMS is used in this work. The BS is responsible for distributing the Secret Key Shares (SKS) among a set of n chunks for CH, CH will perform data gathering from normal nodes and then establishes a route to BS. The scheme with threshold enables secure data transmission to BS. During the routing process, CH will communicate with other CHs to send the packets to BS.BS generates and computes key value and sends it to CH,CH will divide that into different payloads and then shares among the participants by estimating the threshold value.

This work is organized in the following fashion; Sect. 2 describes the related work and problem statement. Sections 3 and 4 describes the proposed system model. In Sect. 5 the performance analysis and relative simulation are conducted. Finally, we draw the conclusion on the proposed scheme in Sect. 6.

2 Related Works and Problem Statement

Many researchers attempted to present security mechanism for WSNs [12–16]. Cryptography based security protocol using public key and other key management methods. These security protocols are attempts to provide security in flat routing for WSNs. The security in hierarchical routing is less addressed than the flat routing for WSNs. Problem in group key management scheme; mutual authentication is performed by using asymmetric key protocol between high and middle powered nodes and establishes links to groups. Once a forwarding node is tampered then security information of entire zone will be leaked. Traditional Shamir's secret key sharing mechanism for hierarchal group based scheme consumes huge storage and computational cost which incurs more networks overhead.

Lu et al. [17] makes use of ID-based digitally signed key for establishing a secure routing for a zone based network. In ID based method, for all the nodes received signal strength (RSS) is computed and then a node with highest value is chosen as region head.. Cluster head communicate directly to base station. The node id will generate public key and private keys without making use of supplementary data transmission techniques in the proposed method. Even though the proposed technique has security efficiency, it exhibits high computational cost. Bertier [18] presented secret key sharing scheme by providing basic secret keys sharing without cryptography between nodes to establish secure communication among neighbor nodes. The author extended work on establishing secret key exchange algorithm, however this scheme consume more energy for key exchange and authentication process which made it unsuitable. Claveirole [11] proposed aggregation based method to secure data on secret sharing to mitigate from DoS attack by splitting message and forwarding these messages through multiple path. This scheme confuses the adversary in finding the actual route. Qin [19] proposed light weighted authentication key management scheme (AKMS), where keys are dynamically generated. Attackers cannot reuse the previous key to cheat. This scheme offers high security with low cost to solve malicious activity in network. This scheme contains three phases, key pre distribution phase where symmetric network key is generated and stored. Network initialization phase, where nodes find its neighbors within communication range and authentication phase involves authenticating and verifying nodes. Chen [20] proposed trust aware low energy security protocol, which considers node's trust values in building topology. This combines trust value, node density and residual energy to select cluster head.

3 Network Model

Network consists of WSNs nodes which are hierarchically clustered. The cluster head is responsible to collect data from cluster members and aggregate the data and forward the aggregated data to BS. Network consists of WSNs nodes which are hierarchically clustered.CH will obtain the payloads from normal nodes (NN) and then relays it to BS. The transmission efficiency is obtained by using more bandwidth and transmission power for CH. The network distribution model is represented in Fig. 1. The BS initially is responsible for distribution of shared secret key k from the sequence $k_0, k_1, k_2 \ldots \ldots k_{n-1} \in \{0, 1\}$ where k represents regular or partitioned secret key. BS is equipped with sufficient energy and resources, it keeps all ID's and Keys. Using Shamir's threshold secret key scheme (t, n) on Lagrange polynomial interpolation.

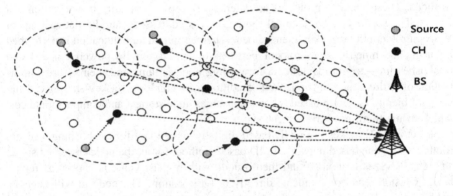

Fig. 1. Network architecture

In threshold secret key scheme BS assigns secret keys and data to each sensor nodes, but does not reveals the secret data. Initially there are p players and a trusted authority $T_a, U = \{p_1, p_2 \ldots .p_n\}$. The method makes use of two phases namely Key generation and construction phase.

3.1 Key Generation Phase

A random polynomial of degree of $f(x)$ of $(t - 1)$ is selected by the trusted authority T_a

$$f(x) = S + a_1 x + \ldots + a_{t-1} x^{t-1} (modP), \tag{1}$$

Consider a finite set of co-efficient with p players represented as $S, a_1, a_2, \ldots, a_{t-1}$ for a condition $secret = f(0)$.

The shares $S_i = f(x_i)$ are computed by the trusted authority and further S_i are privately distributed to each player, which falls under the trusted authority T_a.

3.2 Construction Phase

Shares of $S_1, S_2, \ldots . . S_t$ of, secret key S can be constructed as

$$f(x) = \sum_{i=1}^{t} S_i \left(\prod_{i \neq j} \frac{x - x_j}{x_i - x_j} \right) (modP) \qquad (2)$$

$$f(x) = \sum_{i=1}^{t} S_i \left(\prod_{i \neq j} \frac{x_j}{x_j - x_i} \right) (modP) \qquad (3)$$

The following assumptions are used in modeling of the network

Sensor nodes are static.
Base station assigns unique ID for each sensor.
All sensor nodes are homogenous.
Compromise node reveals all the keys.

4 Proposed Hierarchal Threshold Scheme

We use Shamir's scheme to distribute shares of an initial secret α with threshold among players $P = (p_1, p_2, p_3, \ldots . . p_n)$. Suppose the levels are $L = (l_1, l_2, l_3 \ldots . . l_n)$ with set of players $\{n_1, n_2, n_3, \ldots . n_n\}$ and threshold $\{t_1, t_2, \ldots . . t_n\}$ corresponding to field F.

4.1 Sharing Phase

The BS uses polynomial method for sharing of random secret key with threshold dynamically at each level.

(1) The BS, makes use of polynomial method to generate the shares of random secret β_i with threshold $t \in \min [t_i, t_{i+1}, t_{i+2} \ldots t_m]$.
(2) Cluster members n_i will keep the shares of β_i as their final shares $p = p - \{n_i\}$
(3) The Lagrange method is used to change the threshold dynamically at each level for each level of the sensor node $i \in [i, m-1], \alpha_{i+1} = \alpha_i + \beta_i$ and calculation of $\{\alpha_1, \alpha_2, \alpha_3, \ldots, \alpha_m\}$ happens before α_m.

4.2 Recovering Phase

At recovery phase all secret keys are collected at each level for the master secret key. All secret keys are recovered at base station by solving linear congruence.

(1) Collect the each hierarchy level secrets, $\propto_m$ from level m, β_{m-1} to level $(m-1), \beta_{m-2}$ from level $(m-2)....\beta_1$ to level 1 for the recovery of the master secret.

(2) At every level of hierarchy of WSNs, the recovery of secret is done using

(3) Lagrange interpolation method with $Secret_i = \sum_{j \in \Delta_i} (\gamma_j^{\Delta_i} X \varphi_j)$

(4) All the secret keys are recovered at the base station by solving the linear congruence's $\alpha_{i+1} = \alpha_i + \beta_i$ mod q for $i = (m-1)$ down from level $i = 1$. Hence $\propto_{m-1}, \propto_{m-2}, \ldots, \propto_1$ are used.

4.3 Network Initialization Phase

The network key (n_k) is preloaded for all the nodes in the network. The n_k is a symmetric encryption key generated using Elliptical Curve Cryptography (ECC). By using n_k all the messages are transmitted by the senor nodes. The cluster formation of nodes in hierarchical network and the selection of CH among the nodes in the cluster are done by using LEACH protocol.

By sending its id and current time stamp c_t the CH performs pairwise key generation request k_{req} to BS. Upon receiving the pairwise key generation request BS generates $'p_k'$ pairwise key using one way hashing $'H'$ as

$$P_k = H(CH_i \oplus BS \oplus C_t) \tag{4}$$

BS encrypts the p_k sends to CH_i

$$BS \rightarrow CH_i = k_{reply}(CH_i, BS, E(C_t \| p_k)) \tag{5}$$

4.4 Intra Cluster Pairwise Key Generation

The intra cluster pairwise key is used to communicate between sensor nodes and CH.

The cluster head CH_i soon after elected as cluster head, then the cluster head CH_i checks its Cluster Member (CM) list $CM_{list} = \{CH_{iN_1}, CH_{iN_2} \ldots \ldots CH_{iN_m}\}$ where m represents the total no of nodes present in the list. BS receives the node list from the CH_i of each cluster.

$$CH_i \rightarrow BS : \{CH_i, BS, CM_{list}, C_t\} \tag{6}$$

The combination of pairwise key and one way hash function is used by the base station to compute the cluster key CH_k in such way that $CH_i BS \rightarrow CH_i : [CH_i \| I_{p_k}, (N \| \{CH_{iN_1}, CH_{iN_2}, \ldots, CH_{iN_m}\})]$ And then cluster head CH_i finally sends to its cluster members nodes

$$CH_i \rightarrow N_i : \{CH_i \| CH_{iN_1} \| C_t\} \tag{7}$$

CH_i will share the secret keys S_i to each node N_i in the cluster.

5 Simulation Results

The proposed scheme is evaluated and discussed in this section; our scheme is to solve the security issues and to provide light weighted key management system to reduce the network overhead. Proposed light weighted threshold key scheme (LWKMS) is compared with the Hierarchal group key management scheme (GKMS). The proposed method is evaluated for network parameters like packet delivery ratio, energy consumption and network overhead. The network security issues are analyzed by introducing attacker nodes into the network. The attacker nodes are varied in different rounds. The above said proposed scheme is simulated using event driven simulator NS2 with the network simulation parameters described in Table 1.

Table 1. Network simulation parameters

Network simulation parameters	Values
Deployment area	1000 * 1000 m
No of nodes	80
Bandwidth	2 Mb
Traffic type	CBR
Transmission range	250 m
Attacker nodes	2 to 10
Initial energy	30 J
Propagation model	Two ray model
MAC type	802.11
Protocol	LEACH

The deployment area which is taken into consideration is of dimensions 1000 * 1000 with 80 nodes which are randomly spread in the given area. For each sensor, the transmission range used in 250 m and number of attacker nodes taken into consideration are from 2 to 10. Each of the nodes is equipped with an initial energy of 30 J with propagation model taken into consideration is Two Ray Model with LEACH protocol.

In WSN, the attacks are possible due to open environment and node leaving or joining the network. Attacking the network requires node to be participate in network by doing malicious activities, which intrude the network. Node can also update false information of having shortest route to destinations and generate fake multiple identities. In our proposed scheme, we authenticate false node identities by a Sybil node, where it creates multiple identities and duplicates itself as authentic node. The proposed scheme can efficiently detect malicious node by its authentication and encryption technique.

Figure 2 below shows the detection of malicious activity by dropping the packets. The drop ratio increases in the group key management compared to threshold key scheme. The simulation result of packet delivery ratio is plotted in presence of attacker node, the attacker nodes try to misbehave and drop the packet. Using threshold cryptography the BS reconstructs data sent from sensor nodes, the identification of legitimate node which has shared secret key cannot be replay by malicious nodes to BS. LWKMS reduces error packets and forwards legitimate packet compared to GKMS where the complete group becomes compromise if attacked.

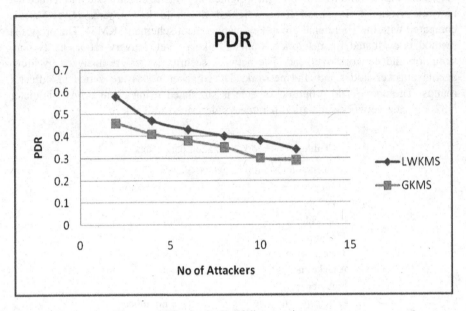

Fig. 2. Packet delivery ratio

In order to prolong the network lifetime node energy consumption has to be optimized, CM has the information about energy levels of other nodes and hence can select CH based on residual energy levels. CH energy depletes as the CH involves in authenticating itself to BS and controlling the CM. Figure 3 shows the average energy consumption of group key management scheme (GKMS) and proposed light weighted key scheme (LWKMS) for LEACH protocol.

The amount of energy consumed during the transmission and reception of data is used to calculate the average energy. The graph of network overhead below shows the average energy consumption of GKMS and LWKMS. Due to more error packets in the cluster energy drain rate increases, when the number of attacker nodes increases. CH filters error packets based on LWKMS and secures the group members and avoids spreading of error packets throughout the network. In GKMS when the attacker node is detected, the CH initiates new key generation procedure to BS which consumes more energy and assigns new keys to group. Proposed LWKMS consume less energy in presence of malicious node, by detecting malicious activity efficiently and does not allow participation of malicious activity in network. The average energy consumption, of the proposed system increases network lifetime. Since the light weighted threshold key management scheme requires time specific mode in authenticating nodes and hence LWKMS Consumes less resource and authenticates efficiently.

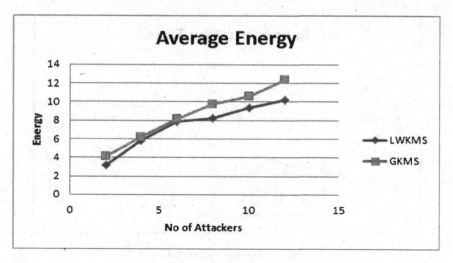

Fig. 3. Average energy consumption

Finally the overhead of the network is evaluated and shown in the network over-head graph as mentioned in Fig. 4. The key length of 256 bit key has been used to generate the graphs of key generation and key management schemes as shown in Fig. 5. LWKMS reduces the network overhead by generating shared keys and authenticating nodes by dynamically changing threshold using Lagrange interpolation, thus uses less resource and increases the network lifetime of the nodes.

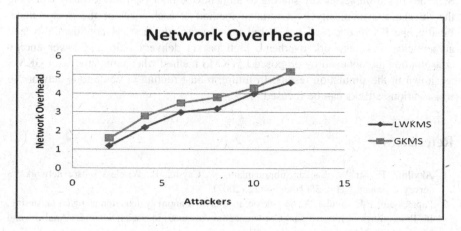

Fig. 4. Network overhead

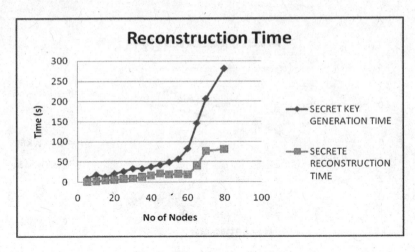

Fig. 5. Key reconstruction time

6 Conclusion

To enhance network security of resource constrained WSN, we propose light weight threshold key management technique using threshold cryptography. The Hierarchical network architecture is employed to provide secure data transmission to BS and node authenticity. We address security issues which increase network overhead in key sharing mechanism. We present LWKMS (Light weighted threshold Key Management Scheme) based on secret key sharing to authenticate nodes at each level by changing the threshold dynamically by Lagrange method at each level of the sensor node. Finally, the BS recovers all the shared keys to provide message confidentiality and authenticity. Less network overhead, high packet delivery ratio and lower energy consumption are obtained by proposed LWKMS method when compared with GKMS as shown in the simulation results. In future, robust routing in ubiquitous network to resist various attacks can be focused.

References

1. Akyildiz, F., Su, W., Sankarasubramaniam, Y., Cayirci, E.: Wireless sensor networks: a survey. Comput. Netw. **38**(4), 393–422 (2002)
2. Papalexakis, E.E., Beutel, A., Steenkiste, P.: Network anomaly detection using co-clustering. In: Proceedings of International Conference on Advances in Social Networks Analysis and Mining (ASONAM), pp. 403–410 (2012)
3. Zhou, L., Haas, Z.J.: Securing ad hoc networks. IEEE Netw. Mag. Glob. Internetworking **13** (6), 24–30 (1999)
4. Cai, Z., Ji, S., He, J.S., Bourgeois, A.G.: Optimal distributed data collection for asynchronous cognitive radio networks. In: Proceedings IEEE 32nd International Conference of Distributed Computing Systems, pp. 245–254 (2012)

5. Ji, S., Cai, Z.: Distributed data collection and its capacity in asynchronous wireless sensor networks. IEEE Trans. Parallel Distrib. Syst. **25**(8), 2113–2121 (2014)
6. Ji, S., Beyah, S., Cai, Z.: Snapshot/continuous data collection capacity for large-scale probabilistic wireless sensor networks. In: Proceedings IEEE INFOCOM, pp. 1035–1043 (2012)
7. Lee, J.C., Leung, V.C.M., Wong, K.H., Cao, J., Chan, H.C.B.: Key management issues in wireless sensor networks: current proposals and future developments. IEEE Wirel. Commun. **14**(5), 76–84 (2007)
8. Zhang, Y.Y., Li, X.Z., Liu, J.M., Yang, J.C., Cui, B.J.: A secure hierarchical key management scheme in wireless sensor network. Int. J. Distrib. Sens. Netw. (2012). Article ID 547471
9. Seyed, H.N., Amir, H.J., Vanesa, D.: A distributed group rekeying scheme for wireless sensor networks. In: Proceedings of the 6th International Conference on Systems and Networks Communications (ICSNC 2011), pp. 127–135 (2011)
10. Bertier, M., Mostefaoui, A., Tredan, G.: Low-cost secret-sharing in sensor networks. In: Proceedings of the IEEE 12th International Symposium on High Assurance Systems Engineering (HASE 2010), pp. 1–9 (2010)
11. Claveirole, T., Dias De Amorim, M., Abdalla, M., Viniotis, Y.: Securing wireless sensor networks against aggregator compromises. IEEE Commun. Mag. **46**(4), 134–141 (2008)
12. Nair, P., Cam, H., Ozdemir, S., Muthuavinashiappan, D.: ESPDA: energy - efficient and secure pattern based data aggregation for wireless sensor networks. In: Computer Communications IEEE Sensors, vol. 2, pp. 732–736 (2006)
13. Ahmad, M., Habib, M., Muhammad, J.: Analysis of security protocols for wireless sensor networks. In: Proceedings of 3rd International Conference on Computer Research and Development (ICCRD), vol. 2, pp. 383–387 (2011)
14. Castelluccia, C., Chan, A.C.-F., Mykletun, E., Tsudik, G.: Efficient and provably secure aggregation of encrypted data in wireless sensor networks. ACM Trans. Sens. Netw. (TOSN) **5**(3), 20 (2009)
15. Pathan, A.K., Hong, C.S.: SERP: secure energy-efficient routing protocol for densely deployed wireless sensor network. Annales des Telecomm **63**(9–10), 529–541 (2008)
16. Lin, K., Lai, ChF, Liu, X., Guan, X.: Energy efficiency routing with node compromised resistance in wireless sensor networks. Mob. Netw. Appl. **17**(1), 75–89 (2012)
17. Lu, H., Li, J., Kameda, H.: A secure routing protocol for cluster-based wireless sensor networks using ID-based digital signature. In: IEEE Global Communication Conference (2010)
18. Bertier, M., Mostefaoui, A., Tredan, G.: Low-cost secret sharing in sensor networks. In: Proceedings of the IEEE 12th International Symposium on High Assurance Systems Engineering (HASE 2010), pp. 1–9 (2010)
19. Qin, D., Jia, S., Yang, S.: A lightweight authentication and key management scheme for wireless sensor networks. J. Sens. **2016**, 9 (2016). Article ID 1547963
20. Chen, Z., He, M.: Trust-aware and low energy consumption security topology protocol of wireless sensor network. J. Sens. **2015**, 10 (2015). Article ID 716468

Denoising Epigraphical Estampages
Using Nested Run Length Count

P. Preethi$^{(\boxtimes)}$, K. Praneeth Kumar, M. Sumukha, and H. R. Mamatha

PES University, Bengaluru, India
{preethip, mamathahr}@pes.edu,
praneeth.kumar6699@gmail.com, sumukhamohan6@gmail.com

Abstract. Denoising in epigraphical document analysis helps in building recognition system for fast and automatic processing. However, it is challenging due to the presence of stone texture as a complex background in input samples. In this paper, a nested run length counting with varying block size of 3 * 3, 5 * 5 and 7 * 7 are applied. Computation is carried out on neighboring pixels of the point of interest and discloses whether it is part of the script on inscription or background based on the count value. If it is part of the background, point of interest is set to background value else set to white. The method is tried and tested on 100 samples of epigraphical Estampages collected from archaeological survey of India. A comparative study is derived on the output of the proposed method and on the nonlinear filters such as median and wiener. Human vision perception has evaluated that proposed method is better than median and wiener filters. The quality measures such as Peak signal to noise ratio and Structural similarity indexes are practiced on the sample output for various filters and proposed method.

Keywords: Epigraphical scripts · Run length count (RLC) · Denoising · Peak to signal noise ratio (PSNR) · Structural similarity index (SSIM)

1 Introduction

History and culture are derived from ancient inscriptions and are scribed using regional script. In India inscriptions are available from 3rd to 17th century in the form of stone carvings (immovable), copper plates, coins and pots. The script used on the inscriptions varies from Brahmi, Hoysala & elongated Hoysala, Poorvada Halegannada, Halegannada and Nadugannada [13]. The processing and preservation of inscriptions are in the hands of Archaeology Department. In the process of preservation, Estampages (a rubbed copy of the stone) is formed on a thick sheet of paper applying black ink and same is circulated among Epigraphers for deciphering. Epigraphers are the philosophers who could read and understand the writings on the inscriptions. Finding epigraphers for reading/ understanding has become difficult as they are few or extinct. Estampages are stored for future research, which are prone to damage due to environmental conditions. Digitization of Estampage as an image to preserve and automating the reading process is the need of today.

© ICST Institute for Computer Sciences, Social Informatics and Telecommunications Engineering 2019
Published by Springer Nature Switzerland AG 2019. All Rights Reserved
N. Kumar and R. Venkatesha Prasad (Eds.): UBICNET 2019, LNICST 276, pp. 198–206, 2019.
https://doi.org/10.1007/978-3-030-20615-4_15

Digitization deals with storing and processing of scanned Estampages, which are the input image for the automatic reading. The scanned images possess irregular rock structure traces, ink spots and distortion as noise. These noises are random in nature and pose a great challenge for further processing. Elimination of noise and isolating the script from the background texture is the focus of the research. Denoised Estampage images are used for segmentation, feature extraction and recognition.

Preprocessing techniques turns out to be a promising step in optical character recognition as the procedure removes outliers, distortion, binarization, low contrast etc., which supports segmentation, feature extraction and recognition processes. Low level entity noise has to be removed from the image to ensure only object of interest is existent. Denoising images involve standard filtering techniques like frequency domain filters and spatial domain filters which are applied to remove Salt and Pepper, Speckle and Gaussian noise. On the grounds of noise level, different types of filters are applied.

Run length encoding or counting is a compression technique which keeps track of same data value in consecutive elements around the pixel of interest and stores the data value along with the count. Keeping track of data values in the consecutive elements describes the feature of the image. In this paper, instead of tracking horizontal or vertical runs, the neighboring data values are tracked and similar data value count are kept in track. This information designates pixel of reference as actual data or noise. Nested Run length counting with varying size kernel of 3 * 3, 5 * 5 and 7 * 7 is implemented. The detailed explanation to the procedure followed is described later.

The paper describes the challenges in Estampage images, the literature survey in understanding different techniques and estimators used in Sect. 2. Section 3 illustrates procedure followed to implement denoising technique. The last section describes the results and discussion.

2 Literature Survey

In the images of Estampages there is no fixed or defined noise, as the texture and ink spitting, mistakes while writing is also considered as the noise. Some of the experiments were conducted on historical documents with similar kind of noises. Below are the survey detailing techniques and noise estimators used in validating the denoising.

In [1] two stage sequential 10 * 10 sized block filtering is applied. The first stage is to flush out the small noise cluster whereas second step is to remove large noise cluster which are now a part of the background. The output of the denoising technique is used as input for the gradient based segmentation. The authors of [6], experimented by applying the morphological filtering techniques on the segmented input for further processing. The inputs considered for experimentation are degraded historical documents.

Arabic historical documents [10] are subjected to contrast stretching filter and manual line by line pixel tracing technique in removing the noise. In [11], handwritten historical document is considered for the noise removal technique. Application of hybrid Iterative global thresholding to remove noise in the Greek historical documents [8], Application of median filters in [9] for filtering Tamil inscriptional images are discussed. The old palm scripts are also considered to be the historical manuscripts, in preserving and processing them, [2] a set theory based morphological operations are applied and the output is compared against the standard filtering techniques such as wiener and median filters. Copper inscriptions are exposed to nonlinear filtering techniques in [7]. The filters like median, harmonic and contra harmonic filters are applied on the images of copper plates and subjected to estimators such as PSNR and SSIM.

Run length coding is applied on the Chinese tablet to remove noise in the image. The rubbings of tablet are considered as the input, where as a preliminary step the image subjected to smoothening and binarization applying Otsu method. A single character from the tablet is the input and the five basic strokes of the Chinese character are considered for calculating the statistics. It is also assumed that the noise is smaller than the strokes. Using horizontal and vertical scan the noise density is estimated [3]. Horizontal and vertical run length count method is used to remove noise in document analysis. The result of the noise removal method is the input for Optical character recognizer. The author validates the efficiency of the algorithm on handwritten document and printed epigraphical images [4].

Understanding the noise characteristics, estimating the noise level and conclusion plays a key role. In [5], the author describes about the existing noise measures with respect to pixel difference based, Correlation based, edge based, context based, spectral distance based and human vision based measures. Human vision system is considered to be the best metric and is implemented by structural similarity index and proves to be the best out of all in his discussion with some example. In [12], author theoretically understand the similarity and difference between peak signal to noise ratio and structural similarity indexing, and finds that PSNR can be derived from SSIM and vice versa.

Survey reveals variant methods applied on different set of input including handwritten documents, manuscripts, images of inscriptions and epigraphical scripts. Each document has dissimilar noise and processed with linear, nonlinear and block filters, noise being estimated using PSNR, SSIM, MSE measures. Existence of random noise, ink spots, stone texture impression in the images of Estampage pose an open challenge in the field of document analysis.

3 Proposed Method

There are many examples of RLC compression technique applied to reduce image dimension. Compression technique cannot be practiced on epigraphical script as reduction of pixel may remove the details of the image. Use of Run length count on the neighboring pixels can describe information such as noise, edge, text and background. Keeping this information, a novel technique - nested run length count algorithm with varying kernel size is designed and applied.

It is noted from the above Fig. 1 and also from the discussion that, there exist a randomized noise and each input image exist with different challenge.

Run length count algorithm is applied on the horizontal and vertical lines of the image. We have proposed a different version where RLC algorithm will work on block of neighboring pixels of greyscale image. The block size is varied from 3 * 3, 5 * 5 and 7 * 7 to achieve better results. An odd sized kernel is intentionally selected as it

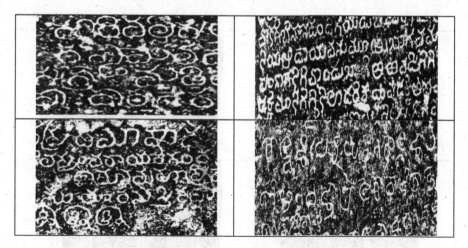

Fig. 1. Depicting the input images majorly having background texture of stone as noise which has considered as preliminary challenge [ASI].

covers all the first, second and third circle neighboring pixels around the pixel of interest. Initially threshold value (by averaging the means) of the image is computed which will be used as a comparative value in deciding the noise level in the neighboring pixels. The marginal pixels of the image are evaluated by considering the out of bound indexing.

Raw input image is first subjected to run length coding algorithm for varying size of the blocks. Each pixel is subjected under 3 * 3 block, covering 9 pixels, where middle pixel pointed by block represents point of input and its remaining 8 pixels are the deciders. Based on computed run length count the value of input pixel is represented as white or black. If white pixel count is maximum than black pixel among 8, the input pixel value is set to white else set to black. The outcome of the 3 * 3 pixel was poor. Hence, changing block size to 5 * 5, 7 * 7 and 9 * 9 was adopted to improvise the Denoise ratio. When 9 * 9 sized kernel was applied on the input, it was removing even the script details. The result of 7 * 7 was comparatively better than 3 * 3, 5 * 5 and 9 * 9. Another problem is, if the number of black pixel is equal to the number of white pixel, then deciding the value of the experimental pixel is tough and random assumption would lead in creating salt and pepper noise. Experimental results are represented in Fig. 2 along with the quality measures.

In proposed nested block model, input pixel value (which is the point of interest) is first compared with 8 neighbors of 3 * 3 block size, if there exists a problem in deciding input pixel value, the same input pixel is subjected for nested experimentation with 5 * 5 block size counting 25 neighboring pixels. The method is continued till block size of 7 * 7 counting 49 surrounding pixels for the conclusion. Experimentation with three nested Run Length Counting has proved with good results and are shown below in Table 1.

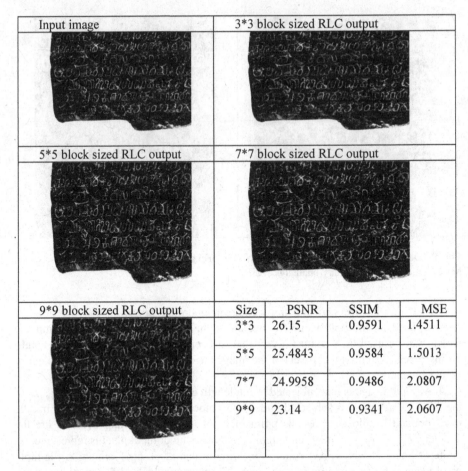

9*9 block sized RLC output	Size	PSNR	SSIM	MSE
	3*3	26.15	0.9591	1.4511
	5*5	25.4843	0.9584	1.5013
	7*7	24.9958	0.9486	2.0807
	9*9	23.14	0.9341	2.0607

Fig. 2. Depicting result of 3 * 3, 5 * 5, 7 * 7, 9 * 9 block sized RLC output along with the PSNR, SSIM and MSE measures for a sample input.

Pseudo code of the Nested RLC is depicted below:

```
I(x, y) is raw input image
Thresholding (I(x, y))
RLC3*3(I(x, y))
If (Count Length with 8 neighbors decides value of I (x, y)) return;
Else RLC5*5(I(x, y))
    If (Count Length with 24 neighbors decides value of I (x, y)) return;
    Else RLC7*7(I(x, y))
        Count Value with 48 neighbors decides the value of I(x, y)
```

The noise estimators are used to validate the work conducted on Estampages and the definition of PSNR, MSE and SSIM are as follows.

Peak signal to noise ratio is the ratio of power of the signal to power of the distorting noise which deteriorates the quality of the image. It is considered as one of the standard noise estimators in both lossless and lossy compression techniques. PSNR value is derived from the mean squared error which is the average squared difference between the estimated values [15].

$$MSE = \frac{1}{mn} \sum_{i=0}^{m} \sum_{j=0}^{n} [I(i,j) - K(i,j)]2 \tag{1}$$

Table 1. shows the output of the nested RLC method

INPUT IMAGE	Measures	OUTPUT IMAGE
	PSNR: 21.5825 MSE: 4.9351 SSIM: 0.92223	
	PSNR: 25.2799 MSE: 3.8771 SSIM: 0.9305	
	PSNR: 22.8620 MSE: 3.7935 SSIM: 0.9358	
	PSNR: 21.5585 MSE: 23.3733 SSIM: 0.8742	

For an image I with m * n dimensions, and noise approximation image K of same size as input image. MSE is computed as in Eq. 1, PSNR as in Eq. 2 where MAX is the maximum possible pixel value in the image.

$$PSNR = 20\log_{10}(MAX) - 10\log_{10}(MSE) \qquad (2)$$

Image quality assessment is also measured in terms of structural similarity index and it is a perception based method and hence closer to human vision system. It is a measure between the two images x and y of size m * n, and SSIM is computed as in Eq. 3 Using which the quality of the output images are estimated. μ_x and μ_y are the average of pixel in image x and y where variance and covariance are represented as σ_x, σ_y and σ_{xy} [14].

$$SSIM = \frac{(2\mu_x\mu_y + C_1) + (\sigma_{xy} + C_2)}{(\mu_x^2 + \mu_y^2 + C_1)(\sigma_x^2 + \sigma_y^2 + C_2)} \qquad (3)$$

Table 1 showcase the input and output images along with computed value of estimators. Input images are also subjected to nonlinear a well-known median and wiener filters and PSNR, SSIM values are recorded. The results are discussed in next section.

4   Results and Discussion

As noise reduction and automation of epigraphical Estampages are new topic of interest, the data samples are collected from the Archaeological survey of India, Mysore. The images considered are of old Kannada Estampages which depicts background stone texture as major noise. These are non-standard random errors and cannot be removed completely by standard filters. The proposed method is compared with median and wiener filters and the results are as shown for 10 images in Table 2.

Table 2. Showing the outcome of the measures applied on the filtered image

Sl. no	Median filters			Wiener filters			Nested RLC filtering		
	MSE	PSNR	SSIM	MSE	PSNR	SSIM	MSE	PSNR	SSIM
1	18.618	26.61	0.942	25.808	29.336	0.952	**4.539101**	**21.58246**	**0.922325**
2	21.890	26.17	0.939	27.351	28.917	0.950	**5.238516**	**21.89441**	**0.9166**
3	21.684	26.92	0.945	27.660	29.045	0.952	**5.508122**	**22.06989**	**0.916554**
4	20.821	26.38	0.943	28.398	28.792	0.952	**5.058379**	**21.89571**	**0.920653**
5	29.876	24.62	0.923	36.8073	27.115	0.939	**9.242608**	**19.64612**	**0.858684**
6	28.376	25.21	0.931	35.0153	27.571	0.943	**8.612306**	**20.18732**	**0.870931**
7	19.535	26.55	0.939	25.8011	29.352	0.949	**4.854342**	**22.02918**	**0.920685**
8	23.139	26.43	0.942	28.538	28.744	0.950	**5.788686**	**21.74733**	**0.910441**
9	15.788	27.29	0.941	21.084	30.444	0.952	**3.793502**	**22.86201**	**0.935805**
10	21.050	27.63	0.950	21.165	30.424	0.958	**5.201315**	**23.1605**	**0.920123**

The experiment is conducted for 100 samples and for all inputs the proposed method has given good results, than median and wiener filters. Human vision could observe better noise removal in proposed method than by standard techniques. The proposed method was also tested on well-known inputs with Gaussian noise and the output is as shown in the Fig. 3. Outcome of the proposed method appears to be distorted.

| Noisy Leena input | Image after Nested RLC | Noisy Cameraman input | Image after Nested RLC |

Fig. 3. The outcome of Nested RLC on Leena and Cameraman images with Noise level of 0.025.

5 Conclusion

A novel method of using Run length counting is used for denoising the epigraphical Estampages to preserve the foundation of history. The proposed method uses a simple 3 * 3, 5 * 5, 7 * 7 neighbors to eliminate the noise based on the run length count of white and black pixels. Application of 9 * 9 sized block had given noisy and inappropriate result when compared with inputs and hence stopped at 7 * 7. The method was tested on 100 samples and could achieve average PSNR as 23.75 and average SSIM of 92.83%. The proposed method is able to remove small noise clusters around the script but the prominent noises are still seen. Our future plan is to extend the preprocessing methods for better filtering of Estampage images.

Acknowledgement. My sincere thanks to The Director and staff members of Archaeological survey of India, Mysore for providing data samples for the research work.

References

1. Baig, A., Al-Ma'adeed, S.A.S., Bouridane, A., Cheriet, M.: Automatic segmentation and reconstruction of historical manuscripts in gradient domain. IET Image Process. **12**, 502–512 (2018)
2. Gangamma, B., Murthy, K.S., Singh, A.V.: Restoration of degraded historical document image. J. Emerg. Trends Comput. Inf. Sci. **3**(5), 792–798 (2012)
3. Zhang, J., et al.: Denoising of Chinese calligraphy tablet images based on run-length statistics and structure characteristic of character strokes. J. Zhejiang Univ. Sci. **7**, 1176–1186 (2006)

4. Karthik, S., Mamatha, H.R., Murthy, K.S.: An approach based on run length count for denoising the kannada characters. Int. J. Comput. Appl. **50**(18), 42–46 (2012)
5. Al-Najjar, Y.A.Y., Soong, D.C.: Comparison of image quality assessment: PSNR, HVS, SSIM, UIQI. Int. J. Sci. Eng. Res. **3**(8), 118–126 (2012)
6. Boudraa, O., Hidouci, W.K., Michelucci, D.: A robust multi stage technique for image binarization of degraded historical documents. In: 5th International Conference on Electrical Engineering. IEEE (2017)
7. Chairy, A., et al.: Image restoration on copper inscription using nonlinear filtering and adaptive threshold. J. Phys: Conf. Ser. **801**, 012043 (2017)
8. Kavallieratou, E., Stamatatos, E.: Improving the quality of degraded document images. In: The Second International Conference on Document Image Analysis for Libraries (DIAL 2006). IEEE (2006)
9. Janani, G., Vishalini, V., Kumar, P.M.: Recognition and analysis of Tamil inscriptions and mapping using image processing techniques. In: International Conference on Science Technology Engineering and Management. IEEE (2016). ISBN 978-1-5090-1706-5
10. Elfattah, M.A., Hassanien, A.E., Mostafa, A., Ali, A.F.: Artificial bee colony optimizer for historical arabic manuscript images binarization. In: 2015 11th International Computer Engineering Conference. IEEE (2015). ISBN 978-1-5090-0275-7
11. Chakraborty, A., Blumenstein, M.: Preserving text content from historical handwritten documents. In: 2016 12th IAPR Workshop on Document Analysis Systems. IEEE (2016). ISBN 978-1-5090-1792-8
12. Horé, A., Ziou, D.: Image quality metrics: PSNR vs. SSIM. In: 2010 20th International Conference on Pattern Recognition DBLP (2010)
13. Soloman, R.: Indian Epigraphy, 2nd edn. Oxford Indian Press (1999). ISBN 0-19-509984-2
14. Keiran, G.: Structural similarity index simplified. Occasional Texts in the Pursuit of Clarity and Simplicity in Research. Series 1, no. 1 (2015)
15. http://www.ni.com/white-paper/13306/en/

Improving Transition Probability for Detecting Hardware Trojan Using Weighted Random Patterns

Kshirod Chandra Mohapatra[✉], M. Priyatharishini, and M. Nirmala Devi

Department of Electronics and Communication Engineering, Amrita School of Engineering, Coimbatore, Amrita Vishwa Vidyapeetham, Coimbatore, India
kshirod_00066@yahoo.co.in,
{m_priyatharishini,m_nirmala}@cb.amrita.edu

Abstract. Computer system security has related to security of software or the information processed. The underlying hardware used for information processing has considered to as trusted. The emerging attacks from Hardware Trojans (HTs) violate this root of trust. The attacks are in the form of malicious modification of electronic hardware at different stages; possess major security concern in the electronic industries. An adversary can mount HT in a net of the circuit, which has low transition probability. In this paper, the improvement of the transition probability by using test points and weighted random patterns is proposed. The improvement in the transition probability can accelerate the detection of HTs. This paper implements weighted random number generator techniques to improve the transition probability. This technique is evaluated on ISCAS 85' benchmark circuit using PYTHON and SYNOPSYS TETRAMAX tool.

Keywords: Transition probability · Hardware Trojan · Weighted random patterns

1 Introduction

The security of computer systems has related to the protection of the software or the information processed. The essential hardware needed for processing the information seems to be trusted. The emerging attacks from the Hardware Trojans (HTs) contravene this root of trust. Increasing dependence on untrusted 3rd party Intellectual properties, CAD tools and decreasing control on the design or fabrication steps of Integrated circuits results in a malicious modification in ICs.

HTs are activated in aberrant conditions as discussed in the paper [1], and the conventional tests are not effectual for the detection of HTs. The furtive nature of HTs implies, most of the time, they are integrated into nets that has less transition probability, or less SCOPE measurements. The inputs to these HTs are fed from the nets (wires) with low transition probability (tp), which in turn influence power and delay analysis. Several techniques for HT have been suggested in the last decade. The techniques are characterized into two types (1) Side-channel analysis [2–6], (2) Logic testing [7–10].

N. Kumar and R. Venkatesha Prasad (Eds.): UBICNET 2019, LNICST 276, pp. 207–217, 2019.
https://doi.org/10.1007/978-3-030-20615-4_16

In the side-channel analysis, the parameters like power, delay, current (both transient and leakage) are analyzed and techniques for Trojan detection are discussed in the paper [2]. In [3] the path delay model is used to detect the HTs by using the separate clock (shadow clock). In [2] uses the power (transient) to detect the Trojans as side channel analysis. Here they conclude that the resolution of the detection of HTs measured directly on the activity rate of HTs and inversely on the activity of the circuit. The method given in [4] based on reordering the scan cells to decrease the activity of the circuit. It helps in magnifying power consumes by HTs, hence total circuit power (transient) is improved, as a result, side channel power consumption improved. In paper [5], another side-channel power consumption technique that uses nonlinear detection method and it shows the differences in nonlinear curves of consumed power between the inflected circuit and reference circuits. In this [5] paper for observation, projection and analysis of different nonlinear functions are proposed. In order to improve the side channel signal analysis, an algorithm is given by the [6]. Here the idea is to decrease the effect of the aberrant points due to the noise the superimposed curve of a signal by a smooth filtering algorithm.

Logical testing is additional way to detect HT. In this method, test patterns are provided to activate hidden HTs. In [7], generated test patterns used to excite the aberrant logic at the internal nodes for multiple times. This statistical approach maximizes the probability of interpolate HT's being triggered and detected by logic testing. In [8] N vectors form a set, and this set has given to the circuit under analysis(CUA) and design circuit, if the CUA and design have same probability signature, implies CUA isn't inflected. In [8], HTs detection based on a method called activation sequence generation. This uses an activation sequence, which activates the HT circuit and this activation effect will propagate to the memory elements or PO's. At PO's the effects can be observe by the designer.

There are methods, which uses both logic testing and side-channel analysis to identify HTs such as [9, 10]. In [9], Principal component analysis (PCA) algorithm is the data processing algorithm used for the detection of Trojans in the circuit. In this the characteristics of the reference circuit and inflected circuit are analyzing by PCA algorithm and corresponding projections are plotted on 3D graph, which gives enough information about the reference circuit and inflected circuit. In [10], demonstrates a new side-channel test generation mechanism. This presents the concept of multiple number of excitations of rare switching (MERS). MERS can expressively improve sensitivity of HTs detection. This approach statistically increases switching activity in an unrecognized HT and amplify the HT effect in the large process variation conditions. In [11], HT detection was based on the improving the transition probability of the internal nodes by weighted input probability. In this method, they found the internal node has less controllability & observability and improved the transition probability using weighted input probability.

As we know that, HTs activated in aberrant conditions, less coverage detection provided by random test pattern and generation and deterministic test pattern generation by ATPG tools. However better results can be obtained for the probability of activation of HTs by increasing tp by means of extra hardware such as DSFF or test points. In [12], insertion of 2:1 mux as the test point is proposed. This paper based on the tp of fan-out cone gates extremely depends on the input probability of applied to logical-gate inputs. Candidate nets are the nets with low tp than user defined threshold tp. For each candidate nets, a 2:1 MUX inserted in its input, which has less transition probability. Again, to optimize the number of insertion of 2:1 MUX in the candidate nets, weighted random patterns (WRP) are applied. In paper [13], gate-level characterization (GLC) approached is used for detection HTs. They have calculated side channel parameter such as power for each test vector applied to inflected circuit.

In [14, 15] given the idea about the weight set calculation for the weighted random generator (WRG). In the paper [14], the basic idea is minimize the variance such that number of test patterns required is less for test the circuit. Paper [15] is based on the fact that, test pattern which have less sampling probability than sampling probability of test pattern from LFSR are deleted and new test set is created.

In this paper, we have compared the different weight set generation scheme from [14, 15] and obtained the corresponding results for more efficient weights set generation algorithm for improving the tp of low probable nets. After successfully generating the weight sets, low tp nets are identified and from these suitable candidates net is observed for insertion of 2:1 mux. After insertion of 2:1 mux and application of weight set, it is observed that there is significant improvement in low tp net. Improved tp of each net for the circuit is an effective way to enhance HTs detection in two ways as follows. (1) As the tp of the nets will increased, results more transitions in the nets, hence the side channel signal analysis of HTs will improved. (2) it allows to fully activated the HTs and observes faulty outputs at POs of circuit.

The rest of the paper organized as follows. In Sect. 2, proposed methodology is discussed, in Sect. 3 comparison of test set based on [14, 15], simulation results are shown in Sect. 4 and Sect. 5 concludes this paper.

2 Proposed Methodology

The flow chart for the proposed methodology shown in Fig. 1. The aim of the proposed methodology is to identify the low probable nets and from these low probable nets the suitable candidate net for insertion of 2:1 multiplexer as test points are determined. In the proposed methodology, generation of weighed random numbers and application of these patterns for obtaining the optimal number of test points for improving transition probability.

Fig. 1. Flow chart for proposed method

2.1 Generating the Circuit's Netlist

For our proposed method, circuit is designed using hardware description language. There are several hardware description language like VHDL, VERILOG, and SYSTEM C. Here circuit is designed using Verilog hardware description language. The netlist for the circuit obtained using SYNOPSYS TETRAMAX tool. For identifying the low tp nets, threshold for tp is provided by the user. In [13], general method is discussed for setting the threshold tp. After setting the threshold for tp, circuit's netlist is analyzed for finding out the low tp nets.

2.2   Determining the Transition Probability for Each Gate

Calculation of transition probability (tp) for each net is done by using Shannon's decomposition theorem. The detailed tp for each gate is given in the below Table 1. Table 1 shows some basic formula to calculate the tp for each basic gate. The basic gates are AND, OR, NOR & NAND. For example consider the AND gate shown in Fig. 2. IT has two primary inputs namely A and B. "Prob0 -> 1" is the transition probability when there is a transition from 0 to 1 and "Prob1 -> 0" is transition probability from 1 to 0. "PA" and "PB" are primary input signal probability. "Probout = 0" and "Probout = 1" are the primary output probabilities being 0 and 1 respectively.

Table 1. Computation of transition probability of basic gates

	$Prob_{0 \to 1} = Prob_{out=0} \times Prob_{out=1}$
AND	$(1 - Prob_A Prob_B) \times Prob_A Prob_B$
OR	$(1 - Prob_A)(1 - Prob_B) \times (1 - (1 - Prob_A)(1 - Prob_B))$
NAND	$Prob_A Prob_B \times (1 - Prob_A Prob_B)$
NOR	$(1 - (1 - Prob_A)(1 - Prob_B)) \times (1 - Prob_A)(1 - Prob_B)$
XOR	$(1 - (P_A + P_B - 2P_A P_B)) \times (P_A + P_B - 2P_A P_B)$

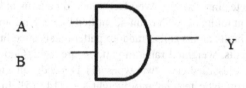

Fig. 2. AND gate

2.3   Identifying Suitable Insertion Point

The Transition probability (tp) of all the nets for the circuit under test are calculated and the low tp nets are extracted from the list. For finding the suitable test points, fan-in cone of the low tp nets is taken. Among all the fan-in cone nets the lowest tp net is considered for test point insertion of 2:1 mux. The below example shown in Fig. 3 described the procedure of finding out the suitable test points. In the below figure two AND gates are shown, the output of the second AND gate has low tp net Y'. By the fan-in cone analysis, one of the inputs of the first AND gate has the lowest tp among all the fan-in nets and this net is suitable for insertion of 2:1 mux as the test point.

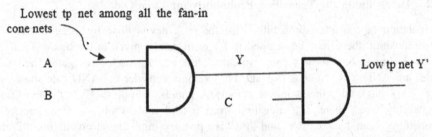

Fig. 3. Low tp example

2.4 Application of Weighted Random Patterns

After identifying test points in the circuit, insertion of 2:1 mux is done on every test points. To reduce the number of 2:1 mux insertion, weighted random patterns are applied as test inputs. Weighted random number patterns are normal random patterns with each of the bit in the test pattern has different weights for being 1. The detailed analysis of weighted random patterns are given Sect. 3.

3 Weighted Random Pattern

Random patterns are generated using LFSR and are used to detect faults that are present in circuits during the testing process. Weighted random patterns are very significant in finding out the stuck at faults, which are un–identified by the random patterns generated by the LFSR. These faults are as called random pattern resistance faults [13]. To detect random resistance faults, weighted random patterns are used. Generation of weighted random patterns are classified into two types (1) Depends on circuit topology and (2) Encode the deterministic test set into weight sets [14, 15]. In proposed method, second one is used.

3.1 Introduction to Weighted Random Number Generator

To test the pattern resistant faults WRPs are proposed. In WRPs, the probability of being logic 1 at each input is biased differently. A WRG is made up with a LFSR and some combinational circuits in order to bias the input probability. Weight calculation logic is used to bias the probability of occurrence of logic value 1 at inputs.

The procedure to generate the WRP is categorized into two types in terms of weight calculation sources; they are (1) structural analysis and (2) deterministic test pattern set. The advantage in (1), it can used in an ATPG process and time taken for generation of weight set is less than the (2). However, sufficient fault content is not guaranteed. The (2) can provide significant test coverage with considerable test length.

3.2   Weight Random Pattern Number Generator Algorithm

The Algorithm 1 is based on identifying the suitable test subset from the deterministic test pattern and this algorithm is repeated until desired fault content is achieved.

Algorithm 1.

Input: Deterministic Test Pattern,
Output: New weight random number patterns

1: Get the deterministic test pattern from any test pattern generator.
2: Create subset from deterministic test set by calculating the conflicts.
3: Calculate weights, Average, sampling probability, variance.
4: Modify the generated weight set by E_i.

Following notations are used to explain the course of the weight set calculation algorithm.

Let a deterministic test pattern 't_j' and a test pattern set be T = {t_1, t2 ... tl}, 'l' is the test length. The ith bit of a deterministic test set be t_j denoted as t[i], and the weight of bit position are denoted as w_i, and is calculated by the Eq. (2).

An ATPG system generates the deterministic test patterns. Then the pattern sets are grouped into different subsets according to the number of conflicts between test patterns. A conflict between 2 test patterns, tj and t_k is defined as $\Delta(tj, tk)$ and given by Eq. (1)

$$\Delta(tj, tk) = \sum_{i=0}^{m} \delta(tj[i], tk[k]) \tag{1}$$

The weights of deterministic test patterns are calculated by (2)

$$wi = \frac{|\{tj \in T | tj[i] = 1\}|}{|\{tj \in T | tj[i] \neq X\}|} \tag{2}$$

The sampling probability 'Pj' of a deterministic test pattern with a weight set is delineate as the probability that the test pattern occurs through the WRP generation cycle and given by the Eq. (3)

$$Pj = \prod_{i=1, tj[i] \neq X}^{m} \{(wi \times tj[i]) + (1 - wi) \times (1 - tj[i])\} \tag{3}$$

Average of the sampling probability is given by (4)

$$A = \frac{\sum_{j=1}^{l} pj}{l} \tag{4}$$

Variance of the sampling probabilities is given by (5)

$$V = \frac{\sum_{j=0}^{l} (Pj - A)^2}{l} \tag{5}$$

To reduce the variance, the effect of modifying the weight of the ith bit is evaluated E_i and given by (6)

$$Ej = \sum_{i=1, tj[i] \neq X}^{m} \{(A - PJ) \times tj[i]) + (Pj - A) \times (1 - tj[i])\} \tag{6}$$

Algorithm 2.

Input: Deterministic Test Pattern,

Output: New weight random number patterns

1: Get the deterministic test pattern from any test pattern generator.

2: Calculate the sampling probabilities of the deterministic test pattern Sp.

3: Calculate the sampling probabilities test patterns from LFSR Splfsr.

4: Remove test pattern from the subset which are Sp<Splfsr

5: Calculate Sp ,weights ,average ,and variance.

6: Modify the reduced subset by E_i

In the Algorithm 2 candidate list include the test patterns which have more sampling probability than the test patterns from LFSR. The idea is that WRP have better sampling probabilities than the LFSR. Weight set and sampling probability are calculated from the candidate list. Weight set calculated form the candidates list are modified in order to reduce the variance of the sampling probability. After the modification the rounding-off the weight set is performed.

The SP of a test pattern with LFSR can is calculated by Eq. (3) with all weights set to 0.5.

3.3 Algorithm for Detection of HTS

The following Algorithm 3 identifying the suitable nets to which 2:1 MUX is inserted.

Algorithm 3.

Input: circuit net list, transition probability threshold (Ttp),

Output: Signal probabilities of candidate nets

1: Compute the signal probabilities S.

2: Compute transition probabilities Tp.

3: Find the minimum transition probability M_{minTp}.

4: Get the fan-in cone Fin.

5: Choose the minimum Tp (from Fin) T_g.

6: Insert HT into MminTp net.

7: Insert 2:1 MUX into Tg.

8: Apply WSP (Weighted Signal Probabilities) test input to the 2:1 MUX.

9: Observe transition on HT.

As we know that Trojans are connected to the low probable nets, so in the proposed work, inputs are provided from the low probable nets to the inserted HT into circuit. After the insertion of 2:1 MUX in the target net, the tp of the candidate nets are improved, therefore we can see improvement in the activation rate in HT.

4 Experimental Results

In this paper, comparison of two different algorithms for generating weight random number is presented and the proposed method is validated using ISCAS benchmark circuits. Table 2 shows the transition probabilities without weighted random patterns. It is observed that the nets N10 and N11 have less tp as compared to other nets in the circuit.

Table 2. Transition Probability without WRP

Nets	Signal prob.1	Signal prob.0	Transition prob.
N10	0.75	0.25	0.1875
N11	0.75	0.25	0.1875
N16	0.625	0.375	0.234
N19	0.625	0.375	0.234
N22	0.53125	0.46828	0.249
N23	0.609375	0.3906	0.238

Table 3 shows the improvement in the transition probability from Algorithm-1. The proposed method in Sect. 2 is applied for the circuit under test and the results are projected in Table 3. It is observed that the nets N10 and N11 which has low tp as shown in Table 1 is improved to the proposed method. The tp of net N11 is improved by 23.1% but N16 tp is drooped by 46.4%. To improve tp of net N16 another test point is inserted in lowest fan-in cone of N16.

Table 3. Transition Probability with WRP one

Nets	Signal prob.1	Signal prob.0	Transition prob.
N10	0.775	0.225	0.174
N11	0.5176	0.4284	0.2448
N16	0.854	0.146	0.125
N19	0.733	0.264	0.1957
N22	0.33815	0.66185	0.224
N23	0.374	0.626	0.2341

Table 4 shows the improvement in the transition probability from Algorithm-2. Here all tp of low tp nets are improved. The tp net N10 and N11 is improved by 10% and 14% respectively. Further improvements can achieved for circuits that are more complex.

Table 4. Transition Probability with WRP two

Nets	Signal prob.1	Signal prob.0	Transition prob.
N10	0.7035	0.2965	0.2085
N11	0.6821	0.3179	0.2168
N16	0.6105	0.3895	0.2377
N19	0.7442	0.2558	0.1903
N22	0.5705	0.4295	0.245
N23	0.5456	0.4544	0.2479

5   Conclusion

In this paper, the two algorithms for generation of weighted random patterns have been successfully implemented. These algorithms are implemented in PYTHON and the deterministic test patterns were obtained from SYNOPSYS TETRAMAX ATPG tool. The experiment is performed on ISCAS-85 C17 circuit. The comparison between the two algorithms is shown in Tables 3 and 4 respectively. When the WRP are applied to the input nets of C17 circuit, it is observed that there is a significant increase in the transition probability as compared to Table 2. Algorithm 2 shows better improvement in transition probability when compared to Algorithm 1. Detection of hardware Trojan will be a part of this paper in future.

References

1. Bhunia, S., et al. Hardware Trojan attacks: threat analysis and countermeasures. Proc. IEEE **102**(8), 1229–1247 (2014). Author, F., Author, S.: Title of a proceedings paper. In: Editor, F., Editor, S. (eds.) CONFERENCE 2016, LNCS, vol. 9999, pp. 1–13. Springer, Heidelberg (2016)
2. Rad, R., Plusquellic, J., Tehranipoor, M.: Sensitivity analysis to hardware Trojans using power supply transient signals. In: Proceedings of IEEE International Workshop on Hardware-Oriented Security Trust (HOST), Anaheim, CA, USA, pp. 3–7 (2008)
3. Cha, B., Gupta, S.K.: Trojan detection via delay measurements: a new approach to select paths and vectors to maximize effectiveness and minimize cost. In: Proceedings of IEEE Design, Automation and Test in Europe Conference Exhibit. (DATE), Grenoble, France, pp. 1265–1270 (2013)
4. Zhou, E., Li, S., Zhao, Z., Ni, L.: Nonlinear analysis for hardware Trojan detection. In: 2015 IEEE International Conference on Signal Processing, Communications and Computing (ICSPCC), Ningbo, pp. 1–4 (2015). https://doi.org/10.1109/icspcc.2015.7338921
5. Zhang, Z., Li, L., Tang, T., Wei, Z.: Side channel analysis of hardware Trojan based on smooth filtering algorithm. In: 2015 8th International Symposium on Computational Intelligence and Design (ISCID), Hangzhou, pp. 192–195 (2015). https://doi.org/10.1109/iscid.2015.253
6. Chakraborty, R.S., Wolff, F., Paul, S., Papachristou, C., Bhunia, S.: *MERO*: a statistical approach for hardware Trojan detection. In: Clavier, C., Gaj, K. (eds.) CHES 2009. LNCS, vol. 5747, pp. 396–410. Springer, Heidelberg (2009). https://doi.org/10.1007/978-3-642-04138-9_28

7. Jha, S., Jha, S.K.: Randomization based probabilistic approach to detect Trojan circuits. In: 2008 11th IEEE High Assurance Systems Engineering Symposium, Nanjing, pp. 117–124 (2008). https://doi.org/10.1109/hase.2008.37

8. Yoshimura, M., Bouyashiki, T., Hosokawa, T.: A hardware Trojan circuit detection method using activation sequence generations. In: 2017 IEEE 22nd Pacific Rim International Symposium on Dependable Computing (PRDC), Christchurch (2017). https://doi.org/10.1109/prdc.2017.40

9. He, C., Hou, B., Wang, L., En, Y., Xie, S.: A novel hardware Trojan detection method based on side-channel analysis and PCA algorithm. In: 2014 10th International Conference on Reliability, Maintainability and Safety (ICRMS), Guangzhou (2014). https://doi.org/10.1109/icrms.2014.710736221-222

10. Huang, Y., Bhunia, S., Mishra, P.: Scalable test generation for Trojan detection using side channel analysis. IEEE Trans. Inf. Forensics Secur. **13**(11), 2746–2760 (2018). https://doi.org/10.1109/tifs.2018.2833059. 1043–1046

11. Devi, N.M., Jacob, I.S., Ranjani, S.R., Jayakumar, M.: Detection of malicious circuitry using transition probability based node reduction technique. http://dx.doi.org/10.12928/telkomnika.v16i2.6812

12. Zhou, B., Zhang, W., Thambipillai, S., Jin, J.T.K., Chaturvedi, V., Luo, T.: Cost-efficient acceleration of hardware Trojan detection through fan-out cone analysis and weighted random pattern technique. IEEE Trans. Comput.-Aided Des. Integr. Circuits Syst. **35**(5), 792–805 (2016). https://doi.org/10.1109/tcad.2015.2460551

13. Karunakaran, D.K., Mohankumar, N.: Malicious combinational Hardware Trojan detection by gate level characterization in 90 nm technology. In: Fifth International Conference on Computing, Communications and Networking Technologies (ICCCNT), Hefei, pp. 1–7 (2014). https://doi.org/10.1109/icccnt.2014.6963036

14. Lee, H., Kang, S.: A new weight set generation algorithm for weighted random pattern generation. In: Proceedings 1999 IEEE International Conference on Computer Design: VLSI in Computers and Processors (Cat. No. 99CB37040), Austin, TX, USA, pp. 160–165 (1999). https://doi.org/10.1109/iccd.1999.808421

15. Kirn, H.-S., Lee, J.K., Kang, S.: A new multiple weight set calculation algorithm. In: Proceedings International Test Conference 2001 (Cat. No. 01CH37260), Baltimore, MD, USA, pp. 878–884 (2001). https://doi.org/10.1109/test.2001.966710

16. Yeap, G.: Practical Low Power Digital VLSI Design. Springer, Heidelberg (1998). https://doi.org/10.1007/978-1-4615-6065-4

Prefix Tree Based MapReduce Approach for Mining Frequent Subgraphs

Supriya Movva, Saketh Prata[✉], Sai Sampath, and R. G. Gayathri

Department of Computer Science and Engineering, Amrita School of Engineering,
Amritapuri, Amrita Vishwa Vidyapeetham, Coimbatore, India
supriya.movva.212@gmail.com, pratasaketh@gmail.com

Abstract. The frequent subgraphs are the subgraphs which appear in
a number, more than or equal to a user-defined threshold. Many algorithms assume that the apriori based approach yields an efficient result
for finding frequent subgraphs, but in our research, we found out that
Apriori algorithm lacks scalability with the main memory. Frequent subgraph mining using Apriori algorithm with FS tree uses adjacency list
representation. FS tree is a prefix tree data structure. It implements the
algorithm in two phases. In the first phase, it uses the Apriori algorithm
to find frequent two edge subgraphs. In the second phase, it uses FS-tree
algorithm to search all the frequent subgraphs from frequent two edge
subgraphs. Scanning the dataset for every candidate is the drawback of
the Apriori algorithm, so the Apriori algorithm with FS-tree is used to
overcome the multiple scanning. This algorithm is also implemented in
an assumption that the data set fits well in memory. In this paper, we
propose parallel map-reduce based frequent subgraph mining technique
performed in a distributed environment on the Hadoop framework. The
experiments validate the efficiency of the algorithm for generating frequent subgraphs in large graph datasets.

Keywords: Frequent subgraph mining · Subgraph ·
Support threshold · Hadoop framework · Map-reduce

1 Introduction

Data mining is a process of discovering patterns in large data sets. One of our
research interests is finding frequent itemsets that occur in large graph datasets.
With the increasing demand on the analysis of large amounts of complex data,
graph mining has become an active and essential theme in data mining. The
task of graph mining is extracting interesting patterns from graphs that describe
the underlying data and could be used further. Mining patterns in biochemical
structures [1,2], anomaly detection, chemoinformatics [3], network flow analysis
and social network analysis [4] are some of the applications of graph mining.

© ICST Institute for Computer Sciences, Social Informatics and Telecommunications Engineering 2019
Published by Springer Nature Switzerland AG 2019. All Rights Reserved
N. Kumar and R. Venkatesha Prasad (Eds.): UBICNET 2019, LNICST 276, pp. 218–232, 2019.
https://doi.org/10.1007/978-3-030-20615-4_17

Frequent subgraph mining is an important research in graph mining to find all the subgraphs that appear frequently in database according to given frequency threshold. There are two different ways for finding frequent subgaphs. (1) Transaction setting [5] (2) Single graph setting [6]. The number of transactions containing the frequent pattern is said to be transaction setting and the number of times the pattern appears in the whole graph is said to be single graph setting. There are many proposed algorithms for finding frequent subgraphs, but all these algorithms are on the assumption that the graph data fits well in memory. As the data size grows memory becomes a problem and computational time rises drastically. Hence, an efficient way to compute large datasets is to process them in parallel by distributing the data among several nodes and combining the results. Distributed computing frameworks like Pregel, Hadoop are popular of their kind.

Map Reduce programming model [7] has been the most successful for mining frequent subgraphs on a distributed computing platform. Hadoop framework uses a distributed file system that is particularly optimized to improve the IO performance while handling Big data. The main reason behind using Hadoop framework for mining frequent subgraphs is its computational performance and efficiency. Another reason is, the higher level of abstraction that it provides, which keeps many system levels hidden from the programmers and allow them to concentrate more on problem specific computational logic.

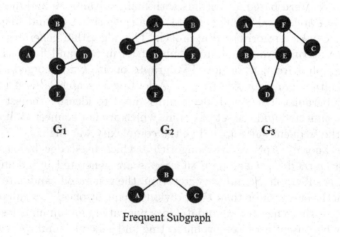

G₁   G₂   G₃

Frequent Subgraph

Fig. 1. Frequent subgraph

Solving the task of Frequent Subgraph Mining (FSM) using Hadoop framework is challenging. In this paper we use Improvised Apriori with frequent subgraph tree Algorithm in distributed computing framework to find the frequent subgraphs. If the input graphs are partitioned over different data nodes, calculating the support count in the data nodes and then finding the frequent subgraphs does not yield an efficient result because of the data set partition. Here, we propose an algorithm that generates all the one-edge candidates and the occurrence count from the given graph data set in the data nodes and then find the frequent subgraphs using support count.

The rest of the paper is framed as follows: Sect. 2 exchanges its views on several works related to Frequent Subgraph Mining. Section 3 presents the proposed approach, important concepts related to the algorithm. Section 4 presents the implementation of the proposed algorithm and the experimental results.

2   Related Work

Extracting or finding frequent subgraphs in a single large graph or set of graphs has been popular in recent times. If the graph dataset is extensive the time and space complexity will be high. Many researchers have implemented many algorithms to find frequent subgraphs in both single and multiple graph settings in an efficient way. Single graph setting has one large graph, and multiple graph setting comprises of a collection of graphs. These frequent itemsets are used for discovering association rules, for extracting common patterns and for classification. Developing algorithms for finding frequent subgraphs is computationally intensive as subgraph isomerism play a vital role throughout the computation. There are two types of approaches for finding frequent subgraphs. (1) Apriori-based algorithms and (2) Pattern-based approach. In this section, we present different Apriori and Pattern based algorithms with many advantages and drawbacks.

Apriori Graph-based Mining (AGM) is an algorithm to find frequent subgraphs [8]. It uses Apriori-based approach. This algorithm generates candidate graphs, merges any two candidate graphs at an instant and finds whether the obtained graph is frequent or not. Two graphs of size k are merged together to form a resultant graph of size $(k + 1)$. A level-wise search is used to find the frequent subgraphs. The AGM algorithm is used to identify the set of graphs which are connected and the set of graphs which are not connected. It efficiently found all the frequent subgraphs, but the complexity was high.

FSG is another Apriori-based algorithm which uses edge based candidate generation method [5]. Candidate subgraphs are generated by adding edge to the previous subgraph. So, in every iteration, the generated candidate subgraph size is exactly one greater than the previous frequent ones. Candidate pruning is also done if the generated candidate does not satisfy minimum threshold. It is very costly because it uses isomorphic testing and generates multiple candidates.

Edge-disjoint path join algorithm [9] abides Apriori-based approach which uses edge disjoint paths as building blocks. The number of disjoint paths is the measuring factor of this algorithm. It also efficiently finds frequent subgraphs, but it is computation intensive.

Fast Frequent subgraph mining (FFSM) considers large dense graphs with fewer labels for finding frequent itemsets. Data sets used here are chemical [10]. It uses the vertical level search strategy to reduce the number of candidate generation. Limitation for FFSM algorithm is that it is an NP-Complete problem. Experimentation showed that FFSM outperformed gSpan.

Molecular Fragments Identification Technique [11,12] is a pattern based approach algorithm used to find regular core structures which are found in all given molecular structures and generates an embedding list. In this algorithm, in every iteration, one more edge is added to the previous frequent subgraph which leads to duplicate candidate generation.

Spanning Tree-based Maximal Graph Mining (SPIN) is a pattern based algorithm. The main aim of this algorithm is to mine subgraphs that are not part of any frequent subgraph [13]. It uses spanning tree approach to discover maximal frequent subgraphs. Pruning technique used in the SPIN algorithm is bottom-up pruning. It saves space by using these techniques.

Temporal pattern subgraph Mining (TSM) finds patterns having temporal information [14]. It uses forward unnecessary checking scheme and backward unnecessary checking scheme to find a frequent temporal graph. It does not generate unnecessary candidates and scans the database once. It is an extension of the DFS search strategy. It is an efficient algorithm for finding patterns which have temporal information.

gSpan algorithm [16] generates a tree-like structure (DFS code tree) over all possible patterns, in which every node represents a DFS code for a graph pattern. The ith level of a code tree contains DFS of all the subgraphs of size (i-1). Each subgraph is generated by adding one extra edge to subgraphs which are present in the previous level of the tree. It preserves the transaction list for discovered graph and pruning is done by deleting nodes which do not satisfy minimal DFS code.

All these algorithms are in assumption that data set fits well in memory, but if data set size is huge, all these algorithms do not give an efficient result, and even though if it can find all the frequent subgraphs, it takes a lot of time and space to find frequent item sets. Hence, some of the researchers implemented a few algorithms in a parallel or distributed environment to find frequent subgraphs in multiple systems in parallel, which give efficient output and reduce both time and space complexities.

There exist some algorithms on adaptive parallel mining for CMP Architectures [18]. Map-Reduce programming model has been used to mine frequent patterns where the transactions in input database are simpler combinatorial objectives such as set or sequence [19,20,22–24]. These algorithms do not implement any method to avoid duplicate candidates generated. Another problem for the iterative approach of Map-Reduce is that it requires many iterations to get the final output.

Frequent subgraph mining using Apriori algorithm with FS tree uses adjacency list representation. It implements the algorithm in two phases. In the first phase, it uses the Apriori algorithm to find frequent two edge subgraphs. In second phase it uses FS-tree algorithm to find all the frequent subgraphs from frequent two edge subgraphs. Scanning the dataset for every candidate is the drawback of the Apriori algorithm, so the Apriori algorithm with FS-tree is used to overcome the multiple scanning. This algorithm is also implemented in an assumption that the data set fits well in memory. In this paper, we implemented the same Apriori algorithm with FS-tree in a distributed environment using the Map-Reduce programming model in a distributed environment to reduce execution time and enhance efficiency.

3   Proposed Work

When a large number of graphs are given as input to the Apriori algorithm, it can lead to inefficient computation of the desired solution. So, dividing the graphs into several non-empty sets with a limited number of graphs in each set and computing them in distributed environment improves time efficiency. In this paper, we propose a two-phase approach to generate all the subgraphs that frequently occur in the graph data set containing a large number of graphs. The proposed method starts with the Data pre-processing, Candidate Generation, Support Counting followed by the phases where these concepts are used.

Let $D = \{G_1, G_2 ..., G_n\}$ be a graph data set where each G_i represents an undirected graph. Let the data set be divided into three sets say, D_1, D_2, D_3 such that $D_1 = \{G_1, G_2 ..., G_i\}$, $D_2 = \{G_{i+1}, G_2 ..., G_k\}$, $D_3 = \{G_{k+1}, G_2 ..., G_n\}$ where i, j, k are any arbitrary values representing the graphs in the data set.

3.1   Data Pre-processing

The graph data set is pre-processed and stored in the form of an adjacency list. Let $D = \{G_1, G_2 ..., G_n\}$ be a graph data set where each G_i represents an undirected graph. Now, each G_i is of the form (V, E) where V is a set of Vertices and E is the set of edges in the graph. Each graph is represented as an adjacency list. The idea of computing the frequent subgraphs is based on the iterative approach of the Apriori algorithm computes the Frequent subgraphs in two steps. One is Candidate Generation, and the other is Support Counting.

3.2   Candidate Generation

A subgraph in a graph is said to be a candidate. To find all frequent subgraphs in a given graph data set, we need to generate all the subgraphs and check whether each one is a frequent subgraph or not. Thus candidate generation is an important step in Frequent Subgraph mining. The candidates are generated as k-edge subgraphs starting from k = 0 which are the vertices. The candidates are thus generated by adding one edge to the previous frequent subgraph. Thus to form a candidate with $k + 1$ edges, we combine two k-edge subgraphs. The two k-edge subgraphs are thus selected such that they have the same $k - 1$ size subgraph. This common subgraph is often referred to as Core of the subgraph. The frequency of each subgraph is also calculated. Algorithm 1 shows the stepwise implementation of Candidate Generation function.

Algorithm 1. Candidate Generation

Input : F_{k+1}, set of k+1 edge frequent subgraphs
Output: C_{k+2}, set of k+2 edge candidate subgraphs along with their count
//s_1 and s_2 are subgraphs such that $s_1 \in F_{k+1}$ and $s_2 \in F_{k+1}$
//C_i is the list of candidate subgraphs of i-edge length and corresponding count
//$s_1 \cup s_2$ defines an operation where a k+2 edge subgraph is formed using k+1 edge subgraphs
//If k<0, s_1 and s_2 are vertices and have no common edges, then $s_1 \cup s_2$ is a valid combination
   iff $s_1 \cup s_2 \in g$

1. **for all** $(s_1, s_2) \in F_{k+1}$
2.   **if** $(s_1 \cup s_2 \in C_{k+2})$
3. $C_{k+2}(s_1 \cup s_2) \leftarrow C_{k+2}(s_1 \cup s_2) + 1$
4.   **else**
5. $C_{k+2} \leftarrow C_{k+2} \cup (s_1, s_2)$
6. $C_{k+2}(s_1 \cup s_2) \leftarrow 1$
7. **end for**
8. return C_{k+2}

The candidate generation can be illustrated using an example. Let the value of k be one. To form a two-edge candidate, Let A-B-C be a two edge subgraph with B as the root. This two edge subgraph can be formed from two one-edge subgraphs A-B and B-C. These subgraphs have a $k-1$ size subgraph, i.e. a vertex B in common. Thus, to form a $k+1$ edge candidate, two K-edge candidates are to be combined with a $k-1$ edge as the core. Figure 2 shows the detailed explanation of candidate generation for the above-stated example.

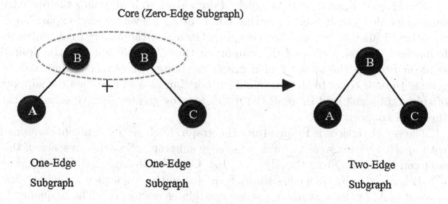

Fig. 2. Example of candidate generation

3.3 Support Counting

Support of a graph is the parameter used to determine whether a graph is a frequent subgraph or not. The total number of times a subgraph is appearing in the graph dataset is termed as the frequency of that graph. Support of a given graph is defined as the frequency of each graph divided by the total number of graphs in the graph data set. To check if a graph is frequent or not, the parameter defined by the user to compare is the threshold support. If the calculated support is greater than or equal to the user-defined threshold support, that graph can be called as a Frequent subgraph. These frequent subgraphs are used to find the subgraphs with more edges added to them.

Mapper

Algorithm 2. Mapper

Input : G: *a graph dataset, σ : minimum support.*
Output: *Set of one-edge graphs with their frequency, adjacency list.*
//C_i: Candidate subgraph set of i length edges
//cg(F_i): Candidate generation function using i-edge frequent subgraphs
//adjacency_list(g): Create adjacency list for graph g
//Reducer(a,b): Send parameters a , b to reducer

1. $C_1 \leftarrow NULL$
2. adj_list $\leftarrow NULL$
3. **while** $g \, \varepsilon \, G$ **do**
4. $F_0 \leftarrow set \, of \, vertices \, in \, g$
5. $C_1 \leftarrow C_1 \cup cg(F_0)$
6.   adj_list $\leftarrow adj\_list \cup adjacency\_list(g)$
7. **end while**
8. Reducer(adj_list, C_1)

The Mapper operates on the block of data given to it and finds the one edge subgraphs along with their repeating count using a level-by-level expansion of the Apriori algorithm. For each sub-graph in a set, the Mapper calculates its frequency. The calculation of the support at this stage will not give the desired solution because the support of a graph calculated at one node may not be greater than or equal to the threshold support but as a whole when the support of sub-graph combined from all the nodes may be greater than or equal to the threshold support.

The set of vertices is formed from the graph. Each vertex is taken, combined with another vertex so as to form a one edge subgraph. Now the presence of this edge can be checked from the adjacency list. Consider an edge A-B. We can check if A-B is an edge by traversing through the list in the Adjacency list whose first element is A. In this way, the one-edge candidates are formed. The frequency of each one-edge is calculated which forms a (key, value) pair where the one-edge candidate is the key, and the frequency of the candidate is the value. Since several blocks of data are being processed at the same time; we achieve computational efficiency. This (key, value) is the output of the Mapper and is given as the input to the Reducer. Algorithm 2 shows the step-wise implementation of Mapper.

Reducer

Algorithm 3. Reducer

Input : adj_list, C_1, σ

Output: *Set of frequent two-edge subgraphs.*

//C_i: Candidate subgraph set of i length edges

//cg(F_i): Candidate generation function using i-edge frequent subgraphs

//$\delta(C_i)$:Count of the graph C_i

//σ : Minimum support threshold

//F.add(C_i): Add element C_i to set F

1. $F \leftarrow NULL$
2. $F_1 \leftarrow NULL$
3. $F_2 \leftarrow NULL$
4. **for** all candidate C_i ε C_1 **do**
5.   Support(C_i) = $\delta(C_1)/T$
6.   **if** Support(C_i) $\geq$ σ **then**
7. F_1.add(C_i)
8.   **end if**
9. **end for**
10. $F \leftarrow F \cup F_1$
11. $C_2 \leftarrow cg(F_1)$
12. **for** all candidate C_i ε C_2 **do**
13.   Support(C_i) = $\delta(C_i)/T$
14.   **if** Support(C_i) $\geq$ σ **then**
15. F_2.add(C_i)
16.   **end if**
17. **end for**
18. $F \leftarrow F \cup F_2$
19. FS-Tree()

The (key, value) pairs received from Mapper nodes are combined in the reducer. It aggregates the frequency of a sub-graph using the key which is the one-edge candidate. Thus the support of each one-edge candidate is calculated. The support calculated is then compared with the threshold support. The candidates whose support is greater than or equal to the threshold are made into a set and are said to be frequent one-edge subgraphs.

Two-edge subgraphs can be formed by combining the frequent one-edge subgraphs with zero-edge subgraph as the core. The two-edge candidates are generated by checking their presence in the adjacency list. The set of frequent two-edge subgraphs is formed by choosing the candidates whose support is greater than equal to the threshold support. This set is given to a tree data structure named as FS-TREE which is built to determine the further frequent subgraphs. Algorithm 3 shows the step-wise implementation of Reducer.

The main disadvantage of the Apriori algorithm is its memory usage. A large number of candidates are generated, and it becomes costly to store and scan them. Hence a tree data structure is used to store the frequent subgraphs. The tree data structure uses the concept of a prefix-tree. The prefix tree is a tree data structure where the children of a node share the common prefix with that node, and the root node is associated with null. The main aim of this tree is to save some amount of memory to store the candidates. Traversal through the tree extracts the frequent subgraphs.

Algorithm 4. FS-TREE

Input : *Frequent two-edge subgraphs.*
Output: *FS-Tree with all frequent subgraphs.*
//F: Set of frequent two-edge subgraphs and one-edge subgraph
//insert(S,T):If T has a child C and S is the one edge expansion of C, then insert S as the child of C.

1. root ← *NULL*
2. **for** all $C_i \in F_2$
3.   insert(C_i,root)
4. **end for**

The input to the data structure is the set of frequent two-edge subgraphs. The root node is created. The frequent two-edge subgraphs are added to the root as children. Thus, the first level of the tree contains all the frequent two-edge subgraphs along with their frequencies. To add a subgraph of more number of edges, those are added as children to the nodes which have the same prefix and then the frequency is incremented. Once, the tree is constructed, each level contains all the frequent subgraphs having the same number of edges along with their support value. On traversing to the higher levels, we can find the frequent subgraphs of a higher number of edges. Thus all the frequent subgraphs can be found. Algorithm 4 shows the step-wise implementation of FS Tree.

The above algorithm can be well represented using an example. Consider the frequent subgraph stated in the Fig. 1. There A-B-C is a frequent subgraph. Let us assume A-B-D is a frequent subgraph. The FSG A-B-D can be obtained by expanding the FSG A-B-C at B, i.e., the edge B-D can be added to A-B-C. This reduces the necessity of two different nodes, and those can be represented using a single node as shown in Fig. 3.

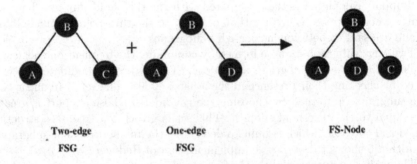

Two-edge   One-edge   FS-Node

FSG   FSG

Fig. 3. Implementation of FS-TREE

4 Experimental Validation and Verification

The algorithm is implemented in Python. The operating system is Ubuntu 16.04. The Hadoop version used is 3.0.0. The experiments were performed on a CPU which possesses a 3.1 GHz quad-core Intel processor with 4 GB memory and 1 TB of storage.

All the values are experimented thrice, and the average values are taken. Following are the results of our experiments, implemented in a Hadoop cluster having four nodes. One node serves as the master node, and the remaining three nodes are the data nodes also known as slave nodes [22].

A set of synthetic graphs is generated to evaluate the performance of the proposed approach. The number of graphs in the data set range from 20 to 5000. Each graph contains 10–14 vertices. Each graph contains 25–30 edges.

Table 1. Number of FSG with varying threshold

Number of graphs in data set	Number of FSG with threshold 0.1	Number of FSG with threshold 0.2	Number of FSG with threshold 0.3
20	417	184	85
50	463	161	75
100	417	141	71
500	344	137	64
2000	312	138	60

Initially, a data set containing 20 graphs is taken. Each graph has at most 13 vertices and 29 edges. The threshold value was set to 0.1. A total of 417 frequent subgraphs including both the one edge and two edge subgraphs are obtained. When the threshold value is increased to 0.2, only 184 frequent subgraphs are obtained in total.

Further, the number of graphs in the data set is increased. A data set with 100 graphs is taken. When the algorithm is implemented with the minimum threshold of 0.1, 417 frequent subgraphs are obtained in total. Upon increasing the threshold value to 0.2, the number of frequent subgraphs decreased to 141. The reason can be illustrated using an example below.

Consider a subgraph G_i. Assume, it is occurring in 15 graphs in the dataset. Let the total number of graphs in the dataset be 100. Hence the support of graph G_i is 0.15. If the minimum support threshold is 0.1, subgraph G_i has supported greater than 0.1 and hence can be stated as a Frequent subgraph. But if the minimum support threshold value is 0.2, the subgraph G_i has support less than 0.2 and hence cannot be called as a frequent subgraph. Thus, with increasing the threshold, many subgraphs may not have their support greater than or equal to the updated minimum support threshold. Thus, with an increasing threshold

Table 2. Experimental results with threshold 0.1

No of graphs in dataset	Apriori (seconds)	Apriori with FS-Tree (seconds)	Apriori with FS-Tree using Hadoop (seconds)
20	10.98321	7.6301	0.194902
50	14.5764	11.9728	0.273901
100	28.9214	19.9214	0.236587
500	178.3206	142.5293	0.925664
2000	2016.65045	2011.093	4.157381

value, the number of frequent subgraphs decrease (Table 1). The term *frequent subgraph* is denoted as FSG.

As the number of graphs increases in the data set, the time of execution increases in the traditional algorithm because of multiple scanning. But, the proposed algorithm takes comparatively very less time which can be concluded from the results in the table below.

Table 2 shows the results for the synthetic graph data set when the threshold value is set to 0.1. The time of execution for 20 graphs in traditional Apriori algorithm is 10.98321 s. When the number of graphs increased to 50, the time of execution in traditional Apriori algorithm is 14.5764 s. The same is the case when the data is tested using Apriori algorithm using FS-TREE and also the Apriori algorithm using FS-TREE implemented in Hadoop.

Table 3. Experimental results with threshold 0.2

No of graphs in dataset	Apriori (seconds)	Apriori with FS-Tree (seconds)	Apriori with FS-Tree using Hadoop (seconds)
20	5.67543	3.3156	0.148771
50	10.1214	9.3213	0.216901
100	21.2494	15.1247	0.161685
500	91.6564	77.53	0.778358
2000	1865.51075	1561.328	3.242671

The time of execution shows a similar pattern for increasing threshold values. When the threshold value is increased to 0.2, the time execution increased with the increase in the number of input graphs (Table 3). The results for the time of execution with threshold 0.3 are briefed in (Table 4).

The time of execution for a given graph, at a given threshold is compared for the Apriori algorithm, improvised Apriori algorithm using FS-Tree in (Fig. 4). The time taken for a traditional Apriori algorithm is an exponential curve, whereas, the time taken by improvising the Apriori algorithm using FS-Tree

Table 4. Experimental results with threshold 0.3

No of graphs in dataset	Apriori (seconds)	Apriori with FS-Tree (seconds)	Apriori with FS-Tree using Hadoop (seconds)
20	3.9860	1.6757	0.138207
50	7.30981	3.4252	0.184441
100	10.0919	7.54593	0.104866
500	72.4203	69.00373	0.473741
2000	1341.1567	1032.199	1.726677

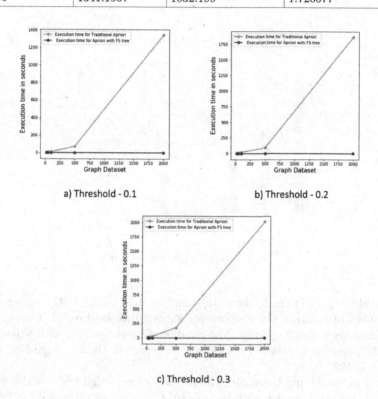

a) Threshold - 0.1

b) Threshold - 0.2

c) Threshold - 0.3

Fig. 4. Execution time vs support threshold

is a linear curve. When the same algorithm is implemented in a distributed environment using Hadoop, the slope of the curve is almost zero. This implies that the time of execution reduced drastically when the algorithm is implemented in Hadoop.

The primary use of FS-Tree is to reduce the space complexity. The tree data structure is built to reduce the number of two-edge candidates. The two-edge candidates sharing common edges can be grouped as discussed in the earlier sections.

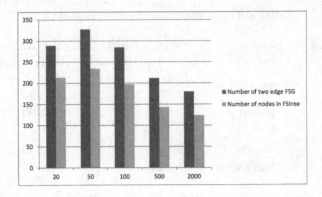

Fig. 5. Graphs with threshold 0.1

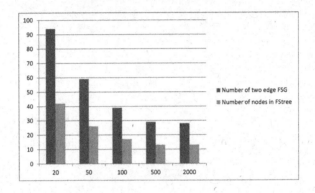

Fig. 6. Graphs with threshold 0.2

The above graph (Fig. 5) shows the number of Two-edge FSG compared with the number of nodes in the FS-Tree for a given threshold of 0.1. Consider, the graph data set with 100 graphs. The number of two-edge FSG with threshold of 0.1 is 285, and the number of nodes used to represent the two-edge FSGs using FS-Tree is 197.

With an increasing threshold, the number of two-edge FSG vs the number of nodes showed a similar pattern (Fig. 6). Consider, the threshold 0.2 for the same data set with 100 graphs. The number of two-edge FSG obtained are 39, and the number of nodes used to represent using FS-Tree is 17. In (Fig. 7), the experimental results for the number of two-edge FSG vs the number of nodes in FS-Tree for threshold 0.3 are shown.

Thus, from the above experimental results, we can state that the space complexity can be reduced using FS-Tree.

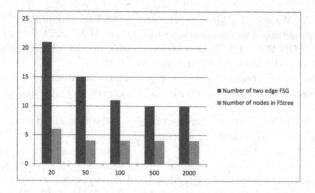

Fig. 7. Graphs with threshold 0.3

5   Conclusion

In this paper, we implemented frequent subgraph mining using FS-tree in a distributed environment using the Hadoop framework. From the experiments, we can conclude that with an increasing number of graphs in the data set, the proposed algorithm takes less time of execution than the traditional Apriori algorithm because the multiple data scans are eliminated. In the traditional algorithm, a large number of candidates are generated. With the FS-Tree approach, once the two-edge candidates are formed, each subgraph is added to the tree as a node. The subgraphs with higher number of edges can be formed using the FS-Tree. Hence the proposed approach generates comparatively less number of candidates than that of the traditional Apriori algorithm. This algorithm can be extended to other distributed frameworks like SPARK or STORM

References

1. Barabási, A., Oltvai, Z.: Network biology: understanding the cell's functional organization. Nat. Rev. Genet. **5**, 101–113 (2004)
2. Lacroix, V., Fernandes, C., Sagot, M.-F.: Motif search in graphs: pplication to metabolic networks. Trans. Comput. Biol. Bioinform. **3**, 360–368 (2006)
3. Borgelt, C., Berhold, M.R.: Mining molecular fragments: finding relevant substructures of molecules. In: Proceedings of International Conference on Data Mining 2002 (2002)
4. Handcock, M., Raftery, A., Tantrum, J.: Model-based clustering for social networks. J. R. Stat. Soc. Ser. (Stat. Soc.) **170**(2), 301–354 (2007)
5. Kuramochi,M., Karypis, G.: Frequent subgraph discovery. In: ICDM01. FSM (2001)
6. Cook, D.J., Holder, L.B.: Substructure discovery using minimum description length and background knowledge. J. Artif. Intell. Res. **1**, 231–255 (1994). 3rd ed
7. Praveena, A., Anitha, B., Rohini, R.: An efficient parallel iterative mapreduce based frequent subgraph mining algorithm. Middle-East J. Sci. Res. 24 (Tech. Algorithms Emerg. Technol.), 524–531 (2016)

8. Inokuchi, A., Washio, T., Motoda, H.: An apriori-based algorithm for mining frequent substructures from graph data. In: Zighed, D.A., Komorowski, J., Żytkow, J. (eds.) PKDD 2000. LNCS (LNAI), vol. 1910, pp. 13–23. Springer, Heidelberg (2000). https://doi.org/10.1007/3-540-45372-5_2
9. Vanetik, N., et al.: Computing frequent graph patterns from semi structured data. In: Proceedings 2002 IEEE International Conference on Data Mining, ICDM-2002 (2002)
10. Huan, J., Wang, W., Prins, J.: Efficient mining of frequent subgraph in the presence of isomorphism. UNC computer science Technique report TR03-021 (2003). FFSM
11. Nguyen, S.N., Orlowska, M.E., Li, X.: Graph mining based on a data partitioning. In: Nineteenth Australasian Database Conference (ADC 2008) (2008)
12. Bhuvaneswari, M., Rohini, R., Preetha, B.: A survey on privacy preserving public auditing for secure data storage. Int. J. Eng. Res. Technol. (2013)
13. Huan, J., Wang, W., Prins, J., Yang, J.: Spin: mining maximal frequent subgraphs from graph databases. In: Proceedings of the 10th ACM SIGKDD International Conference on Knowledge Discovery and Data Mining, pp. 581–586 (2004)
14. Hsieh, H.-P., Li, C.-T.: Mining temporal subgraph patterns in heterogeneous information networks. In: IEEE International Conference on Social Computing/IEEE International Conference on Privacy, Security, Risk and Trust (2010)
15. Thomas, S., Nair, J.J.: Improvised Apriori with frequent subgraph tree for extracting frequent subgraphs. J. Intell. Fuzzy Syst. **32**(4), 3209–3219 (2017)
16. Yan, X., Han, J.: gSpan: graph based sustructure pattern mining. In: Proceedings of 2nd IEEE International Conference on Data Mining, ICDM 2002 (2002)
17. Thomas, S., Nair, J.J.: A survey on extracting frequent subgraphs. In: International Conference on Advances in Computing, Communications and Informatics (ICACCI-2016) (2016)
18. Jeong, B.S., Choi, H.J., Hossain, M.A., Rashid, M.M., Karim, M.R.: A MapReduce framework for mining maximal contiguous frequent patterns in large DNA sequence datasets. IETE Tech. Rev. **29**, 162–168 (2012)
19. Hill, S., Srichandan, B., Sunderraman, R.: An iterative mapreduce approach to frequent subgraph mining in biological datasets. In: Proceedings of the ACM Conference on Bioinformatics, Computational Biology and Biomedicine (2012)
20. Wu, B., Bai, Y.L.: An efficient distributed subgraph mining algorithm in extreme large graphs. In: Wang, F.L., Deng, H., Gao, Y., Lei, J. (eds.) AICI 2010, Part I. LNCS (LNAI), vol. 6319, pp. 107–115. Springer, Heidelberg (2010). https://doi.org/10.1007/978-3-642-16530-6_14
21. Gayathri, S., Radhika, N.: Greedy hop algorithm for detecting shortest path in vehicular networks. Int. J. Control. Theory Appl. **9**, 1125–1133 (2016)
22. Liu, Y., Jiang, X., Chen, H., Ma, J., Zhang, X.: MapReduce-based pattern finding algorithm applied in motif detection for prescription compatibility network. In: Dou, Y., Gruber, R., Joller, J.M. (eds.) APPT 2009. LNCS, vol. 5737, pp. 341–355. Springer, Heidelberg (2009). https://doi.org/10.1007/978-3-642-03644-6_27
23. Di Fatta, G., Berthold, M.: Dynamic load balancing for the distributed mining of molecular structures. IEEE Trans. Parallel Distrib. Syst. **17**, 773–785 (2006)
24. Lin, J., Dyer, C.: Data-intensive text processing with MapReduce (2010)
25. Gayathri, R., Nair, J.J.: ex-FTCD: a novel mapreduce model for distributed multi source shortest path problem. J. Intell. Fuzzy Syst. **34**(3), 16431652 (2018)

A Taxonomy of Methods and Models Used in Program Transformation and Parallelization

Sesha Kalyur(✉) and G. S. Nagaraja

Department of Computer Science and Engineering, R. V. College of Engineering,
VTU, Bangalore, India
Sesha.Kalyur@Gmail.Com, nagarajags@rvce.edu.in

Abstract. Developing Application and System Software in a High level programming language, has greatly improved programmer productivity, by reducing the total time and effort spent. The higher level abstractions provided by these languages, enable users to seamlessly translate ideas into design and structure data and code effectively. However these structures have to be efficiently translated, to generate code that can optimally exploit the target architecture. The translation pass normally generates code, that is sub optimal from an execution perspective. Subsequent passes are needed to clean up generated code, that is optimal or near optimal in running time. Generated code can be optimized by Transformation, which involves changing or removing inefficient code. Parallelization is another optimization technique, that involves finding threads of execution, which can be run concurrently on multiple processors to improve the running time. The topic of code optimization and parallelization is quite vast and replete with complex problems and interesting solutions. Hence it becomes necessary to classify the various available techniques, to reduce the complexity and to get a grasp of the subject domain. However our search for good survey papers in the subject area, did not yield interesting outcomes. This work is an attempt to fill this void and help scholars in the field, by providing a comprehensive survey and taxonomy of the various optimization and parallelization methods and the models used to generate solutions.

Keywords: Taxonomy · Method · Model · Optimization ·
Transformation · Parallelization

1 Introduction

Software development in higher level languages, greatly reduces the burden on the programmer, to seek solutions to problems in the system and application domains. However, translation of programs from source languages to object code, generates inferior, inefficient code due to the inherent nature, of the structure

© ICST Institute for Computer Sciences, Social Informatics and Telecommunications Engineering 2019
Published by Springer Nature Switzerland AG 2019. All Rights Reserved
N. Kumar and R. Venkatesha Prasad (Eds.): UBICNET 2019, LNICST 276, pp. 233–249, 2019.
https://doi.org/10.1007/978-3-030-20615-4_18

of the programming languages. To generate code that is optimal from an execution perspective, cleanup of the translated code is necessary, an activity that is usually referred to as Code Optimization. Code optimization is possible from several perspectives namely, reduction of execution time, reduction of storage requirement or reduction of energy requirement. In the present context, we use the term code optimization to mean code transformation, to improve the running characteristics of the program. We sometimes use the term Optimization to mean either transformation or parallelization. Program transformation includes code changes, that affect a particular aspect of code, such as the instruction count. Program parallelization involves finding concurrent threads of execution, that can be run on separate processing elements.

The Program transformation landscape is quite fertile, and myriad solutions exist. Although the primary goal of all transformation methods, is to improve the running time of the program, the methodology followed by each technique, in reaching the goal is unique. However it is possible to categorize these individual techniques, based on one or more of the following criteria, namely those that target the Instruction Count, Memory Latency, Locality and those that enable other transformations and parallelization.

Program parallelization is a related problem, that is interesting as well, and can be classified along multiple axes. At a very high level the parallelism that is inherent in a program, can be visualized from a code or data perspective, and accordingly we have parallelism that is code centric or data centric. Based on the Programmer Involvement required or Ease of Use, parallelization can be categorized as Manual, Semi-Automated or Explicit and Automated or Implicit. Considering the Granularity of the Parallel Tasks, parallelization can be categorized as Fine Grained or Coarse Grained. Parallelism in a program is contained, in different regions and structures and accordingly can be classified as Loop Level parallelism, Thread Level parallelism or Process Level parallelism. From a performance criteria, parallelization can be classified as Task Level, Instruction Level and Pipeline parallelism. Depending on the Architectural characteristics of the target machine and the resulting Scalability, parallelization can be classified as Shared Memory Parallelization, or Distributed Memory Parallelization. Parallelization could also be categorized, based on the latest emerging trends in the field, as Parallelization by Speculation [1] and Parallelization by Comprehension. Parallelization presents some interesting sub-problems, such as Sub-Program Creation, Orchestration and Distribution which could also serve as criteria for classification.

Since by nature the problems and their solutions, in the field of program transformation and parallelization are non trivial, precise mathematical models are required, to represent the problems and subsequently derive solutions. The range of models used and reported, in the literature is quite vast. We have models based on Trees, Graphs, Machine Learning, Algebra, Statistics, Enumeration, Heuristics among others [2]. From the above presented arguments, it should clear to the reader that the transformation and parallelization domain is exhaustive, and diverse and requires classification and categorization, to simplify and comprehend.

This research work is an effort in this direction and we attempt to fill the void by providing comprehensive taxonomies of the methods and models used in the domain of program transformation and parallelization. Section 2 provides the taxonomy of methods used in program transformation. Section 3 contains the taxonomic details of the methods used in program parallelization. Section 4 is dedicated to a discussion of the taxonomies of various models used in program transformation and parallelization. Section 5 presents the various taxonomies discussed earlier in graphical form, for easy comprehension.

2   Taxonomy of Methods Used in Program Transformation

The domain of Program transformation contains several techniques or methods that can be classified along the following characteristics,

- Instruction Count Reduction
- Locality Improvement
- Memory Latency Reduction
- Parallelization Enablement
- Transformation Enablement.

2.1   Instruction Count Reduction

Instruction count for a given program, is the number of instructions executed, for a certain run of the program. This metric is usually obtained, with the help of dedicated hardware counters present in the architecture. This metric has a direct bearing, on the execution time of the program. So one way to reduce the running time of the program, is to reduce the instruction count.

Table 1 lists several popular transformation methods along with their descriptions, which can be categorized as techniques that aim for the reduction of Instruction Execution Count.

2.2   Locality Improvement

Program Locality is the term used to refer to the program behavior, wherein recently used code and data are once again accessed, in a short time span. Hardware caches are used, to store a subset of the recently used code and datum. Accessing these items once again, can result in a cache hit. Since accessing an item from the cache takes fewer execution cycles, than getting them from memory, this can induce a substantial savings in the run time of a program.

The following table, Table 2 provides a listing of techniques and their explanations, whose primary goal is to improve the Locality behavior of the program, through caching of both code and data.

Table 1. Instruction count reducing transformations

	Method	Description
1	Dead Code Elimination	Removal of code controlled by an expression that always evaluates to false
2	Flow of Control Optimization	Removal of redundant jumps to jump instructions
3	Algebraic Simplification	Replacement of algebraic expressions with simpler ones
4	Reduction in Strength	Replacement of expressions with those that take fewer run cycles
5	Machine Idioms	Replacement of operations by more efficient ones
6	Common Sub-expression Elimination	Eliminate the redundant expressions by saving the result and using the result instead
7	Code Motion	Move an expression that produces a constant value in every loop iteration out of the body or header
8	Induction Variable Strength Reduction	Replace operations that involve induction variables with more efficient ones
9	Partial Redundancy Elimination	Replace redundant expressions by storing results and then using them subsequently
10	Bounds Check Elimination	Costly array access checks are substituted by similar checks at compile time
11	Leaf Routine Optimization	Eliminate or reduce the function prologue and epilogue overheads
12	Shrink Wrapping	A prologue and epilogue overhead elimination technique for non leaf routines

Table 2. Locality improving transformations

	Method	Description
1	Blocking	Split a matrix in to sub-blocks and process a sub-block in its entirety before processing another
2	Changing Data Layout	Rearrange data structures in memory to exploit locality
3	Fusion	Merge two adjacent loops
4	Reindexing	Shift iterations by a constant term
5	Scaling	Shift iterations by a constant factor
6	Reversal	Process the loop in reverse order
7	Permutation	Loops of a loop-nest are processed in the reverse order
8	Skewing	Process iterations at an angle
9	Array Contraction	An array variable in a loop is replaced by a scalar to improve cache locality
10	Strip Mining	Similar to Blocking but targets only a subset of loops in a loop-nest
11	Procedure Sorting	Rearrange procedure code based on its calling relationship and frequency

2.3   Memory Latency Reduction

For programs that do not exhibit good locality, caches cannot improve the running time. Techniques such as Prefetching are employed, whereby an item in memory is fetched in anticipation, before it is actually needed. Such techniques work, by hiding the memory latency from the user.

Redundant Load Store Elimination is a transformation, that falls under the category and involves removal of back-to-back Store followed by Load or vice-versa. Prefetching is another transformation of this kind, which attempts to fetch code and data to the cache in anticipation, before their actual reference. Cache Block Alignment is aimed at eliminating multiple fetch requests to objects, that span two cache lines by alignment, so that the request can be fulfilled in a single request.

2.4   Parallalization Enablement

Techniques such as Loop Unrolling, that prepare code and data to effectively enable the parallelization, which follows this step, can be referred to as Parallelization Enablers. They basically transform code so that they are more parallelization friendly even though they may not produce results right away.

Table 3 lists some transformations, that are parallelization enablers.

Table 3. Parallelization enabling transformations

	Method	Description
1	Loop Unrolling	Replace loop with straight-line code by duplicating the body the required number of times
2	Function Inlining	Replace function calls by the code constituting the function body
3	Fission	Split a loop into two or more resulting loops
4	Tail Recursion Removal	Replace recursive function calls by loop with calls to the function in its body
5	Predicated Execution	Replace the condition and controlled code with speculation and conditional moves
6	Software Pipelining	A compact loop unrolling technique based on the hardware pipelining concept
7	Scalar Privatization	Replace a scalar in a loop with an array so that each iteration has a private copy of the variable
8	Pipelining	Perform parallel execution in pipeline fashion
9	Wave Fronting	Transform inner loops of loop-nest so that the data dependencies are eliminated
10	Successive Over Relaxation	A Parallelization technique for solving simultaneous linear equations
11	Vectorization	Replace operations on array elements with a single vector operation that operates on all array locations

2.5   Transformation Enablement

There are some transformations such as Copy Propagation, which don't offer benefits right away. However other transformations which follow, can benefit from these preparatory transformations. These transformation techniques, can be referred to as Transformation Enablers.

Transformations such as Copy Propagation, Constant Propagation and Pointer Alias Analysis constitute the category of transformations enabling other transformations. Copy Propagation aims to replace the assignee of an assignment by the assigned in subsequent operations. Constant Propagation is a related transformation, that propagates constant values among, a sequence of related variables.

3   Taxonomy of Methods Used in Program Parallelization

The domain of program parallelization offers an interesting ensemble of methods and techniques, which can be grouped as follows,

- Simplicity and Ease of Use
- Performance
- Granularity
- Program Structure and Module
- Scalability
- Novelty
- Orchestration and Management.

3.1   Simplicity and Ease of Use

A Parallelization technique can be viewed, on the basis of how simple or easy it is to implement and use. For instance, manually parallelizing a program is cumbersome to users, compared to the compiler technique which automatically parallelizes a program.

Table 4 categorizes parallelization, based on the criteria of their simplicity and ease of use.

Table 4. Parallelization methods based on simplicity and ease of use

	Method	Description
1	Manual Parallelization	Programmer manually identifies parallel parts of the program and implements parallel code
2	Semi-Automatic Parallelization	Programmer provides informative tags identifying the parallel pieces and the compiler constructs the parallel program
3	Automatic Parallelization	Compiler creates the parallel program after extensive analysis of the given program with out user assistance
4	Explicit Parallelization	It is just an other name for Manual or Semi-Automatic Parallelization [3]
5	Implicit Parallelization	It is a synonym for Automatic Parallelization [4]

3.2   Performance

Parallelization exists at various levels in a program, such as procedures or statements. How we unleash it depends on how much performance we are expecting and the effort we are willing to invest.

Parallelization carried out at the Instruction Level or the level of the Task and inside the hardware instruction Pipeline, fall under this group. Accordingly, Instruction Level Parallelization is the parallelization carried out the level of program statements or instructions. Task Parallelization is realized at the level of procedures or modules. Pipeline Parallelization is conducted at the level of machine instructions.

3.3   Granularity

Granularity is a term which is used to refer, to the size of the structure (abstraction) of a program, such as a module or a procedure. Normally, extracting parallelism from a structure that is coarse grained (large size), is easier than extracting from a structure, that is fine grained (small size).

Parallelization carried out at the task level, can be classified as Coarse Grain Parallelization and parallelization carried out at the statement or instruction level could be termed as Fine Grain Parallelization.

3.4   Program Structure or Module

Parallelism is inherent in program elements, such as Loops and Procedures both normal and recursive. Based on the available source and the statement grouping techniques such as multi-programming and threading we can categorize resulting parallelization.

In Process Parallelization, inherent parallelization is extracted through multiple invocations of the same program, each invocation acting as parallel component of the original program. In Thread Parallelization multiple threads are used, to achieve parallel run of the given program. Loop Parallelization refers to the parallelism that is present and subsequently extracted, by concurrent executions of different group of iterations of the loop.

3.5   Scalability

Certain large scale programs such as those that are numerically intensive, can rigorously test the limits of the executing hardware. Some of the hardware architectures can reach a bottleneck, after running the program of a certain size. To overcome such hardware limits, newer architectures have been proposed to scale the program.

Shared Memory Parallelization and Distributed Memory Parallelization, are two parallelization techniques that can be distinguished, based on the target architecture used to run parallel sub-programs. Shared Memory Parallelization involves a setup where the parallel programs communicate through shared memory. In the case of Distributed Memory Parallelization, the parallel components communicate with the help of explicit Sends and Receive calls.

3.6 Novelty

Published literature, periodically presents novel methodologies, to solve traditional problems. We have such examples in the parallelization domain also, which can serve as a basis for classification of parallelization methods.

This category includes Speculative Parallelization and Parallelization by Comprehension, two techniques that are beneficiaries of seen some recent research activity. Speculative Parallelization is initially carried out without dependence testing, but checks for collision and possible rollback are carried out at a later stage [5]. Parallelization by Comprehension is a parallelization process, based on the concept of algorithm inference.

3.7 Orchestration and Management

Parallelization process is not complete, with out concurrently executing the parallel components identified, during the parallelization phases. The final step in parallelization, is the control and management of the parallel pieces, of the original program which can also serve as a criteria for classifying a parallelization methodology.

Independent of the facilities offered by the modern programming languages, one could classify parallel sub-program generation techniques and the parallelization realized as a result. Program Slicing is a technique for creating sub-programs by splitting the given program. Multi-programming involves creating sub-programs that are replicas of the original program, but executing only a subset of instructions in each replica, which when executed together produce the same result, as executing the original program.

4 Taxonomy of Models Used in Transformation and Parallelization

The domain of transformation and parallelization is rich, in terms of the mathematical models employed, to solve a problem at hand. Here we look at the various models, provide a definition for each modeling technique, and present a comprehensive listing of the use cases for each, in the published literature.

The various Models that are employed in the transformation and parallelization activity, can be categorized along the following criteria,

- Models based on the Tree concept
- Models based on the Graph concept
- Models based on Machine Learning
- Models based on Algebra
- Models based on Statistics
- Models based on Enumeration
- Models based on Heuristics.

4.1 Tree Based Models

Tree is a very basic mathematical model, that is widely used in the optimization domain and Parse tree is a specialized model that falls under this category. It graphically shows how a string is derived in some language [6]. Parse tree has been employed by researchers in implementing optimizations such as the Common Sub-expression Elimination [6].

4.2 Graph Based Models

Graph is the most popular model to solve problems, in the program transformation and parallelization domain. Table 5, provides a description of several models based on the graph concept. The following table, Table 6, provides a listing of their use cases in published literature.

4.3 Machine Learning Based Models

Machine learning offers several opportunities to solve problems, in the domain of transformation and parallelization. Table 7, provides a description of models based on Machine Learning followed by table, Table 8, which lists out their uses.

4.4 Models Based on Algebra

Several models exist in the domain based on the Algebra model. Models based on Integer Linear Programming, Polyhedra, Linear Algebra and Symbolic Algebra fall under this category.

Integer Linear Programming is a system with a set of variables to be optimized, based on a function and a set of constraints. Integer Linear Programming has been used to solve problem such as, finding the Longest path length of a loop-nest, Locality optimization, Loop-nest parallelization, Register allocator optimization [25], Speculative instruction scheduler [1]. Polyhedral models use linear algebra abstractions such as matrices and their operations. [26,27]. Polyhedral models have been used in literature to implement, Code size reduction, Vectorization selection [26], Compute loop iteration counts [28], Identify fusionable loops [29], Improve cache misses [30] Linear Algebra models use matrices, determinants, linear equations and their transformations and vector spaces. Linear Algebra models find use in solving Data Layout Transformation problems. Symbolic Algebra models are a collection of techniques for symbolically manipulating mathematical expressions. Symbolic Algebra has been employed in Power optimization, Floating point to fixed point conversion, Model conditions, loops, and procedures in programs.

Table 5. Description of graph models

	Model	Description
1	Call Graph	Procedures and Modules are nodes and edges represent call information
2	Data Dependence Graph	Nodes are operations and edges are the data values
3	Data Flow Graph	Basic blocks are the nodes and the data paths form the edges
4	Control Dependence Graph	Nodes are executable statements and edges are the dependence on the control node
5	Program Dependence Graph	Operators and operands are the nodes and the dependence is captured in the edges
6	Control Flow Graph	Nodes represent instructions and edges the control transfer
7	Hammock Graph	Are sections of control flow graphs with one entry and one exit node
8	Partition Graph	A graph where nodes are execution sets and edges denote partition relations, between nodes
9	Register Interference Graph	A graph where nodes represent live variables and edges denote overlapping live ranges of variables
10	Bayesian Network	A graph where nodes represent random variables and edges capture the conditional dependencies [7,8]
11	Binary Decision Diagram	Are directed acyclic graphs that correspond to a function that returns a boolean result
12	Finite State Machine	A machine where nodes are states and edges represent the transitions

Table 6. Application of graph models

	Model	Application
1	Call Graph	Detect phase transitions, Program Comprehension, Discover program structure, Procedure call relationship, Loop and array transformations
2	Data Dependence Graph	Critical path reduction, Inter-module dependency detection, Optimum code layout [9]
3	Data Flow Graph	Common sub-expression elimination, Hot path prediction, Parallelization
4	Control Dependence Graph	Detect phase transitions, Program Comprehension, Discover program structure, Procedure call relationship, Loop and array transformations
5	Program Dependence Graph	Automatic program distribution [10]
6	Control Flow Graph	Region detection, Partial redundancy elimination, Edge profiling, Dynamic data dependencies [11]
7	Hammock Graph	Unstructured branch conversion
8	Partition Graph	Hyper-block scheduling
9	Register Interference Graph	Improve thread context switch performance
10	Bayesian Network	Iterative optimization sequence [8]
11	Binary Decision Diagram	Predict path occurrence in Hardware Definition Language [12]
12	Finite State Machine	Behavioural synthesis, Predictor generation

Table 7. Description of machine learning based models

	Model	Description
1	Genetic Algorithm	An Evolutionary method to find the individual of maximum fitness from a random population
2	Genetic Programming	Evolutionary technique to find the most optimized program
3	Simulated Annealing	Search techniques with a stochastic basis
4	Markov Model	A probability model where each event depends in a previous event
5	Hill Climbing	A search technique that starts with a random location, and in a local fashion advances towards goal
6	Artificial Neural Network	A system whose operational characteristics are stored in trained inter-unit connection weights
7	Nearest Neighbor	Labels are generated for unseen features from a set of stored trained features
8	Support Vector Machine	A technique where Kernel functions map features to corresponding classes
9	Linear Regression	A system where a function maps a predictor variable to a response variable [13]
10	Decision Tree	A mapping from a feature (non-leaf node) to a class (leaf-node) [14]

Table 8. Application of machine learning based models

	Model	Application
1	Genetic Algorithm	Reduce code size [15], Register allocation and Instruction scheduling, Instruction template selection [16], Optimize energy consumption [17]
2	Genetic Programming	Super-block scheduling [18], Loop unrolling [19]
3	Simulated Annealing	Compiler tuning [20]
4	Markov Model	Optimization space search
5	Hill Climbing	Numerical analysis
6	Artificial Neural Network	Power draw prediction [21], Graph coloring [22]
7	Nearest Neighbor	Loop unroll prediction
8	Support Vector Machine	Predict benefits of loop unrolling, Combining optimization options [23]
9	Linear Regression	Chip energy optimization [24]
10	Decision Tree	Convert program spatial features for Machine Learning [14]

4.5   Models Based on Statistics

There are several models employed in the domain that are stochastic in nature.

Orthogonal Arrays and Principal Component Analysis are models based on the Statistics model. Orthogonal Arrays measure the influence of a process of independent variables, on response or dependent variables. It has been used to influence Compiler Option Selection. Principal Component Analysis model can be used to prune the program feature space. It has been used to solve Iterative Optimization problems.

4.6   Models Based on Enumeration

When the problems involves search, Enumeration provides several opportunities.

Models based on Branch and Bound, Nelder-Mead Simplex and Enumeration fall under this category. Branch and Bound is a recursive search technique that uses trees [31]. It has been used in the past for Combining Optimization Options [31]. Nelder-Mead Simplex is a multi-dimensional search technique. It has been employed to solve Iterative Parameter Search problems [32]. Enumeration is a search space pruning technique that uses history data. Researchers have used enumeration to implement Optimal Scheduling of Super-blocks.

4.7   Models Based on Heuristics

When exhaustive methods do not provide solutions in a prescribed amount of time, Heuristic methods provide approximate solutions to fill the void.

Heuristics provide approximate solutions to NP-Hard problems and have been used to solve optimization problems, in the domain of translation and parallelization such as Combinatorial Optimization [33].

5   A Graphical Taxonomy of Methods and Models Used in Transformation and Parallelization

This section presents the taxonomy, of the various methods and models used in program translation and parallelization in graphical form.

5.1   A Graphical Taxonomy of Methods Used in Transformation

The various program transformation techniques, that are available today were chronicled earlier. Figure 1 provides a taxonomy of the transformation techniques in graphical form.

5.2 A Graphical Taxonomy of Methods Used in Parallelization

A classification of the various parallelization methods, cited in published literature are presented here in graphical form. See Fig. 2 for details.

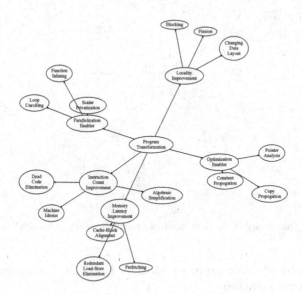

Fig. 1. Taxonomy of methods used in transformation

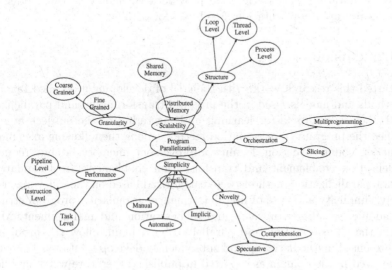

Fig. 2. Taxonomy of methods used in parallelization

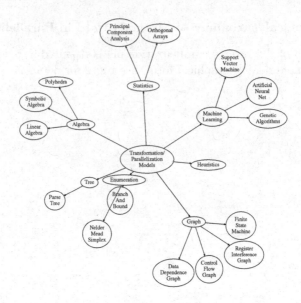

Fig. 3. Taxonomy of models used in transformation and parallelization

5.3   A Graphical Taxonomy of Models Used in Transformation and Parallelization

We discussed the various transformation and parallelization models found in published literature earlier. Here we provide a taxonomy of the models in a hierarchical graph representation. See Fig. 3 for details.

6   Conclusion

We started this research work, with the goal of developing a detailed taxonomy of methods and models, used in the program transformation and parallelization domain, which would foster learning and mastering of the subject area. We classified the program transformation methods along the following axes namely, instruction count reduction, locality improvement, memory latency reduction, parallelization enablement and transformation enablement. In a similar vein, program parallelization methods were categorized based on the following criteria namely, simplicity and ease of use, performance, granularity, program structure and module, scalability, novelty, and orchestration and management. Models used in the transformation and parallelization domain, allow the problems to be represented mathematically and subsequently develop solutions. The various models used in the domain as reported in published literature were classified as follows: models based on the tree concept, models based on the graph concept, models based on machine learning, models based on algebra, models based on statistics, models based on enumeration and models based on heuristics. The outcomes of our research are organized in the form of tables and graphs for easy comprehension. We hope the comprehensive taxonomy we have developed here, will benefit researchers and practitioners alike, and help them in their respective endeavors.

References

1. Winkel, S.: Optimal versus heuristic global code scheduling. In: 40th Annual IEEE/ACM International Symposium on Microarchitecture, MICRO 2007, pp. 43–55, December 2007
2. Kalyur, S., Nagaraja, G.S.: A survey of modeling techniques used in compiler design and implementation. In: 2016 International Conference on Computation System and Information Technology for Sustainable Solutions (CSITSS), pp. 355–358, October 2016
3. Ayguade, E., et al.: The design of OpenMP tasks. IEEE Trans. Parallel Distrib. Syst. **20**(3), 404–418 (2009)
4. Bondhugula, U., et al.: Towards effective automatic parallelization for multicore systems. In: IEEE International Symposium on Parallel and Distributed Processing, IPDPS 2008, pp. 1–5, April 2008
5. Hertzberg, B., Olukotun, K.: Runtime automatic speculative parallelization. In: 2011 9th Annual IEEE/ACM International Symposium on Code Generation and Optimization (CGO), pp. 64–73, April 2011
6. Canedo, A., Sowa, M., Abderazek, B.A.: Quantitative evaluation of common subexpression elimination on queue machines. In: International Symposium on Parallel Architectures, Algorithms, and Networks, I-SPAN 2008, pp. 25–30, May 2008
7. Chin, G., Choudhury, S., Kangas, L., McFarlane, S., Marquez, A.: Evaluating in-clique and topological parallelism strategies for junction tree-based Bayesian network inference algorithm on the cray XMT. In: 2011 IEEE International Symposium on Parallel and Distributed Processing Workshops and Phd Forum (IPDPSW), pp. 1710–1719, May 2011
8. Ashouri, A.H., Mariani, G., Palermo, G., Silvano, C.: A bayesian network approach for compiler auto-tuning for embedded processors. In: 2014 IEEE 12th Symposium on Embedded Systems for Real-Time Multimedia (ESTIMedia), pp. 90–97, October 2014
9. Li, P., Luo, H., Ding, C., Hu, Z., Ye, H.: Code layout optimization for defensiveness and politeness in shared cache. In: 2014 43rd International Conference on Parallel Processing (ICPP), pp. 151–161, September 2014
10. Kalyur, S., Nagaraja, G.S.: ParaCite: auto-parallelization of a sequential program using the program dependence graph. In: 2016 International Conference on Computation System and Information Technology for Sustainable Solutions (CSITSS), pp. 7–12, October 2016
11. Tineo, A., Corbera, F., Navarro, A., Asenjo, R., Zapata, E.L.: A novel approach for detecting heap-based loop-carried dependences. In: International Conference on Parallel Processing, ICPP 2005, pp. 99–106, June 2005
12. Jayaraman, D., Tragoudas, S.: Occurrence probability analysis of a path at the architectural level. In: 2011 12th International Symposium on Quality Electronic Design (ISQED), pp. 1–5, March 2011
13. Vaswani, K., Thazhuthaveetil, M.J., Srikant, Y.N., Joseph, P.J.: Microarchitecture sensitive empirical models for compiler optimizations. In: International Symposium on Code Generation and Optimization, CGO 2007, pp. 131–143, March 2007

14. Malik, A.M.: Spatial based feature generation for machine learning based optimization compilation. In: 2010 Ninth International Conference on Machine Learning and Applications (ICMLA), pp. 925–930, December 2010

15. Zhou, Y.-Q., Lin, N.-W.: A study on optimizing execution time and code size in iterative compilation. In: 2012 Third International Conference on Innovations in Bio-Inspired Computing and Applications (IBICA), pp. 104–109, September 2012

16. Mahalingam, P.R.: Knowledge-augmented genetic algorithms for effective instruction template selection in compilers. In: 2013 Third International Conference on Advances in Computing and Communications (ICACC), pp. 21–24, August 2013

17. Azeemi, N.Z.: Multicriteria energy efficient source code compilation for dependable embedded applications. Innov. Inf. Technol. **2006**, 1–5 (2006)

18. Mahajan, A., Ali, M.S.: Superblock scheduling using genetic programming for embedded systems. In: 7th IEEE International Conference on Cognitive Informatics, ICCI 2008, pp. 261–266, August 2008

19. Leather, H., Bonilla, E., O'Boyle, M.: Automatic feature generation for machine learning based optimizing compilation. In: International Symposium on Code Generation and Optimization, CGO 2009, pp. 81–91, March 2009

20. Zhong, S., Shen, Y., Hao, F.: Tuning compiler optimization options via simulated annealing. In: Second International Conference on Future Information Technology and Management Engineering, FITME 2009, pp. 305–308, December 2009

21. Tiwari, A., Laurenzano, M.A., Carrington, L., Snavely, A.: Modeling power and energy usage of HPC kernels. In: 2012 IEEE 26th International Parallel and Distributed Processing Symposium Workshops PhD Forum (IPDPSW), pp. 990–998, May 2012

22. Wang, X., Qiao, Q.: Solving graph coloring problems based on a chaos neural network with non-monotonous activation function. In: Fifth International Conference on Natural Computation, ICNC 2009, vol. 1, pp. 414–417, August 2009

23. Li, F., Tang, F., Shen, Y.: Feature mining for machine learning based compilation optimization. In: 2014 Eighth International Conference on Innovative Mobile and Internet Services in Ubiquitous Computing (IMIS), pp. 207–214, July 2014

24. Gschwandtner, P., Knobloch, M., Mohr, B., Pleiter, D., Fahringer, T.: Modeling CPU energy consumption of HPC applications on the IBM POWER7. In: 2014 22nd Euromicro International Conference on Parallel, Distributed and Network-Based Processing (PDP), pp. 536–543, February 2014

25. Falk, H., Schmitz, N., Schmoll, F.: WCET-aware register allocation based on integer-linear programming. In: 2011 23rd Euromicro Conference on Real-Time Systems (ECRTS), pp. 13–22, July 2011

26. Trifunovic, K., Nuzman, D., Cohen, A., Zaks, A., Rosen, I.: Polyhedral-model guided loop-nest auto-vectorization. In: 18th International Conference on Parallel Architectures and Compilation Techniques, PACT 2009, pp. 327–337, September 2009

27. Pouchet, L., Bastoul, C., Cohen, A., Vasilache, N.: Iterative optimization in the polyhedral model: Part i, one-dimensional time. In: International Symposium on Code Generation and Optimization, CGO 2007, pp. 144–156, March 2007

28. Lokuciejewski, P., Cordes, D., Falk, H., Marwedel, P.: A fast and precise static loop analysis based on abstract interpretation, program slicing and polytope models. In: International Symposium on Code Generation and Optimization, CGO 2009, pp. 136–146, March 2009

29. Pouchet, L., Bondhugula, U., Bastoul, C., Cohen, A., Ramanujam, J., Sadayappan, P.: Combined iterative and model-driven optimization in an automatic parallelization framework. In: 2010 International Conference for High Performance Computing, Networking, Storage and Analysis (SC), pp. 1–11, November 2010

30. Xue, Y., Zhao, C.: Automated phase-ordering of loop optimizations based on polyhedron model. In: 10th IEEE International Conference on High Performance Computing and Communications, HPCC 2008, pp. 672–677, September 2008

31. Desai, N.P.: A novel technique for orchestration of compiler optimization functions using branch and bound strategy. In: IEEE International Advance Computing Conference, IACC 2009, pp. 467–472, March 2009

32. Lu, P., Che, Y., Wang, Z.: An effective iterative compilation search algorithm for high performance computing applications. In: 10th IEEE International Conference on High Performance Computing and Communications, HPCC 2008, pp. 368–373, September 2008

33. Martí, R., Reinelt, G.: The Linear Ordering Problem: Exact and Heuristic Methods in Combinatorial Optimization, 1st edn. Springer, Heidelberg (2011). https://doi.org/10.1007/978-3-642-16729-4

Time Bound Robot Mission Planning for Priority Machine Using Linear Temporal Logic for Multi Goals

Venkata Beri$^{(\boxtimes)}$, Rahul Kala, and Gora Chand Nandi

Robotics and Machine Intelligence Laboratory,
Indian Institute of Information Technology, Allahabad, Allahabad, India
venkat.beri@gmail.com, rkala001@gmail.com,
gcnandi@gmail.com

Abstract. In this paper, we implement a Linear Temporal Logic-based motion planning algorithm for a prioritized mission scenario. The classic robot motion planning solves the problem of moving a robot from a source to a goal configuration while avoiding obstacles. This problem of motion planning gets complicated when the robot is asked to solve a complex goal specification incorporating boolean and temporal constraints between the atomic goals. This problem is referred to as the mission planning. The paper assumes that the mission to be solved is a collection of smaller tasks, wherein each task constituting the mission must be finished within a given amount of time. We assign the priorities for the tasks such that, the higher priority tasks should be completed beforehand. The planner solves the missions in multiple groups, instead of the classic approach of solving all the tasks at once. The group is dynamic and is a function of how many tasks can be incorporated such that no time deadline is lost. The grouping based prioritized and time-based planning saves a significant amount of time as compared to the inclusion of time information in the verification engine that complicates the search logic. NuSMV tool is used to verify the logic. Comparisons are made by solving all tasks at once and solving the tasks one-by-one. Experimental results reveal that the proposed solver is able to meet the deadlines of nearly all tasks while taking a small computation time.

Keywords: Linear temporal logic · Mission planning ·
Robot mission planning · Model checking · NuSMV

1 Introduction

The problem of robot motion planning is to empower a robot to explore and advance out in a confused hindrance or an obstacle-prone environment. A number of technology applications for *mission planning* and self-governing frameworks [1], (e.g., autonomous vehicle, unmanned air vehicles) require effective procedures that can produce the desired sequence of operations to be done to achieve the user defined mission, correctly and effectively. Over the period of time, the idea of correctness and efficiency has become more and more sophisticated. This results in providing tasks consisting of many other sub tasks with Boolean and temporal constraints, rather than a single goal

© ICST Institute for Computer Sciences, Social Informatics and Telecommunications Engineering 2019
Published by Springer Nature Switzerland AG 2019. All Rights Reserved
N. Kumar and R. Venkatesha Prasad (Eds.): UBICNET 2019, LNICST 276, pp. 250–263, 2019.
https://doi.org/10.1007/978-3-030-20615-4_19

problem constituting the *classical motion planning* problem. The complex goals and several environmental constraints can make a robot wander infinitely in an environment for a given problem statement.

This paper consequently solves the high-level mission planning problem, where the mission is given as linear temporal logic (LTL) formula and develops controllers for the same. It generates the path for the robot which satisfies the given LTL formula. One of the qualities of this system is that it considers assignments in which the conduct of the robot relies upon the data it assembled at runtime. If the task is feasible, then the LTL will be generating a sequence so as to give a path to the robot that accomplishes the mission. There are bisimulation methods which provide a finite transition system to provide an optimal run [2]. The model checking tools NuSMV [3, 4] and LTLMoP [5], provide us the guarantee that the specifications can be guaranteed.

Temporal logic has been used for many complex specifications [6–8]. We construct the problem into a map by partitioning the workspace of the robot [9] and formulating an LTL for its desired behavior. This paper describes the problem of solving a mission planning with the help of LTL specified goals. Metric Temporal logic is another such instance used for obtaining the results in the desired way [10]. Temporal logic has been used for sampling-based motion planning where a multi layered approach has been presented [11]. A mechanism to deal with the large computation time of Temporal Logic is also to use restricted languages and evolutionary techniques to generate iterative solutions [12, 13].

Solving the problem of mission planning hence requires representing the mission as a LTL formula and solving the same using any LTL based verification system. There are two problems that occur in this methodology. First, that the verification of a solution in LTL has an exponential complexity and therefore there is a limited size that the formula can have. Second, the real-life missions can be very complex, requiring time for the robot to compute a solution, however the real-life missions are also real time in nature and beyond a time the solution is needless as the facts requiring the solution may have changed (like the need to have a coffee in a meeting) or a person may volunteer to himself/herself carry the job without the robot.

A typical way of solving the problem is by incorporating timing information associated with the missions and its components thereon for verification. However, the robot first plans and then executes the mission, and the time incurred in the planning stage is significantly high and cannot be assumed to be zero that the current approaches assume. Further, adding time information complicates the search space for a solution in the verification engine and this severely complicates the time.

In this paper, the same problem is solved by decomposition. We assume that a mission is composed of smaller sub-missions called tasks. Each task has its own priority and hence a time within which the task must complete. The search incrementally groups tasks to make a mission, such that the total incurred computation time and expected processing time is within the threshold of time and the solution is hence useful. The grouping also ensures that the number of propositional variables in the LTL formula are small and the computation time as per the exponential complexity of LTL is hence limited.

This paper has been discussed as per the following sections. Section 2 provides a brief about Linear temporal logic. Section 3 discusses the proposed methodology. Section 4 details about the results and simulations. Finally, Sect. 5 concludes the paper.

2 Linear Temporal Logic

Linear temporal logic defines set of logic operators which are bound with a factor of time in contrast to the traditional Boolean logic. The linear temporal logic consists of the operators such as eventually ($\Diamond$), next ($\Box$), always ($\bigcirc$) and until (U). These operators are further described by the assumptions such as safety, liveliness, sequencing and reachability.

The typical LTL operators used are notably used as: Next or $\bigcirc\phi$, meaning ϕ is true in the next moment in time; Always or $\Box\phi$, meaning ϕ is true in all future moments of time; Eventually or $\Diamond\phi$, meaning ϕ is true in some future moment; and Until or ϕ U ψ, meaning ϕ is true until ψ is true. The LTL has some properties with environment assumptions these include:

Safety: Which describes the condition which must be always satisfied, for example like "Always avoid obstacles". The LTL formula negation ($\neg$) is used to describe the conditions $\neg(O_1 \vee O_2 \vee O_3 \vee \ldots \vee O_n)$ U R means eventually reach region R by avoiding all obstacles O_i, $i = 1, 2, \ldots$ n.

Liveness: This specifies that goals which always must be eventually satisfied by some actions in the future (e.g. "if region A is visited then must visit region B infinitely often").

Sequencing: This describes the sequence of goals to be followed in any order. The LTL formula $\Diamond$ specifies that we must visit all regions (i.e. R_1, R_2, R_3, R_4, R_5) as per requirement $\Diamond (R_1 \wedge \Diamond (R_2 \wedge \Diamond (R_3 \vee \Diamond R_4)))$ in given environments.

Reachability: An individual state assume is reachable from any initial present states. Moreover, this kind of goal specification is more useful when the problem is similar corresponds to a single/multi goals without any complex specifications.

3 Proposed Methodology

3.1 Overall Solution Design

The general approach for motion planning comprises of generating the graphical image or representation of the given map from the environment as based on the conditions, mission specification, navigation, control and planning shown in Fig. 1.

Mission Specification describes how we achieve the end goal. For example, it can be to reach a point B from Point A without reaching a particular point C. Mission Planner tells on an overlay how this specific goal can be achieved. Low level planning involves various strategies. The control specification lets us control the robot in the specific directions with the concerned motion.

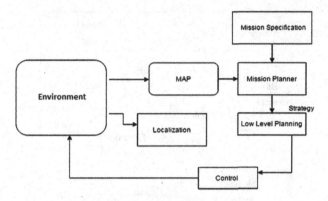

Fig. 1. Overall solution design

Mapping involves looking at the real-world as it is. It depicts the arrangement of the system in the real-world. Localization tells us where the particular object is with respect to the map. It takes into consideration the robots' exact coordinates. The entire real-world system or experimental scenario is represented using a map. Map of real-life environments may 2D or 3D. The map conversion from real-world to workspace environment can happen through camera calibrations, distance information of obstacle to regions, navigable path area, etc.

Path planning can be done in a structured environment or in an unstructured environment. In a structured environment, the obstacles are represented using polygon like figures whereas in the unstructured environment, the size and the shape of the obstacles are not available. This will generate plans only for valid for the LTL specifications and synthesis of the LTL specifications.

3.2 Triangulation

While representing the real-world system for our navigation map in workspace configurations, we first need an efficient technique for representing the complicated world system. Thus, we need to redesign the real-world environmental information for a robotic map. The path from source to goals is fully dependent on how the real-world system is represented.

The original map is assumed to be known with polygons acting as the obstacles. The robot moves in free areas and therefore the free areas are modelled by using triangulation. Triangulation involves the decomposition of the regions into a polygonal area or rather a set of triangles [9, 14]. The area classified as the regions covered by the obstacles which is referred as holes, which is required so that no triangulation happens inside the obstacles, whereas the rest of the region lies to be under triangulation. Each of these triangles or regions serve as a well-connected graph, so that the transitions can be done easily. We consider the map shown in Fig. 2 for all the experiments, which represents a typical map of any home or office scenario. The same map will be used for discussions. The regions of interest are labeled. The given map was triangulated and the result is shown in Fig. 3.

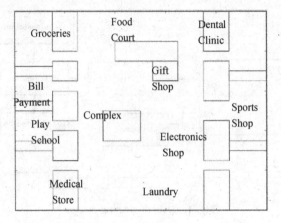

Fig. 2. Pictorial representation of the workspace

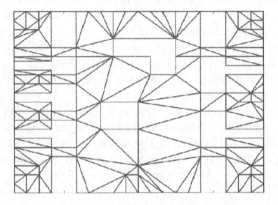

Fig. 3. Triangulated region of the workspace

4 Mission Solver

The main aspect of the problem is solving for a mission. Assume that the mission is given by ψ. In our case we assume that the mission is composed of a group of tasks of the form $\psi = \cup \{<\phi_i, \pi_i, \theta_i>\}$, where ϕ_i is the ith task specified as a LTL, π_i is the priority of the ith task and θ_i is the time within which the task must be completed, otherwise it will be useless to do the task. In the actual implementation the priorities and time thresholds are taken to be related in the sense that a higher priority is given to the tasks with a small time threshold, that is $\pi_i, = rank(\theta_i)$, however in general the two may not always be related and the algorithm is generic for the same.

The proposed algorithm operates in a greedy manner and takes up tasks in the increasing order of priority. Therefore, the higher priority tasks get solved first and have a lesser chance of losing the deadline. The assumption here is that a hard prioritization is followed and a better priority task cannot be compromised to any number of smaller priority tasks. However, the time threshold is soft, meaning that even if a task cannot be completed on time, it must still be completed as early as possible. A group G is defined as an ordered sequence of tasks in the prioritized order, given by $G^k = \cup\,[<\phi_i, \pi_i, \theta_i> : \pi_i \le \pi_{i+1}, \pi_j \le \pi_0 \vee \pi_j \ge \pi_{|G|} \forall <\phi_i, \pi_i, \theta_i> \notin G^k]$. Here G^k denotes the kth group. Let $T^k = t_E + t_P + T^{k-1}$ be the total travel time for the robot to cater to simultaneously solve all the tasks specified in G^k (say execution time, t_E), the time incurred in computing such a plan and division of the group (say planning time, t_P) and the time incurred in planning and executing all previous groups (say T^{k-1}). The constraint is that either all tasks in G^k must adhere to their time thresholds, which is the best possibility; however, in case a task cannot meet its time constraint, then it must be the first and only task in the group so as to specify that there is no way to solve the task within the time threshold, given by $T^k < \max_{j \in Gk}\theta_j \vee |G^k| = 1$. Obviously, each task is solved only once ($G^k \cap G^l = \varnothing \,\forall k \ne l$) and all tasks are solved ($\exists k: <\phi_i, \pi_i, \theta_i> \in G^k$).

The algorithm is then to iteratively build up the groups. Given the group G^{k-1}, the formulation of the group G^k involves iteratively adding in tasks $<\phi_i, \pi_i, \theta_i>$ to G^k until the summation of times $t_E + t_P + T_{k-1}$ is within threshold $\max_{j \in Gk}\theta_j$. A minimum of 1 task is compulsorily added. t_P is the continuous summation over all times in the iterative addition process. Thereafter the group is executed and the information is used for designing the next group. Algorithm 1 gives a pseudo-code of the process.

Algorithm 1: Mission Solver

1: $T^0 \leftarrow 0$, $k \leftarrow 1$
2: $G_1 \leftarrow \varnothing$
3: $t_P \leftarrow 0$
4: for all tasks $<\phi_i, \pi_i, \theta_i>$ in sorted order of priority
5:   add $<\phi_i, \pi_i, \theta_i>$ to G^k
6:   $S_k \leftarrow \text{Plan}(G_1)$ with computation time t
7:   $t_P \leftarrow t_P + t$
8:   if $t_P + t_E(S_k) + T^{k-1} > \max_{j \in Gk}\theta_j$
9:     if $|G^k| > 1$
10:        remove $<\phi_i, \pi_i, \theta_i>$ from G^k
11:        $t^k \leftarrow t_P + t_E(S_{k-1}) + T^{k-1}$
12:     else $t^k \leftarrow t_P + t_E(S_k) + T^{k-1}$
13:     $k \leftarrow k+1$, $G_k \leftarrow \varnothing$
14: Return G^k

---

5   Results and Discussions

For experimentation, we took the tasks given in Table 1 as per the priority assigned to them in the increasing order, the top being more priority. We started off with the tasks and carried out one after the other. NuSMV was used as a model verification tool.

- Task 1: Visit the medical store and pick up medicines and a syringe
- Task 2: Visit the laundry store to collect clothes and get them washed

- Task 3: Visit the dental clinic to check whether the doctor is available or not until an appointment is done.
- Task 4: Visit the office to pay the electricity and phone bills
- Task 5: Visit the Groceries shop to pick the kitchen items and utensils
- Task 6: Visit the Food court and order Chinese and continental food item
- Task 7: Visit the child play school and pick toys
- Task 8: Visit the gifts store and pack gift items dinner set and grinder box
- Task 9: Visit the sports shop and pick up a football and Tennis racquet
- Task 10: Visit the electronics Merchandise and bring appliances AC and a geyser
- Task 11: Visit the shopping complex and bring ties and some clips.

Table 1. Region aliases

S. No	Area	Alias
1	Medical: Medicine	A_1
2	Medical: Syringe	A_2
3	Laundry: Clothes	B_1
4	Laundry: Washing	B_2
5	Play School	C_1
6	Play School: Pick Toys	C_2
7	Bills: Electricity	D_1
8	Bills: Phone	D_2
9	Groceries: Kitchen items	E_1
10	Groceries: Utensils	E_2
11	Food Court: Chinese	F_1
12	Food Court: Continental	F_2
13	Dental Clinic: Doctor available	G_1
14	Dental Clinic: Appointment	G_2
15	Gift store: Dinner Set	H_1
16	Gift Store: Grinder Set	H_2
17	Sports Shop: Football	I_1
18	Sports Shop: Tennis Racquet	I_2
19	Electronics Shop: AC set	J_1
20	Electronics Shop: immersion rod	J_2
21	Complex: Ties	K_1
22	Complex: Clips	K_2

5.1   Simulation Scenario 1

The robot was asked to visit the medical shop to pick medicines and a syringe, followed by visiting a laundry shop and getting the clothes washed, followed by a visit to the doctors clinic until an appointment is being fixed, and visit to the office to pay the electricity bill and phone bill, and then visit to the groceries shop to collect the kitchen items and utensils, followed by a visit to the restaurant to order and collect Chinese and Continental food, next to the child play school and pick some toys, followed by the visit to a gifts store to pack items dinner set and grinder box, subsequently to visit the sports shop to pick a football and a Tennis racquet, followed by a visit to the electronics merchandise shop to book an Air Conditioner and a geyser, and then finally to a shopping complex to bring some clips and ties. The LTL specification for the same was as $((\Diamond A_1 \wedge \Diamond A_2 \wedge \Diamond B_1 \wedge \Diamond B_2 \wedge ((\Diamond C_1) U (\Diamond C_2)) \wedge \Diamond D_1 \wedge \Diamond D_2 \wedge \Diamond E_1 \wedge \Diamond E_2 \wedge \Diamond F_1 \wedge \Diamond F_2 \wedge \Diamond G_1 \wedge \Diamond G_2 \wedge \Diamond H_1 \wedge \Diamond H_2 \wedge \Diamond I_1 \wedge \Diamond I_2 \wedge \Diamond J_1 \wedge \Diamond J_2 \wedge \Diamond K_1 \wedge \Diamond K_2))$.

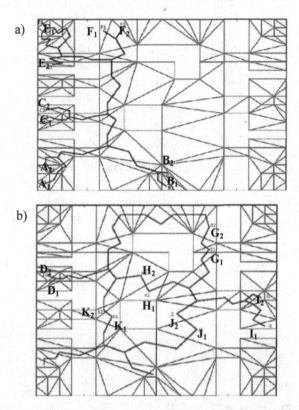

Fig. 4. Output of the algorithm (a) First group (b) Second group

The problem is solved by using the proposed algorithm. The threshold was set to 35 min. The algorithm succeeded by forming 2 groups only. The First group recorded a time of 34.19 min for the path length of 139. The path followed by the robot is shown by Fig. 4(a). Table 2 summarizes the calculations made by the algorithm in the computation of the path. Group 2 primarily incorporates all other tasks and the path is shown in Fig. 4(b) while the calculations are shown in Table 3. The total time required to complete the assigned tasks was 34.26 min. The path length for the tasks to be finished was 137 each assumed to be of a unit path length. Thus, with the proposed algorithm, the total time comes out to be 72.47 min and the path length for the same turns out to be 276 assuming unit lengths each which is less than that of the 290.

Overall with the proposed algorithm the computational time and the path length both turned out to be modestly small, while the algorithm could cater to the time thresholds of most of the tasks.

Table 2. First group with the relative path length

S. No	No. of propositions	Computation time (secs)	Path length	Robot driving time (secs)	Total time (mins)
1	2	151	43	645	10.75
2	4	313	53	795	13.25
3	6	537	83	1245	20.75
4	8	867	93	1395	23.26
5	10	1046	117	1755	29.26
6	12	2434	139	2085	34.19
7	14	3945	151	2265	37.81

Table 3. Second group with the relative path length

S. No	No. of propositions	Computational time (secs)	Path length	Robot driving time (secs)	Total time (mins)
1	2	147	65	975	16.25
2	4	425	86	1290	21.51
3	6	526	104	1560	26.01
4	8	794	122	1830	30.51
5	10	945	137	2055	34.26

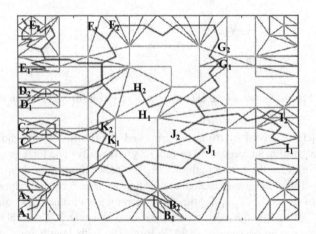

Fig. 5. The Final Path depicting the tasks

In order to compare the approach, two baselines are proposed. The first baseline is a typical implementation of model verification using LTL, in which the entire mission is given as one group to the mission solver, and is called as *all at once* for comparisons. The second baseline is based upon the heuristics that the tasks are already available in some prioritized manner. The baseline takes the missions in a greedy manner, in the increasing order of priority and solves them one by one, called as *one by one* for comparisons.

The results of the first baseline are shown in Fig. 5. The total path length taken to traverse all the satisfying regions avoiding the obstacles was observed as 290. These tasks were performed without having any time constraint. The total time taken for the above specified specification was around 92.51 min for solving 22 proposition variables with 1200 s as the computation time and 4350 s as the robot driving time.

To compare the results, we use 3 metrics path length, total time (planning time and execution time) and number of real time tasks whose time threshold was met. It can be seen that the proposed algorithm performed better in all metrics as compared to the baselines. The number of regions covered by our algorithm within the required threshold was 8 as compared to the others which were 2. The results of the three algorithms are summarized in Table 4. A more detailed view showing every task and the performance on a per task basis can be seen from Table 5.

Table 4. Overall comparisons for scenario 1

	Path length	Total time (mins)	No. of pass
Proposed algorithm	**276**	**72.47**	**8**
One by one	*290*	92.51	*2*
All at once	360	*82.42*	*2*

Table 5. Task level comparisons between algorithms for scenario 1

S. No	Region	Proposed algorithm	One by one	All at once
1	Medical	110, Pass	360, Fail	269, Fail
2	Laundry:	112, Pass	317, Fail	278, Fail
3	Play School	124, Pass	287, Fail	245, Fail
4	Bills:	68, Pass	261, Fail	233, Fail
5	Groceries	26, Pass	237, Fail	188, Fail
6	Food Court:	60, Pass	209, Fail	159, Fail
7	Dental Clinic	38, Pass	184, Fail	139, Fail
8	Gift store:	50, Pass	148, Fail	129, Fail
9	Sports Shop:	98, Fail	110, Fail	87, Pass
10	Electronics Shop	53, Fail	62, Fail	49, Pass
11	Complex:	16, Fail	14, Pass	15, Pass

5.2 Simulation Scenario 2

The robot was asked to dental clinic to check whether the doctor was present or not, followed by a visit to the groceries shop to pick some kitchen items, and then visit the sports shop to find the new cricket bat and new hockey stick has arrived or not, succeeded by a visit to the laundry shop until the visit to the electronics shop to get a washing machine, and visit to the play school to pick the toys for the children, followed by the visit to the complex to get some new pins and ties, and then visit to the gift shop to get some gift items packed. The temporal logic specification for the same is as $(((\Diamond G_1) U (\Diamond G_2)) \wedge \Diamond E_1 \wedge \Diamond E_2 \wedge \Diamond I_1 \wedge \Diamond I_2 \wedge \Diamond B_1 \wedge \Diamond B_2 \wedge \Diamond J_1 \wedge \Diamond J_2 \wedge \Diamond C_1 \wedge \Diamond C_2 \wedge \Diamond K_1 \wedge \Diamond K_2 \wedge \Diamond H_1 \wedge \Diamond H_2)$. The total path length was observed to be 187.

The path length for the tasks to be finished was 137 with our proposed algorithm. With the proposed algorithm, the total time comes out to be 52.34 min with respect to the original time of 69.21 min and the path length turns out to be 137 assuming unit lengths each which is less than that of the 187. Overall, with the proposed algorithm, the computational time and the path length both turned out to be less. The number of regions covered by our algorithm within the required threshold was 8 as compared to the others which were 7. Table 6 shows the comparison of the path lengths when the tasks were carried by proposed algorithm, all tasks taken in go and when a single task at a time for scenario 2. Table 7 gives the calculations on a per task basis.

Table 6. Overall comparisons for scenario 2

Scenario 2	Path length	Total time (mins)	No. of pass
Proposed algorithm	**137**	**52.34**	**8**
One by one	*149*	62.42	7
All at once	187	69.21	1

Table 7. Task level comparisons between algorithms for scenario 2

Region	Proposed algorithm	One by one	All at once
Dental Clinic:	48, Pass	187, Fail	61, Pass
Groceries	72, Pass	170, Fail	171, Fail
Sports Shop:	52, Pass	145, Fail	138, Pass
Laundry:	85, Pass	110, Fail	85, Pass
Electronics Shop:	91, Pass	95, Fail	91, Pass
Play School	72, Pass	81, Fail	72, Pass
Complex:	45, Pass	48, Fail	45, Pass
Gift store:	16, Pass	16, Pass	16, Pass

5.3 Simulation Scenario 3

The robot was asked to dental clinic to check whether the doctor was present or not, followed by a visit to the groceries shop to pick some kitchen items, and then visit the sports shop to find the new cricket bat and new hockey stick has arrived or not, succeeded by a visit to the laundry shop until the visit to the electronics shop to get a washing machine, and visit to the play school to pick the toys for the children followed by the visit to the complex to get some new pins and ties and then visit to the gift shop to get some gift items packed. The temporal logic specification for the same is as $(((\Diamond C_1 \wedge \Diamond C_2) \cup (\Diamond F_1 \wedge \Diamond F_2)) \wedge \Diamond D_1 \wedge \Diamond D_2 \wedge \Diamond J_1 \wedge \Diamond J_2 \wedge \Diamond I_1 \wedge \Diamond I_2 \wedge \Diamond K_1 \wedge \Diamond K_2)$. The total path length was observed to be 125.

The total time required to complete the assigned tasks was 46.25 min. The path length for the tasks to be finished was 137. With the proposed algorithm, the total time comes out to be 46.25 min and the path length for the same turns out to be 125, which is less than that of the 156. Table 8 shows the comparison of the chosen metrics with the baselines for Scenario 3. Overall with the proposed algorithm the computational time and the path length both turned out to be less. The number of regions covered by our algorithm within the required threshold was 6 as compared to the others which were 4 and 3 respectively. A detailed per-task view can be seen in Table 9.

Table 8. Overall comparisons for scenario 3

Scenario 3	Path length	Total time (mins)	No. of pass
Proposed algorithm	**125**	**46.25**	**6**
One by one	*149*	*56.42*	*4*
All at once	156	62.45	3

Table 9. Task level comparisons between algorithms for scenario 3

Region	Proposed algorithm	Single task	All at once
Play School	48, Pass	156, Fail	48, Pass
Food Court:	41, Pass	119, Fail	118, Fail
Bills:	54, Pass	103, Fail	104,Fail
Electronics Shop:	87, Pass	82, Pass	88, Fail
Sports Shop:	35, Pass	50, Pass	53, Fail
Complex:	15, Pass	15, Pass	15, Pass

6 Conclusions

In this paper, we have proposed a solution to the robotics mission planning problem expressed with temporal logic with complex specifications wherein the mission is composed of a prioritized set of tasks, each task has a time threshold within which it must preferably be solved. We have demonstrated that the approach works much faster as compared to the two baselines, solving the complete mission in a go and solving the tasks one by one. This is one of the only papers that defines optimality as a mixture of computation time and execution time of the robot which is a more realistic modelling.

The future work is to actually use the algorithm on a real robot and to ask it to perform the operations. Furthermore, the algorithm may also be extended to the case of multiple robots and task division among the robots is another interesting problem to be looked into the future. The generic temporal logic does not give much scope to design heuristic measures while the problem can best be solved if there are powerful heuristics to attack. This makes the problem challenging.

Another typicality that can be considered is that the robot will interact with the humans and the time for the same cannot be ascertained. This becomes more important considering that the humans may not necessarily be at the workplace but somewhere around as well as their presence or absence is stochastic in nature. So, the robot must be able to locate the human in the vicinity, approach the human and get the needed interaction done along with the human. These are all complex problems.

Acknowledgement. The research is supported by the Indian Institute of Information Technology, Allahabad and the Science and Engineering Research Board, Department of Science and Technology, Government of India through project number ECR/2015/000406.

References

1. Choset, H., et al.: Principles of Robot Motion: Theory, Algorithms, and Implementations. MIT Press, Cambridge (2005)
2. Holzmann, G.: The model checker SPIN. IEEE Trans. Softw. Eng. **25**(5), 279–295 (1997)
3. Cimatti, A., et al.: NuSMV 2: an OpenSource tool for symbolic model checking. In: Brinksma, E., Larsen, K.G. (eds.) CAV 2002. LNCS, vol. 2404, pp. 359–364. Springer, Heidelberg (2002). https://doi.org/10.1007/3-540-45657-0_29
4. Vardi, M.Y., Wolper, P.: An automata-theoretic approach to automatic program verification. In: Logic in Computer Science, pp. 322–331 (1986)
5. Finucane, C., Jing, G., Kress-Gazit, H.: LTLMoP: experimenting with language, temporal Logic and robot control. In: 2010 IEEE/RSJ International Conference on Intelligent Robots and Systems (IROS), 18–22 October 2010, pp. 1988–1993 (2010)
6. Fainekos, G.E., Kress-Gazit, H., Pappas, G.J.: Temporal logic motion planning for mobile robots. In: Proceedings of the 2005 IEEE International Conference on Robotics and Automation, Barcelona, Spain, pp. 2020–2025 (2005). https://doi.org/10.1109/robot.2005.1570410
7. Antoniotti, M., Mishra, B.: Discrete event models+temporal logic=supervisory controller: automatic synthesis of locomotion controllers. In: Proceedings of 1995 IEEE International Conference on Robotics and Automation, Nagoya, Japan, vol. 2, pp. 1441–1446 (1995). https://doi.org/10.1109/robot.1995.525480
8. Kress-Gazit, H., Fainekos, G.E., Pappas, G.J.: Temporal-logic-based reactive mission and motion planning. IEEE Trans. Robot. **25**(6), 1370–1381 (2009). https://doi.org/10.1109/TRO.2009.2030225
9. Shewchuk, J.R.: Triangle: engineering a 2D quality mesh generator and Delaunay triangulator. In: Lin, M.C., Manocha, D. (eds.) WACG 1996. LNCS, vol. 1148, pp. 203–222. Springer, Heidelberg (1996). https://doi.org/10.1007/BFb0014497

10. Karaman, S., Frazzoli, E.: Vehicle routing problem with metric temporal logic specifications. In: IEEE DCC, December 2008

11. Bhatia, A., Kavraki, L.E., Vardi, M.Y.: Sampling-based motion planning with temporal goals. In: 2010 IEEE International Conference on Robotics and Automation (ICRA), 3–7 May 2010, pp. 2689–2696 (2010). https://doi.org/10.1109/robot.2010.5509503

12. Kala, R.: Sampling based mission planning for multiple robots. In: Proceedings of the 2016 IEEE Congress on Evolutionary Computation, Vancouver, BC, Canada, pp. 662–669 (2016)

13. Kala, R.: Dynamic programming accelerated evolutionary planning for constrained robotic missions. In: Proceedings of the IEEE Conference on Simulation, Modelling and Programming for Autonomous Robots, Brisbane, Australia, pp. 81–86 (2018)

14. Ruppert, J.: A delaunay refinement algorithm for quality 2-dimensional mesh generation. J. Algorithms **18**(3), 548–585 (1995)

Author Index

Printed in the United States
By Bookmasters